Confronting the Racist Legacy of the American Child Welfare System

Confronting the Racist Legacy of the American Child Welfare System

The Case for Abolition

ALAN J. DETTLAFF

OXFORD
UNIVERSITY PRESS

OXFORD
UNIVERSITY PRESS

Oxford University Press is a department of the University of Oxford. It furthers the University's objective of excellence in research, scholarship, and education by publishing worldwide. Oxford is a registered trade mark of Oxford University Press in the UK and certain other countries.

Published in the United States of America by Oxford University Press
198 Madison Avenue, New York, NY 10016, United States of America.

© Oxford University Press 2023

Library of Congress Cataloging-in-Publication Data
Names: Dettlaff, Alan J., author.
Title: Confronting the racist legacy of the American child welfare system : the case for abolition / Alan J. Dettlaff.
Description: New York, NY : Oxford University Press, [2023] |
Includes bibliographical references and index. |
Identifiers: LCCN 2023007346 (print) | LCCN 2023007347 (ebook) |
ISBN 9780197675267 (hardback) | ISBN 9780197675281 (epub) |
ISBN 9780197675298
Subjects: LCSH: Child welfare—United States—History. | Racism—United States—History. |
African American children—History. | White people—Race identity
Classification: LCC HV741 .D478 2023 (print) | LCC HV741 (ebook) |
DDC 362 .70973—dc23/eng/20230508
LC record available at https://lccn.loc.gov/2023007346
LC ebook record available at https://lccn.loc.gov/2023007347

DOI: 10.1093/oso/9780197675267.001.0001

Printed by Sheridan Books, Inc., United States of America

To all the abolitionists I've met along the way. Thank you for dreaming and building with me.

Contents

Acknowledgments

When I set out to write *Confronting the Racist Legacy of the American Child Welfare System*, I knew I could never write this book on my own. Not because I didn't have many ideas about abolishing the family policing system, but because I knew that every one of those ideas had been shaped and informed by the amazing colleagues I've worked with over the last several years. *Confronting the Racist Legacy of the American Child Welfare System* would not be possible, either in idea or in writing, without the incredible contributions of my coauthors, Reiko Boyd, Victoria Copeland, Jesse Hartley, Maya Pendleton, and Kristen Weber. Over the last several years, and throughout the writing of this book, I have learned so much from each of you and have been challenged to grow and think bigger and bolder at each step along the way. I will forever be grateful for the experience of working on this with you and for the many ways you've grown and shaped the ideas that ultimately became this collective project.

I am also deeply grateful for the team of abolitionist doctoral students who reviewed every page of this book and contributed incredibly thoughtful ideas and reflections, most of which were immediately incorporated. Brianna Harvey, Bethany Jo Murray, and Noor Toraif, you are each exceptionally brilliant and I can't wait to see all that you go on to do. I'm also very grateful for my research assistants at the Graduate College of Social Work, Jesse Hartley and Aly Jacobs, for all the time and dedication you've given to this project, for helping me stay organized, and for your excellent Internet sleuthing and finding skills. I'm looking forward to following your journeys and continuing to work with and learn from you.

Much of *Confronting the Racist Legacy of the American Child Welfare System* is inspired by the incredible activists and organizers I've met through this work—many of whom have been impacted by the family policing system and are now working to see this system ended. Joyce McMillan, Angela Burton, Shrounda Selivanoff, Lexie Grüber Pérez, and many others—you inspire me daily and I'm so grateful to know you and to be able to contribute to the movement with you. And to the many more that I haven't met, but I know are out there, fighting every day, thank you for all you're doing to dream and build a new world.

I'm also grateful to the many researchers and activists engaging in abolitionist research and organizing that have helped to grow and shape my ideas—Mical Raz, Kelley Fong, Frank Edwards, Laura Briggs, Tina Lee, Kathleen Creamer, Richard Wexler, Nora McCarthy, and many more—thank you for sharing your work and for all you do. I'm also incredibly indebted to and inspired by the abolitionists who have been building and growing this movement for decades—Angela Y. Davis, Ruth Wilson Gilmore, Derecka Purnell, Mariame Kaba, Andrea Ritchie, and many others.

Of course, I wouldn't be an abolitionist or the scholar I am today if I hadn't read *Shattered Bonds* over twenty years ago. Reading *Shattered Bonds* just shortly after leaving the Texas Department of Family and Protective Services, where I had worked as a "child protective services investigator" for many years, changed my life and began my own process of coming to understand the harm I had caused to so many children and families and my own complicity in the racism inherent in this system. Thank you Dorothy Roberts for being a part of my life ever since then and for continuing to share your work and inspiring me and so many others.

To the upEND team at the Graduate College of Social Work—connease Warren, Josie Pickens, Sydnie Mares, and Jaison Oliver—thank you for your dedication to this work and for all you do every day to move this work forward. You've each also done much to grow and shape my ideas as we've engaged in this work together and I'm grateful to be a part of this team with you.

In addition to writing two chapters with me, Victoria Copeland had a huge role in every aspect of this book, from brainstorming ideas, to reading drafts, to endless iterations of the title. I am very grateful to know you and to work with you on so many projects. You are a brilliant thinker and an amazing writer, and I am continually inspired by the ways in which you bring an abolitionist praxis into everything you do.

Finally, to my upEND cofounders—Kristen Weber, Bill Bettencourt, Leonard Burton, and Maya Pendleton—I am so grateful to know you and to be engaged in this work with you. From the early conversations many years ago that became the spark that led to upEND, to the many conversations we've had in the years since, *Confronting the Racist Legacy of the American Child Welfare System* would not be possible without you. Everything that I understand about abolition today has been shaped and informed by our many conversations over the years, and I'm incredibly grateful for your wisdom, your guidance, your fight, and your belief in me and this book. You've read drafts, shared ideas, brainstormed, wordsmithed, and been a source of inspiration that means the world to me. I will forever be grateful not only for how you've helped create this book but also for how you've changed me along the way.

Contributors

Reiko Boyd, PhD, MSW (she/her) is an Assistant Professor at the University of Houston Graduate College of Social Work. Her research focuses on understanding and addressing the consequences of structural racism, promoting Black infant and maternal health, abolition, and structural inequities at the community level. In her work, Dr. Boyd applies a multilevel, strengths-based, life-course perspective that directs attention beyond individual factors to examine and intervene on structures, systems, and conditions to cultivate healthy contexts and increase opportunities for families to thrive in their full potential. Dr. Boyd earned her MSW from the University of California, Los Angeles, and her doctorate in Social Welfare from the University of California, Berkeley.

Victoria Copeland, PhD, MSW is a senior policy analyst, researcher, and organizer who is committed to creating and bolstering noncarceral forms of care and restoration. Their research is situated at the intersections of surveillance studies, social welfare, and Black feminist thought with a particular focus on the ways socio-technical systems play a role in critical decision-making processes. Copeland is currently a founding coeditor of the *Abolitionist Perspectives in Social Work Journal*, and works alongside the Cops off Campus Coalition, Defund MPD Coalition, Stop LAPD Spying Coalition, and Downtown Women's Action Coalition.

Jesse M. Hartley is a doctoral student at the University of Houston's Graduate College of Social Work. Her previous community, educational, and professional experience inspires her research, which examines the impact of historical and present-day structural violence, rooted in White supremacy and anti-Blackness. She explores social work's unwillingness to address the field's complicity in upholding and reinforcing White supremacy in educational and social-welfare spaces. Employing interdisciplinary scholarship, Jesse aims to support the agency of marginalized individuals in the interest of disrupting, dismantling, and ultimately abolishing toxic systems and hegemonic social work practices. Jesse believes social workers, particularly those who are White, must continuously question how our actions maintain the dysfunctional status quo of systems of disenfranchisement—including academia. Jesse holds a Bachelor of Psychology from the University of Southern Mississippi, a Master of Clinical Psychology from Mississippi State University, and a Master of Social Work from Tulane University.

Maya Pendleton is from Richmond, Virginia. She currently lives in Washington, DC where she works with the upEND Movement. She has worked with the upEND movement since its inception. Previously, Maya worked with children and youth living in foster care in the DC area. She graduated from George Washington University's School of Public Policy, studying social policy at the intersection of race and gender.

Kristen Weber (she/her) is an adoptee, parent, attorney, policy advocate, qualitative researcher, and justice seeker. Kristen began her career by providing direct legal services to children and youth captured by the family policing and juvenile punishment systems. She went on to design and lead a multi-year, multi-jurisdiction qualitative review project, known as the Institutional Analysis, to analyze laws, policies, and practices that contribute to poor outcomes for Black and LGBTQ+ families caught up in the family policing system. In 2020, she helped create and launch the upEND movement, an effort focused on abolishing the current family policing system and building many different alternatives that will support the safety, care, and healing of children and youth. Kristen continues to focus on legal, policy, communication, and organizing strategies that increase justice and liberation for children and youth. She is a graduate of Berkeley School of Law and Yale University.

Introduction

It Began with an Intent

The forcible separation of Black children from their parents was first used as a means of controlling Black families in the United States over four hundred years ago as a practice of human chattel slavery. This practice of forcibly and involuntary separating Black children from their families was used by the state as a means of maintaining power and control by a system of White supremacy that is foundational to this country's origins. This foundation was firmly established hundreds of years earlier through the philosophy of settler colonialism upon which the United States began. This philosophy required both the removal and dispossession of the Indigenous population from their land, which included the separation of children from their families, and the importation of forced labor to work in and profit from the land. The philosophy of settler colonialism also firmly established the White settler, and thus Whiteness, as the normalized identity of those who would become citizens of the United States—with all others established as the "Other," disposable and exploitable, whether indigenous or enslaved. This legacy of violence and exploitation that began through settler colonialism and continued through human chattel slavery laid the foundation for the violence and exploitation that occurs today through the modern child welfare system.[1]

Historical evidence suggests that the practice of forcibly separating Black children from their parents during chattel slavery was vast and pervasive, with as few as one-third and as many as two-thirds of enslaved children experiencing some form of family separation.[2] Accounts of these separations written by those who were formerly enslaved describe the devastation and profound loss that accompanied these separations, as well as the cruelty underlying this practice. In some accounts, they tell of infants being sold away solely because their crying annoyed their enslaver, while others tell of infants being beaten to death when they impeded the sale of their enslaved mother.[3]

Confronting the Racist Legacy of the American Child Welfare System. Alan J. Dettlaff, Oxford University Press.
© Oxford University Press 2023. DOI: 10.1093/oso/9780197675267.003.0001

The intent of this practice was clear. Separating children from their parents was the cruelest form of punishment enslavers could enact against Black parents, and it was used to terrorize them into subjugation. Enslavers knew the threat of family separation was more powerful than the threat of physical violence and used this threat to force compliance and quell any notion of rebellion. If enslaved parents disobeyed their enslavers, or demonstrated any indication of dissent, family separation was used as a means of punishment, which served to further regulate their behavior. Fundamentally, the destruction of Black families was the defining characteristic of the horrors of human chattel slavery, and it was the mechanism by which the state maintained Black families' subjugation.

A unique characteristic of this time in history is how clear this intent was to all parties. Enslaved parents knew their children could be taken from them at any moment and submitted themselves to other atrocities to maintain their families. Enslavers knew the effectiveness of this threat and employed it when necessary to maintain order and prevent rebellion. The threat was omnipresent and pervasive with no remedy to prevent separation from occurring. Enslaved individuals were solely considered property—a position sanctioned by the United States Supreme Court—and could be bought, sold, or traded at any time, at the whim of their enslaver. Black parents had no recourse against separation from their children because they were not considered human by law, and thus were legally unable to establish a family.

Another unique characteristic of this time is how clearly horrific the practice of forcible family separations was to all who knew of it. The pain and horror of a child being separated from their mother and sold away to strangers was so visceral that it became the key tool used by abolitionists to unite others in the antislavery movement. Images of babies being torn from their mother's arms at auction blocks were reproduced again and again in pamphlets and newsletters as a means of demonstrating to the public the atrocities and dehumanization of chattel slavery. Even enslavers knew how horrific this practice was—so much so that they denied it even happened.

Ultimately, these images and stories of children violently torn from their mothers by their enslavers are what brought the horrors of chattel slavery to the public consciousness. The effectiveness of this message was so powerful in the antislavery movement that some Southern states moved to ban the practice of family separation as a means of assuring the public they were making necessary reforms, while still maintaining the underlying architecture of the institution. Yet, during hearings for the Thirteenth Amendment to the United States Constitution, it was clear the horrors of family separations had moved the state to this point. The separation of children from their parents was a moral and societal failure and could only be ended through abolition of the system that enabled it.

Following the abolition of slavery through passage of the Thirteenth Amendment in 1865, laws and policies, as well as government systems to implement these policies, were formed with the specific intent of solidifying the White supremacy that was now threatened by abolition. Specifically, laws and policies were created to reinforce inequity and maintain social control through the continued subjugation of Black people.

Beginning in 1865, strict laws referred to as Black codes were passed to severely limit the freedoms of Black people outside a system of enslavement. Black codes denied voting rights, prohibited interracial relationships, restricted where Black people lived, and restricted employment for the purpose of preventing wealth accumulation. Violation of any of these codes came with large fines as a further means of preventing wealth. Black codes also made it a crime for Black people to be unemployed and turned crimes that were formerly misdemeanors into felonies when they were committed by Black people. This aspect of the codes was specifically designed to result in mass incarceration of the formerly enslaved for the purpose of recreating a system of enslaved labor through convict leasing. Black codes also allowed the forced apprenticeship, or indentured servitude, of Black children against their parents' will if those parents were deemed unfit or unable to care for their children. Thus, through criminalization and incarceration, convict leasing, and indentured servitude, Black children and adults continued to be enslaved for the exploitation of Black labor necessary for capitalist accumulation.

The intentional subjugation of Black Americans continued to be reinforced by the state through subsequent Supreme Court decisions and legislation that followed. The Supreme Court's *Plessy vs. Ferguson* decision of 1896 affirmed the constitutionality of racial segregation, legally maintaining the segregation that began through the Black Codes. Following this decision, Jim Crow Laws were passed across the country that not only cemented the restrictions in the Black Codes, but also mandated segregation in businesses, schools, and all public spaces, and in many states simply denied access to certain public spaces for Black people. Jim Crow Laws also significantly limited where Black people lived, often restricting them to neighborhoods with inferior schools and other public services.

The accumulated effects of this state-sanctioned subjugation were not only intentional—they have worked to achieve their intended purpose. From the Black Codes that immediately followed the abolition of slavery to the Jim Crow Laws that were fully upheld as constitutional through 1964, the lasting consequences of these laws include racial residential segregation; an increasing wealth gap; unequal access to quality education, housing, employment, and health care; and a system of policing and punishment that disproportionately surveils and incarcerates Black Americans. Today, significant racial disparities exist across nearly all measures of social functioning and political power including income, employment, educational attainment, home ownership, and wealth. Thus, although constitutionally protected oppression ended through passage of the Civil Rights Act in 1964, the intended effects of this oppression—the maintenance of White power and the subjugation of Black Americans—were achieved and endure.

It is within the context of the need to protect White supremacy that the origins of the modern child welfare system emerged. Since its earliest origins, the child welfare system has been designed to maintain the superiority of White Americans while maintaining the oppression of Black Americans by first excluding Black children from services during the late 1800s and early 1900s when services focused largely on poverty relief, and later through intentional over-inclusion when services shifted to surveillance and separation of families due to challenges they faced resulting from poverty in the 1960s. Today, more than half of all Black children in America are investigated by child welfare authorities,[4] and Black children are forcibly and involuntarily separated from their parents at rates nearly double those of White children.[5] In some states, Black children are forcibly separated from their families at rates more than three times those of White children.[6] Thus, while the history of separating Black families in the United States began during chattel slavery as a means of maintaining their oppression, the oppression of Black families is now maintained by a vast government system of social control that knowingly inflicts harm on Black families through the same act of forcible family separation—an intervention the state refers to in language devoid of trauma as "removal." While the system purports these separations are based on the need for protection, the outcome is the same—the subjugation of Black families at the hands of the state for the purpose of maintaining White power.

Just as the family separations used during slavery led to significant trauma and harm, the harms that result from today's separations at the hands of the state are vast and last across generations. An abundance of research shows that the act of forcibly separating children from their parents results in significant and lifelong trauma, regardless of how long the separation lasts. This is true when parents are incarcerated, when children are separated from their parents by immigration authorities, and when children are forcibly taken by state child welfare systems.[7] Following the initial trauma of being seized from their parents, children continue to experience immense harm as they are sent to live with strangers and receive little to no information on whether they will ever be returned home. As a result, children who spend time in foster care experience severe hardships as adults including poverty, houselessness, joblessness, substance use, mental health concerns, and involvement in the criminal punishment system.[8] The state is well aware of these outcomes. And the state is aware these outcomes occur disproportionately for Black children.

The destruction of Black families by the child welfare system also serves as a mechanism to weaken Black communities and weaken their collective political power. The disproportionate separations of Black families at the hands of the state across generations has led to decades of intergenerational trauma and harm that act to maintain their collective oppression. Poverty, houselessness, joblessness, incarceration—each are the outcomes of child welfare intervention—and each are the outcomes that have maintained the oppression of Black Americans in the United States since the abolition of slavery. Thus, just as family separations and the threat of family separation were used to quell any notion of rebellion during the time of their enslavement, family separations are similarly used today to quell an uprising by maintaining the conditions that facilitate Black Americans' oppression while solidifying the continuation of White supremacy.

What distinguishes the family separations of today from those that occurred during chattel slavery is that today's separations occur under a guise of benevolence. Despite the well-documented harms that result to Black children and families through child welfare intervention, the system has largely avoided scrutiny due to a highly coordinated and successful campaign to frame child welfare intervention as not only helpful for families in need, but also a fundamentally indispensable intervention for children who are being harmed. Although this myth is widely held among the public, it is far from the reality of how and with whom the system intervenes.

The reality of child welfare intervention is that less than one fifth of children who are forcibly taken from their parents have experienced any form of physical or sexual harm.[9] Rather than protecting children from harm, the child welfare system forcibly separates hundreds of thousands of children from their families for reasons largely related to racialized poverty. Every year, nearly 70 percent of children who enter foster care are seized from their parents due to a vague and expansive category referred to as "neglect,"[10] defined by most states as a failure to provide for basic needs including food, clothing, education, and shelter.[11] The inability to meet these needs is largely due to poverty and related concerns of houselessness and joblessness, which disproportionately impact Black families due to the policies put in place by the state since the abolition of slavery to ensure this would result. The determination of neglect and the need for family separations are then influenced by racialized narratives of poverty based on long-standing racial stereotypes and deep-seated biases that subsequently result in disproportionate separations of Black families.

How and with whom the child welfare system chooses to intervene further demonstrate its purpose. As its patterns of family separations demonstrate, the child welfare system is largely a system that responds to families living in poverty. Yet if the system were intended to assist families living in poverty, it would provide supports in the form of direct financial assistance and other material resources to aid families in meeting their children's needs. Instead, when parents experience poverty and are unable to meet their children's needs, they are held responsible for "neglect" and their children are taken from them. Throughout the modern history of the child welfare system, these parents have been disproportionately Black. This individualization of blame for living in poverty, particularly for Black families living in poverty, both absolves the state from addressing the problem of poverty and maintains the White supremacy from which the child welfare system originated. Rather than taking action to address the disproportionate rates of Black families living in poverty, the state responds to this problem by disproportionately taking away their children and subjecting them to the harm and oppression that result. Thus, rather than aiding Black families living in poverty, child welfare intervention, and the resulting harms, ensures Black families remain in poverty.

The horror of family separation was the defining characteristic of human chattel slavery that both maintained its existence for decades and ultimately led to its abolition. The threat of having a child taken away and sold off on a whim instilled a terror among the enslaved that maintained compliance and prevented a rebellion like no other threat could. And the excruciating pain and grief experienced by thousands of parents whose children were taken from their arms reverberated across communities—if enslaved parents had not experienced the horror of separation themselves, they knew of others who had.

The depth of this horror and the inhumanity of this practice were so strong that they became the catalysts for the abolition movement in the 1850s. Despite all the horrors of slavery—the physical and mental horrors of branding, bondage, flagellation, rape, and other acts of torture, along with the moral horrors of defining humans as property and denying all aspects of freedom—it was the horror of separating babies from their mothers' arms that became the collective moral and spiritual outrage that fueled the abolitionist movement and ultimately, the start of the Civil War.

This moral and spiritual outrage over the cruelty of family separations was felt again in the United States in May 2018 when the administration of President Donald Trump announced a "zero-tolerance" policy intended to expedite criminal prosecution of any unauthorized migrant seeking to enter the United States through its southern border, including those legally seeking asylum.[12] Soon after the policy was announced, it became clear that unauthorized parents traveling with children were being targeted under this policy and separated from their children. Upon separation, children were held in detention facilities while their parents were jailed and criminally prosecuted. Although the Trump administration denied that there was a specific policy to separate families, it became clear through multiple reports that family separations were specifically being used as a punishment against migrating parents and as a means to deter further migration.[13] The administration had even hinted nearly a year prior that it was considering family separations as a deterrent if other measures to curb migration were not successful.[14]

The public response to these separations was immediate and harsh. Media outlets began reporting that children were being held in a series of cages with chain-link fencing. Images were disseminated of young children in overcrowded facilities, sleeping on concrete floors, with only foil blankets to cover them.[15] A viral audio clip was released where sobbing children who had been separated from their parents could be heard screaming "Mami" and "Papa" while guards were overheard making jokes about them.[16] Scholars and activists pointed to the connections between the family separations occurring under the zero-tolerance policy and those that were done during the time of slavery—as well as to other periods in history including Indian boarding schools and Japanese internment camps.[17] Once again, images of babies being torn from their mothers' arms were displayed across media outlets. Dozens of protests were held drawing thousands of people demanding that family separations cease immediately. In June 2018, two months after the zero-tolerance policy was announced and following immense public pressure, Donald Trump signed an executive order halting family separations.[18] In total, nearly three thousand families were separated during the two months this practice was in effect.[19] And although the practice was officially discontinued, public outrage persisted as children remained held in detention facilities and it became clear that the administration lacked any process of reuniting children with their parents.

There is a disconnect in our public consciousness. During the era of human chattel slavery the horror of family separation was known to all. The cruelty of this practice and the grief and trauma that resulted was felt so strongly by all Americans that the practice of family separations became the issue that ultimately led to slavery's abolition. Similar responses to the cruelty and trauma of family separations have occurred throughout our country's history, most recently during the Trump administration's blatantly cruel practice of forcibly separating children from their migrating parents as a means of curbing immigration at the southern border. During this brief period of extensive family separations, the trauma children experienced following separation was so clearly painful and visceral, both legal and medical experts proclaimed the trauma caused to children due to family separation was tantamount to torture.[20] Yet the child welfare system forcibly separates over 200,000 children from their families every year in every state across the country and these separations go largely unnoticed.

Similarly, the use of family separations for the specific purpose of maintaining White supremacy has been clear throughout our history. During the era of slavery, family separations were used both as punishment to force compliance and as a deterrent to quell rebellion. Beyond simply an act of cruelty, the primary purpose of family separations was to maintain the subjugation and enslavement of Black Americans through the cruelest form of punishment their enslavers could employ. Following the abolition of slavery, decades of Black Codes and Jim Crow Laws allowed family separations to continue through the incarceration of Black parents and forced indentured servitude of Black children, both for the purpose of maintaining their oppression and to recreate a system of labor exploitation that prevented any form of wealth accumulation among Black families.

It is not a coincidence that during the same decade that saw the end of Jim Crow Laws through passage of the Civil Rights Act and the expansion of voting rights through the Voting Rights Act, child welfare systems across the country shifted their models of practice from one that focused primarily on poverty relief for White Americans to one that focused on surveillance, investigation, and separation of families living in poverty. This shift in focus, bolstered by the rapidly expanding use of foster care as a response to children living in poverty, resulted in a rapid growth of Black children in foster care and the beginning of what the system now refers to as "racial disproportionality," or the overrepresentation of Black children among children in foster care. This phenomenon has existed since the 1960s when the shift in child welfare services occurred.[21]

Today, the oppression of Black Americans is maintained through a vast system of social control with enormous power to surveil, regulate, and punish families. At every stage of child welfare decision-making, Black children are significantly overrepresented due to racist ideologies that reinforce the idea that families must be regulated or made to fit into norms created by those in control of society. The idea of a White, middle-class parenting standard against which all other families are judged has been embedded in modern child welfare policy since the 1960s. Due to these racist policies, as well as explicit and implicit biases among decision-makers, Black children are significantly more likely to be reported to child protection hotlines than White children and significantly more likely to be the subject of a child welfare investigation than White children. In fact, it is estimated that more than half of all Black children in the United States will be the subject of a child welfare investigation by the time they turn eighteen.[22] Once investigated, Black children are significantly more likely than other children to be forcibly separated from their parents and placed in foster care. Once again, the extent of child welfare interference in the lives of Black families is stark. A recent study in California showed that one out of every eight Black children born in the state is seized from their parents by child welfare agents before their eighteenth birthday.[23]

As stated previously, the harm that results from this level of forcible family separation is immense. The very factors that maintain the oppression of Black Americans in the United States—poverty, houselessness, unemployment, low educational attainment, extreme rates of arrest and incarceration—each are the outcomes that result from the trauma of family separation and foster care. Every actor within the child welfare system knows of these outcomes, yet they have done nothing to fundamentally alter their practice of family separations. Thus, today's child welfare system acts as one of the United States' most powerful agents of racial oppression by knowingly and purposely perpetuating the conditions that facilitate this oppression. This has been the purpose of the child welfare system since its earliest origins and remains its purpose today.

What distinguishes the oppression that results from today's family separations from the oppression that resulted from separations during slavery is that it remains largely unknown outside of child welfare circles. For decades, the child welfare system has hidden behind a cloak of benevolence, masquerading as a system needed to protect children at risk of serious harm. Media depictions of extremely rare cases of serious harm have led a public to believe these are the cases wherein child welfare systems are regularly intervening, when in reality child welfare systems are surveilling and terrorizing poor Black families solely because they are poor. The harm that results to hundreds of thousands of children as a direct consequence of family separation is hidden by "success stories" propped up by both the system and the media, where we are fooled into believing that foster care "saved" these few young people who have now gone on to experience success. What we don't see are the thousands of children who exit foster care directly to homelessness, the thousands of former foster children who are forced to engage in sex work and petty crime to survive, and the thousands of former foster children now in prison.

The harmful and racist outcomes produced by the child welfare system demand that we ask critical questions. Can we continue to condone the forcible separation of Black children from their families given all we know of the harm that results? Can we continue to ignore the history of family separations in this country and the trauma this practice continues to produce? Eliminating the harm and oppression that result from child welfare intervention will only be realized when the forcible separation of children from their families is no longer viewed as an acceptable practice in a society that truly values children. Given the history of family separation in the United States, we must begin to consider the consequences of state-sanctioned separation of Black children from their parents in a society plagued with racist violence and the pervasive inequities that exist across every aspect of our health and social service systems. Further, the practice of forcibly and involuntarily separating children from their families must be understood through the history from which it came, and the trauma that family separation continues to produce must lead to a demand that this practice end.

Following the murders of George Floyd and many others at the hands of the police in 2020, many in this country experienced what has been called a "racial awakening." Although the violence inflicted on Black Americans by the police was known to most Black people, the brutality of the murder of George Floyd captured on video and the resulting protests against police violence led to many Americans having a new understanding of the problem of violence and racism in policing. This awakening led to subsequent calls to defund the police and others calling for complete abolition of policing. What was once a largely unknown movement to abolish prisons and policing due to the harm and oppression they produce had now fully extended into the national consciousness, as well as broadened to include other systems of oppression such as Immigration and Customs Enforcement. Yet child welfare systems were largely left out of these conversations. This cannot continue.

Many will push against including child welfare systems in these conversations. They will point to poverty and other factors outside of child welfare systems as the drivers of Black families' disproportionate involvement in this system. They will perpetuate racist ideas such as "disproportionate need" to explain why Black families should continue to be overinvolved in this system. Others will point to "unintended consequences" of policies such as mandatory reporting laws that disproportionately harm Black families. Yet when a system knows these harmful consequences are occurring, and it continues to operate in ways that cause harm, at what point do we question whether these consequences are unintentional? At what point do we acknowledge that the system was designed to maintain the oppression of poor Black families and is operating exactly as intended? And at what point do we accept that abolition of a harmful oppressive system is the only way to end the harm and oppression it produces?

The harm and oppression inflicted on Black children and families by the child welfare system has been known by the system for decades. In response, the child welfare system has been engaged in an endless cycle of reforms in attempts to quell any concerns that occasionally arise through judicial or legislative reviews. Yet these reforms ultimately stall or fail altogether because they intentionally avoid addressing the underlying problem of child welfare intervention. Reforms have failed to result in meaningful change because they have focused primarily on system improvements, while the foundational practice upon which the child welfare system is built—the forcible and involuntary separation of children from their parents—has remained unchanged. In other words, these efforts have failed because they have focused on improving a harmful system rather than eliminating harm.

Thus, the vision for the future of the child welfare system must be a vision of abolition. The racist origins of family separation and the racist intents upon which the child welfare system is built are so deeply rooted in its policies and structures, they cannot simply be revised or reformed. Rather, they must be eliminated as a means of confronting the racist history of the system and the harms it has produced. Thus, abolition of the child welfare system involves the complete elimination of the existing system, which is built on a model of surveillance and separation, as well as a fundamental reimagining of the ways in which society cares for and supports children, families, and communities. Abolition involves simultaneously dismantling the racist policies and structures that produce harm and building resources and supports designed by families and communities that promote the safety and well-being of children in their homes. Importantly, this does not mean the creation of a new government system or a stronger welfare state—this means the creation of a new society where the concept of welfare does not exist because all families have what they need to thrive. In this way, abolition is not about simply ending the child welfare system, it is about creating a new society where the need for a child welfare system is obsolete.

This may appear radical to some, and it is intended to be. Abolition of harmful systems that perpetuate racial oppression is our only path forward if we are to truly achieve a just and healthy society. As a system and as a society, we have accepted forcible separation and the destruction of families as the only solution for children in need of "protection," while turning a blind eye to the oppression and racial terror that result. But we only accept this for some families. As a system and as a society, we need to ask ourselves—Why do we continue to inflict harm when we could instead provide help and support? What prevents us from providing parents with the resources they need to ensure their children can thrive, instead of separating children from their parents and providing those resources to strangers to raise other parents' children?

In calling for abolition, it is important to acknowledge that there are extreme cases of harm to children that occur in society. It is also important to acknowledge that child welfare agencies are often unable to prevent harm to children—even with their coercive power of family separation—and often this harm occurs to children under their supervision. Recognizing this, abolition seeks to understand why we live in a society where such harm occurs and how we can support the creation of a society where such harm does not occur. Abolition does not mean abandoning the need to protect children. It means building new ways of protecting and supporting families that eliminate coercive systems of surveillance and punishment. This is the work of abolition. And this is the work I hope this book leads you to join.

Confronting the Racist Legacy of the American Child Welfare System is designed to provide an understanding of the harm and oppression that result from the modern child welfare system. Throughout the remainder of this book, I will refer to the child welfare system as the family policing system. This term was coined by two UCLA doctoral students, Victoria Copeland and Brianna Harvey,[24] and I believe it more accurately reflects the roles this system plays in the lives of families, which include surveillance, regulation, and punishment, all roles associated with policing rather than children's welfare.

The issue of intent is an important premise of this book. *Confronting the Racist Legacy of the American Child Welfare System* is designed to demonstrate that the harm and oppression that result from the family policing system is not the result of "unintended consequences" or of factors outside the system itself. Rather, the harm to and oppression of Black children and families is the clear intent of this system and the clearly foreseeable result of the policies that have been put in place over decades. These policies were put in place as intentional means of maintaining the subjugation of Black families and the power of White supremacy by creating the conditions among Black families that facilitate their oppression.

Finally, *Confronting the Racist Legacy of the American Child Welfare System* is designed to demonstrate that the intended outcomes of family separations during the time of human chattel slavery—the subjugation of Black Americans and the maintenance of White supremacy—are the same intended outcomes of the family separations done today through the family policing system. What distinguishes contemporary family separations from those that occurred during slavery is that today's separations occur under a façade of benevolence, a myth that has been perpetuated over decades by those in power that family separations are necessary to "save" the most vulnerable children. As a result, the public ignores or simply fails to recognize the harm that results from this practice. Yet this has not always been the case in our history. The horror and terror associated with family separations during slavery were known to all, so much so that recognition within the public consciousness of the pain and trauma experienced by enslaved Black mothers and their children became the pivotal factor that facilitated slavery's abolition. This collective understanding of the inhuman and barbaric act of separating mothers from their children has moved the nation to act in other times throughout our history as well. What if this shared understanding was understood once again? What if we could see past the mirage of benevolence and recognize family separations for what they truly are—state-directed, state-sponsored terror? This book is dedicated to moving us closer to that reality.

Notes

1. Both Black and Indigenous children have been significantly harmed by the child welfare system and both Black and Indigenous children are overrepresented in the child welfare system. Although the experiences of Black and Indigenous children in the United States, and the racism and oppression they face, are linked due to the history of settler colonialism, the experiences of Black and Indigenous children in the child welfare system, and the reasons for their overrepresentation, vary greatly. This book chooses to focus on the experiences of Black children and families to ensure these experiences are covered thoroughly and are not conflated with the unique issues impacting Indigenous children and families, which warrant their own thorough coverage. For additional resources on the experiences of Indigenous children and families in the child welfare system, see Theresa Rocha Beardall and Frank Edwards, "Abolition, Settler Colonialism, and the Persistent Threat of Indian Child Welfare," *Columbia Journal of Race and Law* 11, no. 3 (July 2021): pp. 533–574, https://doi.org/10.52214/cjrl.v11i3.8744; and Claudette Grinnell Davis, Allison Dunnigan, and Bailey B. Stevens, "Indigenous-centered Racial Disproportionality in American Foster Care: A National Population Study," *Journal of Public Child Welfare* (January 2022), https://doi.org/10.1080/15548732.2021.2022565.

2. Estimates of family separations that occurred during slavery vary, with most conservative estimates suggesting at least one-third of enslaved children experienced family separation; for example, see Michael Tadman, *Speculators and Slaves: Masters, Traders, and Slaves in the Old South* (Madison: University of Wisconsin Press, 1989). However, recent data suggests this may be a gross underestimation; see for example, "Family Separation Among Slaves in America Was Shockingly Prevalent," *The*

Economist, June 18, 2022, https://www.economist.com/interactive/graphic-detail/2022/06/18/slave-trade-family-separation.

3. Heather Andrea Williams, *Help Me To Find My People: The African American Search for Family Lost in Slavery* (Chapel Hill: University of North Carolina Press, 2012).

4. Hyunil Kim, Christopher Wildeman, Melissa Jonson-Reid, and Brett Drake, "Lifetime Prevalence of Investigating Child Maltreatment Among US Children," *American Journal of Public Health* 107, no. 2 (February 2017): pp. 274–280, https://doi.org/10.2105/AJPH.2016.303545.

5. Youngmin Yi, Frank R. Edwards, and Christopher Wildeman, "Cumulative Prevalence of Confirmed Maltreatment and Foster Care Placement for US Children by Race/Ethnicity, 2011–2016," *American Journal of Public Health* 110, no. 5 (May 2020): pp. 704–709, https://doi.org/10.2105/AJPH.2019.305554.

6. Emily Putnam-Hornstein, Eunhye Ahn, John Prindle, Joseph Magruder, Daniel Webster, and Christopher Wildeman, "Cumulative Rates of Child Protection Involvement and Terminations of Parental Rights in a California Birth Cohort, 1999–2017," *American Journal of Public Health* 111, no. 6 (June 2021): pp. 1157–1163, https://doi.org/10.2105/AJPH.2021.306214.

7. Kristina Lovato, Corina Lopez, Leyla Karimli, and Laura S. Abrams, "The Impact of Deportation-Related Family Separations on the Well-Being of Latinx Children and Youth: A Review of the Literature," *Children and Youth Services Review* 95 (December 2018): pp. 109–116, https://doi.org/10.1016/j.childyouth.2018.10.011; Shanta Trivedi, "The Harm of Child Removal," *New York University Review of Law & Social Change* 43 (2019): pp. 523–580, https://scholarworks.law.ubalt.edu/all_fac/1085/; Christopher Wildeman, Alyssa W. Goldman, and Kristen Turney, "Parental Incarceration and Child Health in the United States," *Epidemiologic Reviews* 40, no. 1 (2018): pp. 146–156, https://doi.org/10.1093/epirev/mxx013.

8. Joseph J. Doyle, Jr. and Anna Aizer, "Economics of Child Protection: Maltreatment, Foster Care, and Intimate Partner Violence," *Annual Review of Economics* 10 (August 2018): pp. 87–108, https://doi.org/10.1146/annurev-economics-080217-053237; Sue D. Hobbs, Daniel Bederian-Gardner, Christin M. Ogle, Sarah Bakanosky, Rachel Narr, and Gail S. Goodman, "Foster Youth and At-Risk Non-Foster Youth: A Propensity Score and Structural Equation Modeling Analysis," *Children and Youth Services Review* 126 (July 2021), https://doi.org/10.1016/j.childyouth.2021.106034; Peter J. Pecora, Jason Williams, Ronald C. Kessler, A. Chris Downs, Kirk O'Brien, Eva Hiripi, and Sarah Morello, *Assessing the Effects of Foster Care: Early Results from the Casey National Alumni Study* (Casey Family Programs, December 2003), https://www.casey.org/national-alumni-study/.

9. U.S. Department of Health & Human Services, Children's Bureau, *The AFCARS Report: Preliminary Estimates for FY2020 as of October 04, 2021—No. 28* (Washington, DC: October 4, 2021), https://www.acf.hhs.gov/sites/default/files/documents/cb/afcarsreport28.pdf.

10. U.S. Department of Health & Human Services, Children's Bureau. *The AFCARS Report: Preliminary Estimates for FY2020 as of October 04, 2021—No. 28.*

11. Child Welfare Information Gateway, *Definitions of Child Abuse and Neglect* (U.S. Department of Health and Human Services, Children's Bureau, March 2019), https://www.childwelfare.gov/topics/systemwide/laws-policies/statutes/define/.

12. William A. Kandel, *The Trump Administration's "Zero Tolerance" Immigration Enforcement Policy* (Congressional Research Service, February 2021), https://sgp.fas.org/crs/homesec/R45266.pdf.

13. "Q & A: Trump Administration's 'Zero-Tolerance' Immigration Policy," *Human Rights Watch,* August 16, 2018, https://www.hrw.org/news/2018/08/16/qa-trump-administrations-zero-tolerance-immigration-policy.

14. Julia Edwards Ainsley, "Exclusive: Trump Administration Considering Separating Women, Children at Mexico Border," *Reuters,* March 3, 2017, https://www.reuters.com/article/us-usa-immigration-children-idUSKBN16A2ES.

15. Nomaan Merchant, "Hundreds of Children Wait in Border Patrol Facility in Texas," *Associated Press,* June 18, 2018, https://apnews.com/article/north-america-tx-state-wire-us-news-ap-top-news-border-patrols-9794de32d39d4c6f89fbefaea3780769.

16. Ginger Thompson, "Listen to Children Who've Just Been Separated From Their Parents at the Border," *ProPublica,* June 18, 2018, https://www.propublica.org/article/children-separated-from-parents-border-patrol-cbp-trump-immigration-policy.

17. DeNeen L. Brown, "'Barbaric': America's Cruel History of Separating Children From Their Parents," *The Washington Post,* May 31, 2018, https://www.washingtonpost.com/news/retropolis/wp/2018/05/31/barbaric-americas-cruel-history-of-separating-children-from-their-parents/. For an exceptional overview of the history of family separations in the United States, see Laura Briggs, *Taking Children: A History of American Terror* (Oakland: University of California Press, 2020). For a comprehensive historical account of Indian Boarding Schools, see David Wallace Adams, *Education for Extinction: American Indians and the Boarding School Experience, 1875–1928,* 2nd ed. (Lawrence: University Press of Kansas, 2020). For an exceptional account of Japanese Internment Camps and social workers' role in these camps, see Yoosun Park, *Facilitating Injustice: The Complicity of Social Workers in the Forced Removal and Incarceration of Japanese Americans, 1941–1946* (New York: Oxford University Press, 2020).

18. Kandel, *The Trump Administration's "Zero Tolerance" Immigration Enforcement Policy.*

19. Kandel, *The Trump Administration's "Zero Tolerance" Immigration Enforcement Policy.*

20. Amanda Holpuch, "Trump's Separation of Families Constitutes Torture, Doctors Find," *The Guardian,* February 25, 2020, https://www.theguardian.com/us-news/2020/feb/25/trump-family-separations-children-torture-psychology.

21. See Andrew Billingsley and Jeanne M. Giovannoni, *Children of the Storm: Black Children and American Child Welfare* (New York: Harcourt Brace Jovanovich, 1972).

22. Kim et al., "Lifetime Prevalence of Investigating Child Maltreatment Among US Children."

23. Putnam-Hornstein et al., "Cumulative Rates of Child Protection Involvement and Terminations of Parental Rights in a California Birth Cohort, 1999–2017."

24. Author's conversation with Victoria Copeland and Brianna Harvey, April 12, 2022.

1

Family Separation as Terror

Today's family policing system forcibly separates over 200,000 children from their parents every year. A disproportionate number of these children are Black.[1] Many of these children will never see their families again as their parents' legal rights to them will be permanently severed. Year after year, Black families are destroyed, and year after year this destruction occurs with little public acknowledgment or concern. This normalization of children forcibly separated from their parents at the hands of the state results from a society that has not yet fully reckoned with its complex history of enslavement and genocide—one that reinforces a moral distancing that attempts to diminish the connections between our history and our present. Rather than seeing family separations as part of an enduring legacy of violence against Black families, many have used this moral distancing to justify the family policing system's current use of family separations, leaving its historical connections to enslavement unaddressed or deliberately ignored. Consequently, these separations continue and are often accompanied by violent acts of surveillance and punishment. Our inability to bridge the connections between the violence inflicted on Black families during slavery and the violence inflicted on Black families today by the family policing system allows this violence to continue. Understanding family separations as a continuum rather than a historical artifact is an essential act of naming this violence and working toward its end.

During slavery, White enslavers made use of family separations for several reasons, including the punishment of enslaved people for noncompliance, as well as for acquiring labor or to pay off debts. Although family separation may in some ways appear less violent when compared to the multitude of other terrorizing experiences that occurred on plantations, the violence of family separation has been described by Black people as even more harrowing. The narratives retold by Black families during enslavement show the extent of fear, dread, and sorrow that stemmed from the separation of families, so much so that the threat of separation was frequently used to force compliance of those enslaved by their enslavers. These threats of separation

Confronting the Racist Legacy of the American Child Welfare System. Alan J. Dettlaff, Oxford University Press.
© Oxford University Press 2023. DOI: 10.1093/oso/9780197675267.003.0002

occurred in attempts to force obedience, especially when there was abuse and assault occurring by enslavers and traders. Henry Bibb, who was formerly enslaved, recalled a time in which his wife was sexually assaulted and beaten by a trader who threated to sell his wife and child if she did not submit.[2] These types of threats were frequently used to justify violence and maintain order among those who were brutally enslaved.

For most Black families the threat of separation would become a reality. Once separated, families had to live with the trauma of loss, without the time or ability to outwardly express this grief. Enslavers often punished those who grieved or showed signs of emotional attachment to their children. In her book, *They Were Her Property: White Women as Slave Owners in the American South*, Stephanie Jones-Rogers writes:

> White women separated enslaved mothers from their children and placed their own infants at the breasts of these women. They compelled enslaved women to suckle their white children shortly after these mothers had lost their own. They denied enslaved women the right to publicly express their grief. In short, they perpetuated acts of maternal violence against these enslaved mothers, and the slave market made this violence possible.[3]

Enslavers' regard toward enslaved Black parents ranged from ignoring their grief, to punishing their grief, to using their grief against them for compliance. The individual treatment of the enslaved by their enslavers worked in tandem with and through the slave market to ensure a continuum of violence and terror. For Black mothers, this meant that their humanity was constantly tormented by White enslavers who used their grief and enslaved status against them, with many White enslavers believing Black mothers were not worthy of keeping their children. Martha Griffith Browne, a formerly enslaved woman, shared one of her memories of this in her narrative. She writes:

> Oh, I have often marveled how the white mother, who knows, in such perfection, the binding beauty of maternal love, can look unsympathizingly on, and see the poor black parent torn away from her children. I once saw a white lady, of conceded *refinement*, sitting in the portico of her own house, with her youngest born, a babe of some seven months, dallying on her knee, and she toying with the pretty gold-threads of its silken hair, whilst her husband was in the kitchen, with a whip in his hand, severely lashing a negro

woman, whom he had sold to a trader—lashing her because she refused to go *cheerfully* and leave her infant behind. The poor wretch, as a last resource, fled to her Mistress, and, on her knees, begged her to have her child. "Oh, Mistress," cried the frantic black woman, "ask Master to let me take my baby with me." What think you was the answer of this white mother? "Go away, you impudent wretch, you don't deserve to have your child. It will be better off away from you!" Aye, this was the answer which, accompanied by a derisive sneer, she gave to the heart-stricken black mother.[4]

The agonizing pain that Black families endured through family separation and the grief that followed were described by several enslaved people as unyielding and insurmountable. Mary Prince, a formerly enslaved person also recounted her experiences of grief as a child who was separated from her family, stating:

Oh dear! I cannot bear to think of that day,—it is too much.—It recalls the great grief that filled my heart, and the woeful thoughts that passed to and fro through my mind, whilst listening to the pitiful words of my poor mother, weeping for the loss of her children. I wish I could find words to tell you all I then felt and suffered. The great God above alone knows the thoughts of the poor slaves' heart, and the bitter pains which follow such separations as these. All that we love taken away from us—Oh, it is sad, sad! and sore to be borne!—I got no sleep that night thinking of the morrow . . .[5]

Martha Griffith Browne recalled experiencing this grief as a child as well, writing, "[D]espite the entreaty of Master Ed, the cries of mother, and the feeble supplication of my grandfather, I dared to cast one look behind, and beheld my mother wallowing in the dust, whilst her frantic cries of 'save my child, save my child!' rang with fearful agony in my ears."[6]

Mothers' and children's descriptions of separation often showed there were few adequate words that could reveal the pain of losing one's most intimate family member. Many of the stories shared by enslaved Black people show that this pain and grief was often drawn out, depending on the process by which enslavers allowed those enslaved to be informed of the separations. Often, enslavers would prohibit enslaved people from seeing their families before separation as a means of forcing compliance and maintaining order. Those who were able to see their families off recollected the immense grief that overcame them, grief that endured a lifetime. James Watkins recalled this in his narrative, saying:

> I, of course, sympathised very deeply with my poor mother, particularly as at this time two sisters and a brother of mine were sold by Mr. Ensor; also a cousin, a girl nearly white, and a daughter of my Aunt Comfort. This was a sore trial to my poor mother and aunt, and I thought they would never see through their grief at parting with their children, which proved to be for ever, as they never saw them more.[7]

He added,

> My mother and I were only allowed about half an hour to take leave of those whom we were about to lose forever. I shall never forget the parting as long as I live; I really thought it would have killed my mother, and have no doubt but her health and spirits then received such a shock as she will never re-cover from.[8]

As can be seen from these accounts, the grief experienced by separation, and the shock that came from the violence of being separated, were carried by Black people for their entire lives and for generations thereafter. Many Black families desperate to be reunited with their families found ways to escape the plantation, only to work all day and night to afford to buy the freedom of their family members. Other Black families risked returning to their old planta-tions just to see their parents or children again. Many Black families died trying to escape together or perished trying to reunite with their families. Many families were never to be reunited again.

The stories from enslaved people shed light on the horrors of children and parents, cousins and aunts, and communities being torn apart. These horrors impacted not only the ability of Black people to maintain a sense of familial bonds, but it was also an attempt to break down the power of Black communities. Without familial and community bonds, Black people were assumed to have less chance of communicating with one another and revolting against their enslavers. These efforts to control and manipu-late Black communities continue today with family separations being a key mechanism of this control. Today, Black families continue to live in fear of the state's power of family separation and are left with no sufficient answers when separations occur, just as Martha Browne shared in her recollection of being enslaved:

> There I lay through the remaining hours of the night, wearily thinking of mother and home. "Sold," I murmured. "What is it to be sold? Why was I sold? Why separated from my mother and friends? Why couldn't mother come with me, or I stay with her? I never saw Mr. Peterkin before. Who gave him the right to force me from my good home and kind friends?" These questions would arise in my mind, and, alas! I had no answers for them.[9]

Though circumstances have shifted since the enslavement of Black people, many communities find there are no answers that justify separating families and communities. The insufficient and cavalier answers that the family policing system provides to these questions continue to demonstrate that Black families do not benefit from separation. The purpose of family separation instead has continued to serve those who have power and those who seek economic and social benefit from the system. This is the continuum that remains in the afterlife of slavery.

Narratives of Black Parents and Family Separations

Enslavers were keenly aware of the horrors of family separations. This is precisely why they were done. Forcibly separating children from their parents was the harshest form of discipline enslavers could inflict to demonstrate their dominance and to force compliance. Even the threat of selling one's children away was enough to terrorize an enslaved parent into submission. The horrors of these separations were seen again and again by enslavers and the pain and trauma that resulted from these only served to prove their effectiveness.

While enslavers largely denied that family separations occurred (because they were aware of how these separations appeared), they also created their own counternarratives in attempts to weaken the impact these portrayals might have. These counternarratives also served to relieve their own sense of guilt and responsibility by building on long-standing and firmly established myths about the differences between themselves and the enslaved. In her book, *Help Me To Find My People,* Heather Andrea Williams recounts the story of Thomas Chaplin, a young enslaver who, faced with financial difficulties, was forced to sell ten of his enslaved people to alleviate his debt. The impact of this sale was clear to Thomas, as he wrote in his diary,

> Nothing can be more mortifying and grieving to a man than to select out some of his Negroes to be sold. You know not to whom, or how they will be treated by their new owners. And Negroes that you find no fault with—to separate families, mothers & daughters, brothers & sisters—all to pay for your own extravagances.

While he clearly knew the impact these separations would have on those who were being sold and those who remained behind, after the sale and upon seeing the pain and harm that resulted, he attempted to quell these feelings for himself, writing, "The Negroes at home are quite disconsolate, but this will soon blow over. They may see their children again in time."[10]

This myth of enslaved people simply being able to move past the separation of a child or other loved one was widely disseminated at the time. It arose both as a direct response to tales of family separations, as well as part of a much broader societal narrative that had been crafted over decades to justify and rationalize the forced enslavement and barbarous treatment enslaved people endured.

For many, these ideas originated in the writings of Thomas Jefferson in his justifications for slavery. In these writings, collected in *Notes on the State of Virginia*, published in 1785, decades before the birth of Thomas Chaplin, Jefferson wrote extensively on the inferiority of Black people "in the endowments both of body and mind,"[11] and particularly argued that this inferiority was not solely a consequence of their enslavement but rather the result of inherent differences between Blacks and Whites. Specifically regarding these differences, Jefferson wrote the ideas that would later be echoed by Chaplin—"Their griefs are transient. Those numberless afflictions, which render it doubtful whether heaven has given life to us in mercy or in wrath, are less felt, and sooner forgotten with them. In general, their existence appears to participate more of sensation than reflection."[12]

Decades later, these ideas largely influenced both the perpetuation of human chattel slavery and the ambivalence toward this institution by much of the public who were not directly exposed to the horrors that slavery entailed. In 1858, lawyer and secessionist Thomas R. R. Cobb published *An*

Inquiry into the Law of Negro Slavery in the United States of America, a treatise on the legality of slavery that has since been described as "the culmination of decades of scholarship on pro-slavery thought."[13] In this text, Cobb echoes the sentiments of both Jefferson and Chaplin, minimizing any potential harm that might result from family separations stating,

> His passions and affections are seldom very strong, and are never very lasting. The dance will allay his most poignant grief, and a few days blot out the memory of his most bitter bereavement. His natural affection is not strong, and consequently he is cruel to his own offspring, and suffers little by separation from them.[14]

At the same time, Cobb perpetuates the idea that these separations rarely happen, writing, "The young child is seldom removed from the parent's protection, and beyond doubt, the institution prevents the separation of families, to an extent unknown among the laboring poor of the world."[15]

Beyond Cobb's simultaneous justification and minimization of family separations, *An Inquiry Into the Law of Negro Slavery* served to perpetuate long-standing myths and falsehoods about enslaved individuals as well as enslaved parents. These myths were specifically designed to denigrate and dehumanize enslaved Black people as being fundamentally different from and inferior to White Americans, as well as to justify the need for government intervention, by means of enslavement, to regulate and control their behavior. Of the enslaved, Cobb wrote, "Another striking trait of negro character is lasciviousness. Lust is his strongest passion; and hence, rape is an offence of too frequent occurrence. Fidelity to the marriage relation they do not understand and do not expect, neither in their native country nor in a state of bondage."[16] Of enslaved Black women specifically, he wrote,

> An evil attributed to slavery, and frequently alluded to, is the want of chastity in female slaves, and a corresponding immorality in the white males. To a certain extent this is true; and to the extent that the slave is under the control and subject to the order of the master, the condition of slavery is responsible. Every well-informed person at the South, however, knows that the exercise of such power for such a purpose is almost unknown. The prevalence of the evil is attributable to other causes. The most prominent of these is the natural lewdness of the negro.[17]

In these passages, we see Cobb repeatedly reference the "lasciviousness" and "lewdness" of enslaved Black people, and particularly that of Black women, which was in direct contrast to the moral values of the time. We also see Cobb squarely place the blame for the rape of enslaved women on the women themselves due to their "natural lewdness," thus absolving their White owners of any responsibility.[18] Because of their "lasciviousness," Cobb questions their fidelity to, or even understanding of, the institution of marriage as one that is beyond their capacity. Through these passages, Cobb firmly establishes the enslaved—particularly Black women—as out of control, driven by their lustful desires and potentially dangerous to the White men of America if they are not kept under control. Beyond this, Cobb directly addresses Black parents' inability to raise their children without oversight from their White masters, writing:

> The inability of the slave parents to control and govern their own children from the intervention of another power, the master's, has been considered an evil of this social system. Theoretically it is; practically it is not, for two reasons: first, the master never interferes with but rather encourages such government; it is an aid to him. And, second, unless the child in some way interferes with the comfort or wishes of the parent, the negro has no disposition to control his waywardness or his vices.[19]

Although the culmination of these narratives fulfilled a particular purpose at the time of their writing—to justify Black individuals' continued enslavement and to dispel any concerns about the appropriateness of their enslavement—the ideas contained within these narratives—the "lewdness" of Black individuals, and particularly Black women, their disregard for the marital relationship, their inability to control their children without intervention from their White "master," and their lack of feeling or concern when their children were separated from them—each of these ideas formed the origins of the narratives that were used by the state over the decades that followed to justify intrusive state intervention into the lives of Black families both as a means of regulating their behavior and as "protection" against their influence on White families. Thus, although the denigration of Black parents, and specifically Black mothers, originated during chattel slavery, these narratives and practices have been systematically expanded on and relied upon by the state as a means of maintaining and justifying oppression through to today.

How Family Separations Facilitated
the Abolition Movement

Despite the horrors of human chattel slavery that are apparent to all now, and were apparent to some then, many White Americans held a largely indifferent view toward the institution of slavery and toward the lives of the enslaved in the early 1800s. For some this was a matter of being socialized during a time when Black people were viewed by many as being fundamentally different than them—for many, enslaved people were viewed as property rather than full fellow humans—to the point where they simply did not consider the problematic aspects of the practice. Among others, many were swayed by the narratives of enslavers who commonly described their enslaved people as "happy and contented," as well as decades of constructed narratives that enslaved people simply lacked the same capacity for feelings and emotions that they had. Others, both consciously and not, created false narratives for themselves to avoid thinking of the horrors of the practice or to justify their lack of attention and action against it. Descriptions abound of curious White Americans, who after witnessing the horrors of auction blocks, documented sentiments such as "The [n-----s] don't mind it at all but try their best to show off to the best advantage . . . I did not see a tear in any of their eyes but they everyone seemed in fine spirits and laughing and joking," or "I must say that the slaves did not display as much feeling as I had expected."[20]

Yet despite the indifference that existed among many, there was a growing population who abhorred the existence of slavery and began to organize to see the practice end. The abolitionist movement, led by White abolitionists in the North where slavery had been outlawed since 1804, began to organize in the early 1830s and included prominent figures such as social reformer William Lloyd Garrison and influential writer Harriet Beecher Stowe, as well as formerly enslaved people such as Frederick Douglass. Abolitionists called for the immediate and unconditional end to slavery and cited both the moral and spiritual horrors of slavery in their calls for abolition. Abolitionists' primary strategy to end slavery was through persuasion—by exposing the indifferent public to the horrors of slavery and convincing them of the moral and spiritual rightness of their causes. Thus, in many ways, the abolitionist movement was less a political campaign and more a public relations effort designed to ignite outrage among the public, which could then be used to bring about political change.

One of the primary tools abolitionists relied upon to spread their message was abolitionist literature, which included abolitionist newspapers, magazines, pamphlets, and annual almanacs. This literature was disseminated widely by abolitionist organizations and contained personal narratives, essays, and other forms of reporting, all documenting the horrors of slavery, including the brutal treatment of the enslaved and the various means of torture inflicted on them. Abolitionist literature sought to demonstrate both the inhumanity of slavery and the sin of slavery that allowed this level of brutality to exist. Yet of all these messages, it was the harrowing accounts of family separations—of children being torn from their enslaved mothers' arms—that outraged the public and began to break through the indifference of the time. This was recognized from the earliest days of the movement, as seen in an early essay in *The Anti-Slavery Record*, which knowingly asked, "Do the mothers of our land know that American slavery, both in theory and practice is nothing but a system of *tearing asunder the family ties?*"[21]

As a result of the effectiveness of this message, issue after issue of abolitionist literature contained personal accounts of family separations, counter arguments to pro-slavery narratives about family separations, and direct appeals to action. The 1840 edition of the *American Anti-Slavery Almanac* contained the following:

> One of my neighbors sold to a speculator a negro boy, about 14 years old. It was more than his poor mother could bear. Her reason fled, and she became a perfect *manine*, and had to be kept in close confinement. She would occasionally get out and run off to the neighbors. On one of these occasions she came to my house. With tears rolling down her cheeks, her frame shaking with agony, she would cry out, *'don't you hear him—they are whipping him now, and he is calling for me.*[22]

Many of these accounts were accompanied with graphic illustrations of enslavers tearing children away from their mothers (see Figure 1.1). The text accompanying this image states:

> Children, see those two little boys! see that child under the man's arm! See that poor woman with chains on her wrists, stretching out her hand toward the little babe! She is their MOTHER. The boys are crying. They have seen their dear mother for the last time. See how she tries to reach them. She

Figure 1.1 From *American Anti-Slavery Almanac* 1838. Schomburg Center for Research in Black Culture, Manuscripts, Archives and Rare Books Division, The New York Public Library.

would go after them, but her hands and feet are chained, and that wicked man holds her back. How *he* looks!

Do they take the children away because she was unkind to them, or could not take care of them? No, the man who is driving the boys with a hickory stick is a slaveholder. So he came and paid money to the man who is quietly smoking a cigar, and bought them. The hearts of the mother and children are broken, but the slaveholders pity them not. Do you ask if this is true? Yes; children are torn from their parents, and parents from their children, every day, at the south.[23]

Many of these accounts also included direct appeals to action, as seen in this story from the 1838 edition of the *American Anti-Slavery Almanac*:

In Kentucky there lived a wicked woman, a slaveholder, and a member of the Presbyterian church. One of her slaves was the mother of two children, 7 and 9 years old. The woman sold the mother to another slaveholder, and did not let her know it. When she was seized, she shrieked and cried, and the children cried when they saw their mother torn from them, but the slaveholder did not regard their cries. He chained their mother, and drove her away, where she never saw her children again.

Can slaves be happy, when they are all the time exposed to such cruel separations? There are 600,000 children in the U.S. every moment liable to be torn from their mothers. Children, do you think slavery is right? What do thieves and robbers do? Who is a robber, if the man who takes children from their mothers and sells them is not a robber?

Children, pray for the wicked slaveholder, and for the heart-broken slave. Can you do anything to free the poor slave children, so they may not be torn from their mothers and sold? Yes, you can try to convince all your neighbors and playmates that it is wicked to rob the innocent of liberty. When everybody believes this, there will be no more slaves in the world.[24]

In addition to these accounts of family separations and appeals for direct action, abolitionist writers were also careful to acknowledge and challenge the counterarguments presented by enslavers and other pro-slavery members of society. Many of these arguments addressed the long-standing narrative that enslaved people did not have the capacity to feel the same emotions toward their children as White Americans did. One personal account entitled, "Can Slaves Feel?" stated:

Some years since, when traveling from Halifax, in North Carolina, to Warrenton in the same state, we passed a large drove of slaves on their way to Georgia. Before leaving Halifax, I heard that the drivers had purchased a number of slaves in that vicinity, and started with them that morning, and that we should probably overtake them in an hour or two. Before coming up with the gang, we saw at a distance a colored female, whose appearance and actions attracted my notice. I said to the driver, (who was a slave,) 'What is the matter of that woman, is she crazy?' 'No, massa,' said he, 'I know her, it is _____. Her master sold her two children this morning to the soul-drivers, and she has been following along after them, and I suppose they have driven her back. Don't you think it would make you act like you was crazy, if they should take your children away, and you never see 'em any more!' By this time we had come up with the woman. She seemed quite young. As soon as she recognized the driver, she cried out, 'They've gone! they've gone! The soul-drivers have got them. Master would sell them. I told him I could'nt live without my children. I tried to make him sell me too; but he beat me and drove me off, and I got away and followed after them, and the drivers whipped me back—and I never shall see my children again. Oh! what shall I do!' The poor creature shrieked and tossed her arms about with maniac wildness—and beat her bosom, and literally *cast dust into the air,* as she moved towards the village. At the last glimpse I had of her, she was nearly a quarter of a mile from us, still throwing handfuls of sand around her with the same phrenzied air.[25]

Others included appeals to readers directly challenging the logic that a mother could not care for her child, as well as invoking the spiritual bond of a mother to her child given by God:

[W]e are told these blacks do not care! they sing and dance as before—they are hard and callous to the tender feelings that belong to civilized life. Alas, it is the heart of this nation that is callous! The great God has planted in the heart of the mother an affection for her offspring which floods cannot drown—under the trampling hoofs of oppression it only grows the stronger. The fabric of human society is reared on this very principle . . . . The voice of the whole animate creation cries out against this separation of families, as treason against nature.[26]

While these accounts of the destruction of enslaved families slowly began to shift the public perception toward slavery, it was Harriet Beecher Stowe's *Uncle Tom's Cabin* that ultimately broke through the public apathy and dispelled the carefully constructed myth that enslaved people were unfeeling and lacked human emotions. Published in 1852, after a forty-week serialization in the abolitionist newspaper *The National Era,* the novel *Uncle Tom's Cabin* sold out its first printing almost immediately and became the second-bestselling book of the nineteenth century, only surpassed by the Bible. The book contained many moving stories that depicted the horrors of slavery, but at the heart of the story are Eliza and George Harris, an enslaved couple who learn their infant son Harry has been sold away from them. Rather than allow this to happen, Eliza and George run away with their son to prevent this sale from occurring. This escape features several harrowing sequences of Eliza, George, and Harry on the run from their enslavers, including the widely known escape across the treacherous Ohio River with her enslavers in close pursuit, which was etched in the minds of readers afterward:

A thousand lives seemed to be concentrated in that one moment to Eliza. Her room opened by a side door to the river. She caught her child, and sprang down the steps towards it. The trader caught a full glimpse of her, just as she was disappearing down the bank; and throwing himself from his horse, and calling loudly on Sam and Andy, he was after her like a hound after a deer. In that dizzy moment her feet to her scarce seemed to touch the ground, and a moment brought her to the water's edge. Right on behind they came; and, nerved with strength such as God gives only to the desperate, with one wild cry and flying leap, she vaulted sheer over the turbid current by the shore, on to the raft of ice beyond. It was a desperate leap—impossible to anything but madness and despair; and Haley, Sam, and Andy, instinctively cried out, and lifted up their hands, as she did it.

The huge green fragment of ice on which she alighted pitched and creaked as her weight came on it, but she staid there not a moment. With wild cries and desperate energy she leaped to another and still another cake; stumbling—leaping—slipping—springing upwards again! Her shoes are gone—her stockings cut from her feet—while blood marked every step; but she saw nothing, felt nothing, till dimly, as in a dream, she saw the Ohio side, and a man helping her up the bank.[27]

This passage was later described by author and historian Fergus Bordewich as "The single most memorable passage in the novel, indeed in all nineteenth century literature to readers of the day and one that inspired countless previously neutral Americans to embrace the cause of abolitionism."[28] The novel, and particularly its depictions of family separations, had such an impact on turning the previously apathetic public against slavery and fueling the abolition movement it was alleged that President Abraham Lincoln, upon meeting Harriet Beecher Stowe in 1862, stated, "So you're the little woman who wrote the book that made this great war."[29]

Thus, despite all the horrors of human chattel slavery, of which there were many, it was the unthinkable act of seizing a child away from its mother that brought the public to see past the narratives created by enslavers of the unfeeling, unemotional—even compliant—enslaved person. It was the violent act of tearing families apart that exposed the institution of slavery as one that was no longer tenable in a humane society that upheld the family unit and the right to family autonomy as matters of both divine and natural law. Ultimately it was the inhuman act of separating families that humanized the condition of the enslaved and brought about the realization that reform could never be sufficient for an institution that had reached this level of inhumanity—that improvements could never end the violence that had been firmly established as the norm—and that the only way to ensure this violence would never again be perpetrated on another family was complete and total abolition.

The Government Response to Family Separations and the Thirteenth Amendment

On January 1, 1863, President Lincoln issued the Emancipation Proclamation, directed to the ten states remaining in rebellion to the Union, stating, "I do order and declare that all persons held as slaves within said designated States, and parts of States, are, and henceforward shall be free."[30] While this effectively freed nearly all the enslaved, it was not certain the Proclamation would withstand legal challenges post-war, which had not yet been concluded at this point. Thus, an amendment to the Constitution was initiated to ensure the abolition of slavery was permanently enshrined in the Constitution.

As hearings commenced for the Thirteenth Amendment in 1864, it was clear that legislators had been deeply impacted by the widespread accounts of family separations and had every intention of being responsive to the outrage associated with those separations. Over the course of these deliberations, the arguments developed over decades by abolitionists citing both the horrors of family separations and the fundamental right to family integrity, were cited again and again by legislators. Many of these legislators particularly emphasized the fundamental and inalienable rights of family autonomy and family integrity that slavery denied. Representative John Farnsworth of Illinois stated, "What vested rights so high or so sacred as a man's right to himself, to his wife and children, to his liberty, and to the fruits of his own industry? Did not our fathers declare those rights inalienable?"[31] Similarly, Representative John Kasson of Iowa stated,

> There are three great fundamental natural rights of human society which you cannot take away without striking a vital blow at the rights of white men as well as black. They are the rights of a husband to his wife—the marital relation; the right of father to his child—the parental relation; and the right of a man to the personal liberty with which he was endowed by nature and by God, and which the best judicial authorities of England have for a hundred years declared he could not alienate even by his own consent.[32]

In denouncing the cruel deprivation of these rights, Senator Jacob Howard of Michigan delivered a particularly moving speech, stating,

> What is a slave in contemplation of American law, in contemplation of the laws of all the slave States? We know full well; the history of two hundred years teaches us that he had no rights, nor nothing which he could call his own. He had not the right to become a husband or a father in the eye of the law, he had no child, he was not at liberty to indulge the natural affections of the human heart for children, for wife, or even for friend . . . . He stood upon the face of the earth completely isolated from the society in which he happened to be; he was nothing but a chattel, subject to the will of his owner, and unprotected in his rights by the law of the State where he happened to live. His rights, did I say? No, sir, I use inappropriate language. He had no rights; he was an animal, he was property, a chattel.[33]

Other legislators focused particularly on the divine right to family as given by their creator that could not be denied to any human. Senator James Harlan of Iowa stated, "Another incident [of slavery] is the abolition practically of the parental relation, robbing the offspring of the care and attention of his parents, severing a relation which is universally cited as the emblem of the relation sustained by the Creator to the human family."[34] Representative Ebon Ingersol of Illinois expressed his support for the amendment, stating,

> I am in favor of the adoption of this amendment because it will secure to the oppressed slave his natural and God-given rights. I believe that the black man has certain inalienable rights, which are as sacred in the sight of Heaven as those of any other race . . . . He has a right to the endearments and enjoyment of family ties; and no white man has any right to rob him of or infringe upon any of these blessings.[35]

Further, in challenging the idea espoused by some that slavery itself was of divine origin, Representative Thomas Shannon of California stated,

> Who will dare make, in this enlightened age, the assertion that the fruits of slavery are divine? . . . What divinity in whipping women for protesting when their virtue is assailed? What divinity in tearing from the mother's arms the suckling child, and selling them to different and distant owners? Where is there one fruit of this tree that any man will dare to call divine?[36]

Finally, in an impassioned speech to the Senate floor, Senator Henry Wilson of Massachusetts, clearly moved by the horrors of family separations, envisioned the day when the Thirteenth Amendment became law, stating,

> Then, sir, when this amendment to the Constitution shall be consummated the shackle will fall from the limbs of the hapless bondman, and the lash drop from the weary hand of the taskmaster. Then the sharp cry of the agonizing hearts of severed families will cease to vex the weary ear of the nation, and to pierce the ear of Him whose judgments are now avenging the wrongs of centuries. Then the slave mart, pen, and auction-block, with their clanking fetters for human limbs, will disappear from the land they have brutalized . . . . Then the sacred rights of human nature, the hallowed family relations of husband and wife, parent and child, will be protected by the guardian spirit of that law which makes sacred alike the proud homes and lowly cabins of freedom.[37]

The Thirteenth Amendment to the United States Constitution was passed by the Senate in April 1864. After an initial failed attempt and much deliberation, the amendment was passed by the House of Representatives in January 1865. Members of the House openly wept upon its passage and Black spectators, who had previously been unable to attend Congressional sessions, cheered and wept from the galleries. On December 6, 1865, seven months after the end of the Civil War, the amendment was ratified by twenty-seven of the then thirty-six states and became law, stating "Neither slavery nor involuntary servitude, except as a punishment for crime whereof the party shall have been duly convicted, shall exist within the United States, or any place subject to their jurisdiction."[38] Thus, the movement begun decades earlier by an impassioned body of abolitionists saw their hopes realized with a constitutional amendment abolishing the practice of human chattel slavery and along with it, the forcible separation of enslaved families. The movement that began largely as a public relations campaign to raise awareness about the horrors of human chattel slavery, and particularly the horrors of family separations, moved an entire country to recognize these horrors, ultimately leading to a civil war to guarantee freedom for all and to permanently end the practice of state-sanctioned, state-designated family separations.

Yet, as we now understand, just as the Thirteenth Amendment did not end slavery, it also did not end family separations. The power of the White elite, and the overarching foundation of White supremacy that had been firmly established through centuries of government-sanctioned terror and oppression would not allow that. The Thirteenth Amendment, for all that it guaranteed to ensure the emancipation of the formerly enslaved, contained a vast loophole—*except as a punishment for crime*—that allowed an extensive system of laws and statutes, referred to as the Black Codes, to recreate a system of forced, unpaid labor that the abolition of slavery had eliminated. Although the Black Codes governed all aspects of Black lives, their defining feature was a broad set of vagrancy laws that allowed Black people to be arrested for minor infractions and subsequently incarcerated and committed to involuntary labor. Specifically, the Black Codes made it a crime for Black people to be homeless or unemployed, thus criminalizing poverty among a population of formerly enslaved people who had been barred from owning any form of goods or property, and subjecting them to arrest and involuntary labor through a system of convict leasing whereby states leased prisoners in ball and chain to private mines, railways, and plantations—a system later described by journalist Douglas Blackmon as "slavery by another name."[39]

Similarly, the Black Codes allowed endless family separations to continue through the forced apprenticeship of any Black child whose parents were deemed "vagrants" or otherwise "destitute." In certain states, Black codes gave former enslavers first rights to compulsory apprenticeship of Black children, even without parental consent. Although termed as "apprenticeships," these forced placements similarly replicated enslavement—Black children were forced to provide free labor for their captor, faced severe discipline and punishment for failure to comply, and were subject to arrest and incarceration if they attempted to escape. In total, tens of thousands of Black children were forcibly separated from their families and forced into servitude in the years following their supposed emancipation.

Hence, we see the power of White supremacy and a government built on this foundation. As Black Americans attained a level of freedom that could potentially jeopardize the White supremacy upon which the country was founded, the White supremacist government responded in ways to ensure their continued subjugation and oppression. We will see this pattern continue in subsequent chapters. Yet we also see a period in our history where a public was motivated to act. We see a time in our past where the public was motivated by a collective and shared outrage—an outrage against families being systematically torn apart by their government—an outrage that ultimately forced that government to respond. This time in our history can now be viewed as evidence—evidence of what can happen when we realize our collective power, and our collective power demands something better for our families and for our future.

Notes

1. For data on the number of children entering foster care, see U.S. Department of Health & Human Services, Children's Bureau, *The AFCARS Report: Preliminary Estimates for FY2020 as of October 04, 2021—No. 28* (Washington, DC, October 4, 2021), https://www.acf.hhs.gov/sites/default/files/documents/cb/afcarsreport28. pdf. Data on racial disproportionality may be found at Charles Puzzanchera, Moriah Taylor, Wei Kang, and Jason Smith, *Disproportionality Rates for Children of Color in Foster Care Dashboard* (National Council of Juvenile and Family Court Judges, February 28, 2022), https://ncjj.org/AFCARS/Disproportionality_Rates_for_Childr en_of_Color.aspx.
2. Henry Bibb, *Narrative of the Life and Adventures of Henry Bibb, an American Slave* (New York: Published by the Author, 1849), https://docsouth.unc.edu/neh/bibb/ bibb.html.
3. Stephanie E. Jones-Rogers, *They Were Her Property: White Women as Slave Owners in the American South* (New Haven, CT: Yale University Press, 2019), p. 122.
4. Martha Griffith Browne, *Autobiography of a Female Slave* (New York: Redfield, 1857), p. 75, https://docsouth.unc.edu/neh/browne/browne.html.
5. Mary Prince, *The History of Mary Prince, a West Indian Slave* (London: F. Westley and A. H. Davis, Stationers' Hall Court, 1831), p. 3, https://docsouth.unc.edu/neh/prince/ prince.html.
6. Browne, *Autobiography of a Female Slave*, p. 16.
7. James Watkins, *Narrative of the Life of James Watkins, Formerly a "Chattel" in Maryland, U.S.; Containing an Account of His Escape from Slavery, Together with an Appeal on Behalf of Three Millions of Such "Pieces of Property," Still Held Under the Standard of the Eagle* (Bolton: Kenyon and Abbatt, 1852), p. 11, https://docsouth.unc. edu/neh/watkin52/watkin52.html.
8. Watkins, *Narrative of the Life of James Watkins*, p. 12.
9. Browne, *Autobiography of a Female Slave*, p. 21.
10. Heather Andrea Williams, *Help Me To Find My People: The African American Search for Family Lost in Slavery* (Chapel Hill: University of North Carolina Press, 2012), pp. 93, 97.
11. Thomas Jefferson, *Notes On the State of Virginia* (Philadelphia: Pritchard and Hall, 1785), p. 143, https://www.masshist.org/thomasjeffersonpapers/notes/index.php.
12. Jefferson, *Notes On the State of Virginia*, p. 139.
13. Alfred L. Brophy, *University, Court, & Slave: Pro-Slavery Thought in Southern Colleges & Courts & the Coming of Civil War* (New York: Oxford University Press, 2016), p. 228.

14. Thomas R. R. Cobb, *An Inquiry into the Law of Negro Slavery in the United States of America* (Philadelphia: T. & J. W. Johnson & Co., 1858), p. 39.

15. Cobb, *An Inquiry into the Law of Negro Slavery*, p. ccxviii.

16. Cobb, *An Inquiry into the Law of Negro Slavery*, p. 40.

17. Cobb, *An Inquiry into the Law of Negro Slavery*, p. ccxix.

18. For more on the Jezebel, and other, stereotypes and its implications for Black women today, see Carolyn M. West, "Mammy, Sapphire, and Jezebel: Historical Implications of Black Women and Their Implications for Psychotherapy," *Psychotherapy* 32, no. 3 (Fall 1995): pp. 458–466.

19. Cobb, *An Inquiry into the Law of Negro Slavery*, p. ccxx.

20. Original letters as cited in Williams, *Help Me To Find My People*, pp. 106–107. The authors of this chapter have chosen not to use one word present in the original quote but rather have replaced this with [n-----s] so as not to take away from the severity of the original quote.

21. "The Disruption of Family Ties," *The Anti-Slavery Record* 2, no. 3 (March 1836): p. 9.

22. Francis Hawley, "Selling a Mother from Her Child," *American Anti-Slavery Almanac* 1, no. 5 (1840): p. 15.

23. "Separating Parents from Children," *American Anti-Slavery Almanac* 1, no. 3 (1838): p. 16.

24. "Separating Parents from Children," *American Anti-Slavery Almanac* 1, no. 3 (1838): p. 17.

25. Theo. D. Weld, "Can Slaves Feel?" *American Anti-Slavery Almanac* 1, no. 6 (1841): p. 21.

26. "The Disruption of Family Ties," *The Anti-Slavery Record* 2, no. 3 (March 1836): pp. 9–10.

27. Harriet Beecher Stowe, *Uncle Tom's Cabin* (Boston: John P. Jewett & Company, 1852), pp. 94–95.

28. Fergus M. Bordewich, *Bound for Canaan: The Epic Story of the Underground Railroad, America's First Civil Rights Movement* (New York: Amistad, 2006), p. 371.

29. Cindy Weinstein, "Introduction," in *The Cambridge Companion to Harriet Beecher Stowe*, edited by Cindy Weinstein (Cambridge: Cambridge University Press, 2004), p. 1.

30. "Transcript of the Proclamation," National Archives, January 1, 1863, https://www.archives.gov/exhibits/featured-documents/emancipation-proclamation/transcript.html.

31. *Congressional Globe*, 38th Congress, 2nd session, January 10, 1865, p. 200, https://memory.loc.gov/ammem/amlaw/lwcglink.html#anchor38.

32. *Congressional Globe*, 38th Congress, 2nd session, January 10, 1865, p. 193, https://memory.loc.gov/ammem/amlaw/lwcglink.html#anchor38.

33. *Congressional Globe*, 39th Congress, 1st session, January 30, 1866, p. 504, https://memory.loc.gov/ammem/amlaw/lwcglink.html#anchor39.

34. *Congressional Globe*, 38th Congress, 1st session, April 6, 1864, p. 1439, https://memory.loc.gov/ammem/amlaw/lwcglink.html#anchor38.

35. *Congressional Globe,* 38th Congress, 1st session, June 15, 1864, p. 2990, https://mem ory.loc.gov/ammem/amlaw/lwcglink.html#anchor38.

36. *Congressional Globe,* 38th Congress, 1st session, June 14, 1864, p. 2948, https://mem ory.loc.gov/ammem/amlaw/lwcglink.html#anchor38.

37. *Congressional Globe*, 38th Congress, 1st session, March 28, 1864, p. 1324, https://mem ory.loc.gov/ammem/amlaw/lwcglink.html#anchor38.

38. Thirteenth Amendment, Constitution of the United States, https://constitution.congr ess.gov/constitution/amendment-13/.

39. Douglas A. Blackmon, *Slavery by Another Name: The Re-Enslavement of Black Americans from the Civil War to World War II* (New York: Doubleday, 2008).

2

A Racist Foundation

The social conditions of the nineteenth century led to the early beginnings of the modern child welfare system. From the nineteenth to the twentieth century, the United States shifted from a rural, agricultural society to a manufacturing, industrial society, undergoing both industrialization and urbanization. The social makeup of American society also shifted during this time, as the result of a massive wave of immigration. Between 1800 and 1910, millions of immigrants from Eastern and Western Europe migrated to the United States—mostly to northern cities along the East coast. Migrants coming to the United States during this time coincided with a rapidly industrializing society. The Industrial Revolution brought about rapid production that depended on the labor of occupants of these northern cities. Immigrants thereby became the mainstay of the industrial workforce.

Coming to the United States during the Industrial Revolution, these migrants often worked in factories in urban cities. This Industrial Revolution fundamentally shifted economic conditions for workers. Unlike artisans and farmers who could rely on themselves for food and clothing by growing much of what they needed, factory workers were dependent on wages to provide for food, clothing, and shelter. Thus, when migrants came to urban areas, they relied heavily on factory jobs to support their families. Over time, as migrant workers became more dependent on wages, their quality of life lessened. Living conditions were poor for migrants, with many living in crowded tenement homes. Migrants who did work labored for long hours and without extended family networks to help with child care. As a result, many children cared for themselves, or roamed the streets, while their parents worked. The sudden death or illness of migrant workers had many implications for their families, including a significant loss of wages, which could quickly cause a family to become homeless.

Thus, while the rapid industrialization of urban cities created an economic boom, it also relied on a workforce living in precarity. Mass production created an easier, more comfortable life for the upper classes, yet the laborers producing these goods dealt with unsanitary working conditions, crowded

Confronting the Racist Legacy of the American Child Welfare System. Alan J. Dettlaff, Oxford University Press.
© Oxford University Press 2023. DOI: 10.1093/oso/9780197675267.003.0003

neighborhoods, and greater financial insecurity than ever before. Moreover, workers were disposable to employers. The massive wave of immigration and perilous living conditions made it so employers could always find new workers for low cost. No unions existed at the time—thus, employers held all the power. The precarious conditions experienced by adult workers in turn produced conditions that were equally precarious for their children.[1]

With parents working continuously or parents falling ill due to terrible living and working conditions, children were often left alone to fend for themselves. Consequently, the living conditions of poor and working-class people created certain "social ills" that more elite urban dwellers found threatening to their way of life. Elites worried that people living in poverty would commit crimes against them, and they worried that a growing disenfranchised population might soon pose a political threat to the existing social order. Therefore, wealthier residents of northern cities concluded they had to do *something* about the expanding "dangerous class" of people in northern cities.[2] In particular, addressing the increasing number of homeless or unattended children wandering the streets became an urgent need for members of the upper class. In describing this problem in his treatise, *The Dangerous Classes of New York*, Charles Loring Brace wrote:

> Something must be done to meet the increasing crime and poverty among the destitute children of New York . . . [who] hardly seem able to distinguish good and evil . . . .Immigration is pouring in its multitude of poor foreigners, who leave these young outcasts everywhere abandoned in our midst. For the most part, the boys grow up utterly by themselves. No one cares for them, and they care for no one. Some live by begging, by petty pilfering, by bold robbery . . . . They sleep on steps, in cellars, in old barns, and in markets . . . . They cannot read; they do not go to school or attend a church. Many of them have never seen the Bible. Every cunning faculty is intensely stimulated. These boys and girls, it should be remembered, will soon form the great lower class of our city. They will influence elections; they may shape the policy of the city; they will assuredly, if unreclaimed, poison society all around them. They will help to form the great multitude of robbers, thieves, vagrants, and prostitutes who are now such a burden upon the law-respecting community.[3]

As a solution to this, Brace established a private charity, the Children's Aid Society, and created what became known as the Orphan Train Movement.

Brace believed that poor children could be "saved" if they were taken away from their current circumstances and surrounded by new circumstances. Specifically, he wrote,

> [T]he cheapest and most efficacious way of dealing with the "Dangerous Classes" of large cities, is not to punish them, but to prevent their growth; to so throw the influences of education and discipline and religion about the abandoned and destitute youth of our large towns; to so change their material circumstances, and draw them under the influence of the moral and fortunate classes, that they shall grow up as useful producers and members of society, able and inclined to aid it in its progress.[4]

Importantly, Brace believed that these children could assimilate into society and become productive members of it, because although they were immigrants, they were still of European descent. Sending children away from their current environments to live with other White families allowed the wealthy to feel as though they were "saving" children from terrible conditions while also ensuring that immigrant children assimilated into a capitalist society by becoming productive workers. Children who boarded the orphan trains often went to Protestant families living in rural areas, serving similarly to indentured servants, earning their stay through the labor they provided. Rather than change the social conditions that produced poverty, Brace hoped that taking children from their impoverished communities would change the trajectory of their lives.

Thus, between 1854 and 1929, Brace and the Children's Aid Society facilitated the migration of an estimated 200,000 children from New York City and other urban cities to the South, Midwest, and even California. Through the Orphan Train Movement, Brace and the Children's Aid Society relocated these children, separating them from their families, as a solution to the poor living conditions immigrants experienced in the 1900s.[5] Thus, the Orphan Train Movement or "placing out" became the solution to the rampant child poverty that existed in the nineteenth century. Instead of addressing the working conditions working-class people faced that produced perilous living conditions, separating children from their families and communities allowed the wealthy to keep the adult workforce intact while hopefully molding their children into productive members of society.

The concept of "placing children out" is a colonial one, as placing out originated in France and Great Britain. In the 1700s, poor children in France were ordered to go to French colonies in North America. Similarly, the British government sent women and children to serve as additional labor during the colonization of Canada and Australia. Born out of this legacy of colonialism, Brace saw the orphan trains as a solution to the rapidly growing poverty in urban areas—orphan trains were seen as a humane way to handle poor children and the problems they produced. Brace also believed that placing out children would instill in them the values of hard work through the labor they provided throughout the rapidly expanding rural Midwest. In other words, the orphan trains were a way to discipline poor children into becoming productive members of a capitalist society, while also aiding in the spread of capitalism across the entire continent.

Yet, although Brace and the Children's Aid Society argued that they were saving poor children from terrible conditions, the Orphan Train Movement was more about eliminating poor people from society without changing the conditions that made them poor. That is, instead of being focused on how poor living conditions were impacting poor children, the Orphan Train Movement was primarily concerned with how poor people's presence would impact society. Brace referred to poor migrant children as "the dangerous classes," showing his fear of losing control of the growing population of poor children and families in urban areas. Therefore, the orphan trains served dual purposes. They separated "undesirable" members of society by creating an institution specifically for poor families while also serving a capitalist ideology by reinforcing hard work and personal responsibility as a solution to poverty. Importantly, making orphans work for housing and food also reinforced the idea that only those who work are deserving of help.

Intentional Exclusion of Black Children

When the Orphan Train Movement began in 1853, Black children were the property of their enslavers. Thus, the early origins of what would eventually become the "child welfare" system, including the Orphan Train Movement, entirely ignored the needs of Black children because they were not even considered human. In many ways, chattel slavery acted as a de facto "child welfare" system for Black children given that the majority of Black children in the United States were forcibly held within this institution. Further, as noted by W. E. B. DuBois and others, slavery performed certain social welfare functions for Black children,[6] although this was solely for the purpose of capitalist accumulation rather than a concern for children's "welfare." Yet the presence of slavery allowed what would become known as the "child welfare" system to emerge as one solely focused on the needs of White children, a focus that would remain for the next century. As Billingsley and Giovannoni noted in *Children of the Storm*, "The very existence of slavery meant that child welfare institutions could develop in this country without concern for the majority of Black children; this factor alone ensured an inherently racist child welfare system."[7]

Yet, following the abolition of slavery in 1865, Black children continued to be intentionally excluded from the Orphan Train Movement and other "child saving" movements of the time.[8] This was due to both Brace's own views about Black children, as well as the general philosophy of the child-saving movement and where those efforts focused. For Brace, he also understood that the operations of the Children's Aid Society were entirely dependent on funding from wealthy White donors, and he did not want to be viewed as a sympathizer of Black causes, particularly due to the lack of support for Black emancipation among most in the White elite class.[9] He also understood that taking in Black children would largely be unacceptable to most rural White families. However, it was Brace's own racist beliefs that likely influenced the intentional exclusion of Black children from the Children's Aid Society and the Orphan Train Movement. In much of Brace's writings, he referenced the inferiority of certain races, generally believing that White Europeans were superior to those of African descent. As one of Brace's biographers, Stephen O'Connor, states, "nothing explains the scarcity of black children as thoroughly as simple racism, within and outside the CAS."[10]

Yet, as this quote references, this was not a view shared solely within the Children's Aid Society or confined to the Orphan Train Movement. The broader child-saving movement that began in the mid-1800s and included other charitable organizations, as well as the Settlement House Movement led by Jane Addams, focused primarily on providing services to White, European immigrant children with the goal of molding them into future American citizens. Similarly to the Orphan Train Movement although an aspect of the child-saving movement focused on rescuing White children from poverty, the movement was largely one focused on social control and regulation of the poor for the purpose of instilling certain behaviors related to citizenship and autonomy. Thus, while the altruism of these efforts can be debated, the intent was clearly one of providing aid for the purpose of citizen-building among the population of European immigrant children who would become the future adults of the United States.

These charitable efforts did not extend to Black children. In contrast to the hopes of the child savers, Black children were viewed by society as unamenable to these efforts. As sociologist and historian Geoff K. Ward states, "A two-pronged denial of black humanity and democratic standing negated black youth and community claims to rehabilitative ideals. Black youths were rendered unsalvageable and undeserving of citizen-building ambition, while black adults were disempowered in the deliberations of a white-dominated parental state."[11] Thus, Black children were intentionally excluded not only from the earliest formations of what would become known as the "child welfare" system in the United States, but also from related child-saving efforts of the time, because they were deemed wholly unworthy of them and fundamentally incapable of achieving their intended goals.

Instead, Black children in need of aid remained unhoused or were relegated to local almshouses, a loose system of publicly run homes for those who were mentally ill, disabled, or otherwise without means to care for themselves. By all accounts, the almshouses were deplorable facilities, yet this was the only aid available for Black children, as well as for Black adults. Although both private and government-run orphanages eventually replaced the use of almshouses for abandoned or orphaned White children, Black children remained explicitly excluded from these institutions.[12] For example, in 1816, the Orphan Society of Philadelphia was established, "To rescue from ignorance, idleness and vice, destitute, unprotected and helpless children, and to provide for them that support and instruction which may eventually render them valuable members of the community."[13] However, "To be admitted, a boy or girl needed to be white, fatherless, [and] the child of legally married parents."[14]

Continued Separation and Enslavement of Black Children

Unlike immigrant children who were new to the United States, the position of Black children in the country had already been established through chattel slavery. European immigrant children could be saved from their poor parents and become moral, productive citizens through various child-saving movements, including the orphan trains. In contrast, Black children were not seen as deserving of these services, because the role of

Black children in the United States, as defined by slavery, had been to labor for the production of capital. Even after the abolition of slavery the treatment of Black children mirrored the treatment they had received during slavery. Instead of receiving the aid provided to White children for the purpose of citizen-building, poor Black children were regulated by social and racial control.

Following the formal abolition of slavery in the United States, White southerners continued to depend on slavery, or slavery-like institutions, to control both the behavior of Black people and their labor. In addition to controlling the movement of Black people and regulating their relationships, the Black Codes, which were enacted into law in every Southern state in 1865 and 1866, were developed for the purpose of controlling, and continuing to force, Black labor. For Black adults, this meant enslavement through incarceration and the forced labor allowed by the Thirteenth Amendment. For Black children, this meant enslavement through forced "apprenticeships" with White enslavers that mirrored the conditions of slavery and the forced labor it included.

In the period after slavery, orphans were defined as children without parents or children of unwed parents. Formerly enslaved peoples' marriages were not honored, allowing many Black children to assume an orphan status even while having parents. Moreover, White enslavers and others who remained pro-slavery did not believe that Black parents could raise their own children without White supervision. As a result, Southern states passed laws that allowed Black children to enter forced apprenticeship arrangements that recreated the master-slave relationship. For example, in November of 1865, Mississippi passed a law that required sheriffs to identify Black children who were either orphaned or whose parents could not care for them and force them into apprenticeships with White masters or mistresses.[15] In certain states, such as Alabama, these laws even gave former enslavers first rights to compulsory apprenticeship of Black children, even without parental consent.[16]

In Maryland, forced apprenticeships of Black children began immediately upon emancipation on November 1, 1864. Existing law in Maryland prior to emancipation already allowed for the seizure and apprenticeship of any free Black child upon the finding of a judge that it would be "better for the habits and comfort of the child that it should be bound as an apprentice to some white person."[17] Within one day following emancipation, a local marshal, Andrew Stafford, warned his supervisor that former enslavers were "endeavoring to intimidate colored people and compel them to bind their children to them." Former enslavers began flooding courthouses and filing petitions to apprentice Black children under the guise that their parents were unable to properly care for them. Local courts announced publicly that they would give preference to former enslavers when these petitions were made. Within just days after emancipation, former enslavers had captured nearly three thousand formerly enslaved Black children and forced them into apprenticeships. In an effort to advocate for these children, one White citizen wrote to his neighbors:

> On friday there was upwards of hundred young Negroes on the ferry with their old Masters draged away forseble from there parents for the purpose of Having them Bound . . . In the Name of Humanity is there no Redress for these poor ignorant downtrodden wreches—Is this is it not Involinterily Slavery?

Yet despite the advocacy of some, it was clear that local judges were siding with former enslavers, declaring parents unfit with little to no evidence and returning their children to their enslavers. Another White advocate concluded in a letter to local officials,

> The colored people here can take care of their own children and are willing to do it . . . But the people here, or a great many of them, don't seem satisfied unless they have negroes . . . the original owners of slaves cannot do without servants, as they have been used to some one and don't want to pay any person for their labor.

Andrew Stafford, the local marshal, again appealed to his supervisor, stating, "In plain terms, the Rebels here are showing an evident determination to still hold this people in bondage."[18]

In addition to forced apprenticeships, a growing system of incarceration also allowed for the re-enslavement of Black children. The broader child-saving movement that was active during this time also brought about the formation of the juvenile legal system, or what is often referred to as the "juvenile justice" or "juvenile delinquency" system. As part of the efforts of the child savers, the first juvenile court was established in Chicago, Illinois in 1899, and by 1928, all but two states had established judicial systems to address issues of juvenile "delinquency" and juvenile "dependency."[19] Although the early focus of the "juvenile justice" system was similar to the broader goals of the child-saving movement—the assimilation of European immigrant children whose parents were unable to care for them into the dominant White and Christian culture—this changed dramatically during the early- to mid-1900s. Due to the widespread exclusion of Black children from other emerging "child welfare" services, as well as the closure of most almshouses during this time, juvenile delinquency institutions, or "reformatories," became another mechanism for the continued enslavement of Black children. While poor White children were cared for in private or government-run orphanages or other charitable institutions, Black children were sent to state delinquency institutions because they were not allowed entry into these other facilities. This was noted by the New York City Children's Court in 1925, which stated,

> The situation in regard to the inadequate facilities for institutional care of colored delinquent children is an unfortunate one. The Children's Court is confronted almost daily with its inability to deal constructively with colored children under sixteen years of age who are in need of custodial care by reason of the scarcity of institutions willing to accept such children.[20]

Changes to legal definitions of delinquency during this time further exacerbated the rise of Black children now being incarcerated. For example, in New York in 1924, certain behaviors that were once considered by the juvenile court as "neglect" such as truancy, waywardness, or disorderly conduct, were reclassified as "delinquency." Whereas cases formerly considered "neglect" were handled by benevolent, private institutions or charities, cases now considered "delinquency" were subject to incarceration in a juvenile detention facility, resulting in a rapid increase of Black children labeled as "delinquent" and incarcerated.[21] Of the rapid disparities that arose following these changes, Billingsley and Giovannoni wrote,

> That Black children are and were more readily shunted to the less desirable system can be concluded from little thought. Now, as then, because he is Black, the Black child is more likely than the white child to be poor. Because he is poor, he is more likely to be in need of care outside his family. But because he is Black, he is, today as in 1830, less likely to be cared for in the same manner as the white child . . . He is thus more likely to be labeled

a "delinquent" because that is the system of child welfare that is most available to him.[22]

Once incarcerated, Black youth were not excluded from the convict
leasing programs that forced them into labor along with the Black adults
incarcerated under the Black Codes (see Figure 2.1). Black children, often
as young as ten years old, were sold to White plantation owners to pick
cotton or grow sugar—just as they had during chattel slavery—or they were
sold to White-owned private corporations to build railroads or work in
mines. This work was both dangerous, and in many cases, deadly. Further,
according to many scholars, the brutality experienced through the convict leasing system was even greater than the brutality of human chattel
slavery.[23] Historian Geoff Ward states, "Coupled with a disregard for black
humanity and civil rights, the economic principles of convict leasing
reduced black convicts to a form of chattel less valued than the enslaved

Figure 2.1 "Juvenile Convicts at Work in the Fields"—1903. Detroit Publishing
Company photograph collection, Library of Congress Prints and Photographs
Division.

laborers they replaced. Brutal mistreatment, terrible working conditions, and high death rates resulted."[24]

What distinguished the treatment of those subjected to convict leasing from their treatment during slavery was the lack of investment by their former enslaver. Whereas enslavers needed to minimally ensure the ongoing health of their enslaved people to continue to produce labor, incarcerated children and adults were a fully replenishable source of this labor, which made room for the brutality that ensued. This is made clear in this statement of a lessee in 1883, "Before the war we owned the negroes . . . If a man had a good [n-----] he could afford to take care of him; if he was sick get a doctor. He might even put gold plugs in his teeth. But these convicts; we don't own 'em. One dies, get another."[25]

Thus, in the decades following the abolition of slavery, we see a system of White supremacy organized to maintain nearly every aspect of slavery that had been lost through abolition. Whether through forced apprenticeship or incarceration, within days following emancipation, we see Black children forcibly separated from their parents and returned to slavery both for the purpose of benefitting capital and to maintain their subjugation. We also see a system of White supremacy organizing to expand its power through the citizen-building efforts of the child-saving movement that intentionally excluded Black children from these efforts. This would continue through the early 1900s until a series of policy changes coalesced to bring about the modern family policing system and with it, a new means for Black oppression and Black family destruction.

The Philosophy of White Saviorism

The child-saving movement of this time was undergirded by a philosophy of White saviorism that is maintained today in the systems created by the child savers, including the family policing system. According to Anthony Platt, author of *The Child Savers*, the seminal account of this movement, "the child savers viewed themselves as altruists and humanitarians dedicated to rescuing those who were less fortunately placed in the social order."[26] Written in 1969, this characterization of the child savers provides an apt description of the philosophy of White saviorism. White saviorism is the belief that wealthier White people can save those who are less fortunate than them, often with a specific focus on children living in poverty. White saviorism ignores, while simultaneously perpetuating, the oppressive structures and systemic social conditions that lead to both poverty and racism, and rather focuses on "saving" individuals from their circumstances. Importantly, White saviorism also posits that only White people can improve other's lives. That is, White saviorism maintains the conditions that deny people's autonomy and self-determination, constructing a society where only White people possess the means and resources to position themselves as the "helpers."

The Orphan Train Movement, which formed the basis for the modern family policing system, is a clear example of the philosophy of White saviorism. When the Orphan Train Movement began, wealthier White people took poor immigrant and American children from their communities in order to "save" them. The Orphan Train Movement was not concerned with the root causes of the poverty these children were experiencing, and it did nothing to address these causes, thus perpetuating the idea that certain individuals can be saved from their circumstances. Within this philosophy, the individuals became the problem rather than their circumstances.

Because White saviorism is rooted in White supremacy, a main component of White saviorism is assimilation into White dominant culture. Within the Orphan Train Movement, poor children and immigrants were relocated to homes where they could learn "the traditional American values of family, home and hard work."[27] Because these children were of European descent, even though they were immigrants, the child savers believed they could still be assimilated into western, White-dominant culture. In 1854 Brace wrote about the children the movement intended to save, describing them as "mostly the children of foreign parents—poor Irish or German— yet they are in all their peculiar traits distinctively *American*: quick, keen, excitable and inquisitive, with nervous motion, and generally a native type of feature."[28] These children were not quite White within the understanding of that time but they were proximate enough to White to undergo Brace's project of assimilation. Unlike Black children who were excluded from this movement, wealthy White people operating and maintaining the Orphan Train Movement believed that poor and immigrant children could be individually saved from their conditions if only they assimilated into White Protestant culture. As part of this assimilation, these children could also be developed into good workers with the hope of re-entering society, and unlike their parents and other adults around them, contribute to the economy and benefit capital.

As the modern family policing system began to develop in the mid-1900s following the end of the Orphan Train Movement, the system began to include the Black children it had previously excluded. Yet, while the racial makeup of the family policing system changed, its roots in White saviorism did not. Similar to the Orphan Train Movement, today's family policing system routinely and disproportionately separates Black children from their families and communities, while doing nothing to address the root causes of the issues Black communities face. These children are then often placed into White foster homes. The same idea that children can be saved through assimilation into White dominant culture exists. Further, within the family policing system, Black foster and adoptive parents are routinely marginalized and discriminated against, reinforcing the ideology of White saviorism— only White people can and should help children. Thus, when viewed through the White gaze, the family policing system is able to perpetuate the myth that it is a benevolent helping system. White people look at the system and feel compassion for the poor Black children it is saving, while also being grateful a system such as this exists.

Thus, the model of the modern family policing system, as it was during the Orphan Train Movement, serves the purpose of reinforcing the idea that individuals are the cause of their hardships, as opposed to the systemic reasons that create poverty, houselessness, and other scarcities that are a product of capitalism. The family policing system exists to both maintain poverty and to maintain society's acceptance of poverty. These ideas will be further explored in the following chapters.

Notes

1. Stephen O'Connor, *Orphan Trains: The Story of Charles Loring Brace and the Children He Saved and Failed* (Chicago: University of Chicago Press, 2001).
2. Charles Loring Brace, *The Dangerous Classes of New York, and Twenty Years' Work Among Them* (New York: Wynkoop & Hallenbeck, 1872), p. i, https://archive.org/details/dangerousclasses00bracuoft.
3. Brace, *The Dangerous Classes of New York*, pp. 90–92.
4. Brace, *The Dangerous Classes of New York*, pp. ii–iii.
5. O'Connor, *Orphan Trains*.

6. Andrew Billingsley and Jeanne M. Giovannoni, *Children of the Storm: Black Children and American Child Welfare* (New York: Harcourt, Brace, Jovanovich, 1972); W. E. B. DuBois, *Black Reconstruction in America 1860–1880* (New York: The Free Press, 1935).

7. Billingsley and Giovannoni, *Children of the Storm*, p. 24.

8. For more on the child-saving movement, see Anthony M. Platt, *The Child Savers: The Invention of Delinquency* (Chicago: University of Chicago Press, 1969).

9. O'Connor, *Orphan Trains*.

10. O'Connor, *Orphan Trains*, p. 211.

11. Geoff K. Ward, *The Black Child-Savers: Racial Democracy and Juvenile Justice* (Chicago: University of Chicago Press, 2012), p. 10.

12. Billingsley and Giovannoni, *Children of the Storm*.

13. "Constitution of the Philadelphia Orphan Society: With Rules for the Regulation of the Board of Managers and the Asylum" (Philadelphia, 1845), https://archive.org/details/constitutionofph00orph/page/n1/mode/2up.

14. "Orphan Society of Philadelphia Records" (The Historical Society of Pennsylvania, 2003), p. 3, https://hsp.org/sites/default/files/legacy_files/migrated/orphansocietyfin dingaid.pdf.

15. "Black Codes of Mississippi, 1865," Thirteen, accessed October 21, 2022, https://www.thirteen.org/wnet/slavery/experience/legal/docs6.html.

16. W. E. B. DuBois, *Black Reconstruction in America*.

17. Otho Scott and Hiram M'Cullough, compilers, *The Maryland Code: Public General Laws and Public Local Laws* (Baltimore: John Murphy, 1860), p. 38, https://msa.maryl and.gov/megafile/msa/speccol/sc2900/sc2908/000001/000145/html/index.html.

18. For more on the forced apprenticeships of Black children following slavery, including more from the texts of the letters cited in this chapter, see Herbert G. Gutman, *The Black Family in Slavery and Freedom, 1750–1925* (New York: Vintage, 1977), pp. 402–412.

19. Platt, *The Child Savers*.

20. Joint Committee on Negro Child Study in New York City, *A Study of Delinquent and Neglected Negro Children before the New York City Children's Court, 1925* (New York: Joint Committee on Negro Child Study in New York City in Cooperation with the Department of Research of the National Urban League and the Women's City Club of New York, 1927), p. 1, http://name.umdl.umich.edu/ABL6603.0001.001.

21. Michaela Christy Simmons, "Becoming Wards of the State: Race, Crime, and Childhood in the Struggle for Foster Care Integration, 1920s to 1960s," *American Sociological Review* 85, no. 2 (2020): pp. 199–222, https://doi.org/10.1177/000312242 0911062.

22. Billingsley and Giovannoni, *Children of the Storm*, pp. 32–33.

23. See, for example, Mark Colvin, *Penitentiaries, Reformatories, and Chain Gangs: Social Theory and the History of Punishment in Nineteenth-Century America* (New York: St. Martin's Press, 1997); and David M. Oshinsky, *Worse Than Slavery: Parchman Farm and the Ordeal of Jim Crow Justice* (New York: Simon & Schuster, 1999).

24. Ward, *The Black Child-Savers*, p. 68.

25. Leon F. Litwack, *Trouble In Mind: Black Southerners in the Age of Jim Crow* (New York: Alfred A. Knopf, 1998), p. 273. The authors of this chapter have chosen not to use one word present in the original quote but rather have replaced this word with [n-----] so as not to take away from the severity of the original quote.

26. Platt, *The Child Savers*, p. 3.

27. Malgorzata Gajda-Laszewska, "Securing Homes: Orphan Trains as a Way of Curing Ills of the Late 19th Century America," *Kultura Popularna* 4, no. 58 (2018): pp. 29–30.

28. Charles Loring Brace, "Walks Among the New York Poor," *New York Daily Times*, March 21, 1854, p. 2, https://www.nytimes.com/1854/03/21/archives/walks-among-the-newyork-poor.html?searchResultPosition=2.

3

A Racist Transformation

When Welfare Was White

At the turn of the nineteenth century, the Progressives—a group of White middle-class women that included many of those involved in the child-saving movement—entered the political arena with a gender-focused platform aimed at upholding the sanctity of Anglo-Saxon motherhood and "uplifting" those not currently meeting the values and standards of Whiteness. "What women must do . . . is to survey their national situation, not from the narrow point of view of reforming the surface morals of their countrymen, but from the stand-point of experts in race improvement"[1] noted one White reformer, while others proposed policies to "safeguard the race."[2] Considering the sociopolitical context of the early 1900s, which included postemancipation indentured servitude for Black children, the Jim Crow regime, and as Ida B. Wells-Barnett concluded, public lynchings as resistance to any Black progress, it was clear which *race* was to be protected. For White supremacy, and White womanhood, to reign supreme, there needed to be an Other—and Black women were forced into this position.

Challenging existing public relief and private charity models, the Progressives advocated for state-sponsored social insurance that would preserve the role of motherhood in the home for those deemed "deserving." In this context, the "deserving poor" were those who could not be individually blamed for their poverty, but rather this poverty was outside their control. Much like the architects of modern-day welfare, aid for these mothers came with conditions that would not impact their White middle-class womanhood but would create a precedent for governmental control and policing of poor and non-White mothers. These regulations ultimately "brought motherhood under surveillance, as juvenile courts, local governments, and relief agencies investigated home conditions and women's morality."[3] Even though Black mothers were excluded during the early years of aid, as reformers believed only European immigrant women could be properly assimilated and "Americanized," these White-led reform regulations laid a foundation

Confronting the Racist Legacy of the American Child Welfare System. Alan J. Dettlaff, Oxford University Press.
© Oxford University Press 2023. DOI: 10.1093/oso/9780197675267.003.0004

that would later harm and destroy Black families. Holding positions of power as social workers, welfare administrators, and health officers, these reformers became the judges of morality and arbitrators of eligibility for those outside their race and class.

The Progressives' political advocacy was supported by the 1909 White House Conference on the Care of Dependent Children held to address the estimated 93,000 children in orphanages and 50,000 children in foster homes, most of whom were White and in these placements due to extreme poverty resulting from the death or disability of their father.[4] President Theodore Roosevelt, in his message to Congress that accompanied the conference transcript stated:

> Home life is the highest and finest product of civilization. Children should not be deprived of it except for urgent and compelling reasons. Surely poverty alone should not disrupt the home. Parents of good character suffering from temporary misfortune, and above all deserving mothers fairly well able to work but deprived of the support of the normal breadwinner, should be given such aid as may be necessary to maintain suitable homes for the rearing of their children. The widowed or deserted mother, if a good woman, willing to work and to do her best, should ordinarily be helped in such a fashion as will enable her to bring up her children herself in their natural home.[5]

Concurrently, Roosevelt was leading an obsessive campaign to increase the birth rates of "native white stock" declaring "unless the average woman, capable of having children, has four, the race will not go forward."[6] Using the alarmist term "race suicide" popular with eugenicists and writing, "there are communities which it would be to the interest of the world to have die out,"[7] it should be clear his concern was specifically with White mothers. During this era, Black women and children were either intentionally excluded from this social "progress" or their less-than-human status in the eyes of Whites did not even rise to the level of "worthy versus unworthy."

Declaring existing types of aid such as almshouses "an unqualified evil" that "should be forbidden everywhere by law,"[8] the sentiments expressed by the President and roughly 150 attendees (only two of whom were Black) echoed prevailing beliefs that moral character must be a foundational standard of eligibility for aid and that keeping White children in their home with their mothers benefited society. "Except in unusual circumstances, the home should not be broken up for reasons of poverty, but only for considerations of inefficiency or immorality" was noted in a summary of the conference that was unanimously accepted by those in attendance.[9] A former settlement worker turned journalist wrote, "Every year thousands of American children are torn from their mothers to be given to strangers. Not because those mothers are bad. Only because, through no fault of their own, they are poor."[10]

Undergirding the goal of helping these children was, as always, the economic interest of society: "it is actually cheaper in dollars and cents to maintain children in their own home than to support them in institutions and, 'homemade' children cared for by their own mothers, have the best chance of becoming healthy, normal citizens."[11] Illinois and Missouri took the lead in establishing Mothers' Pension (also called Widows' Pension and Mothers' Aid) and by 1935, all but two states had adopted legislation that provided financial relief for mothers. Payers of state taxes, from which the funds were mostly drawn, were appeased by the notion of an "elite" program only available to those considered "deserving."[12] Widows were the primary recipients of aid, but states ultimately broadened their scope to any mother with dependent children.

To ensure the program remained only for those deemed "deserving," what became known as "suitable home" requirements were an intentional effort by states to ensure aid was only provided to families who demonstrated "moral fitness."[13] Vague or nonexistent definitions of fitness provided caseworkers with wide discretion. As political scientist Gwendolyn Mink noted:

> Discretion meant, for example, that black mothers, barred from eligibility in some southern states, were elsewhere denied entitlement by policy managers. Further, both law and discretion invited pension agencies to police their clients regularly to enforce fitness: evidence of smoking, lack of church attendance, poor hygiene, male boarders, or faulty budgeting could result in withdrawal of a mother's allowance.[14]

Echoing the rhetoric of the reform movement, worthiness continued to be rooted in White middle classness and morality. Given that in 1931, some 96 percent of the almost 47,000 recipients of Mother's Pensions were White while only 3 percent were Black, there was no question who was deemed worthy of support. North Carolina, the only Southern state that provided such aid, supported only one Black family.[15]As Mink further stated, "For mothers who did not meet the criteria of Anglo-Saxon morality, denial of pensions represented a form of political eugenics."[16]

Prior to 1935, aid through Mother's Pensions was provided solely at the state level. However, bolstered by the economic downturn of the Great Depression and movement toward more progressive public aid, passage of the 1935 Social Security Act (SSA) marked the federal government's first entry into providing cash assistance to those living in poverty. Aid to Dependent Children (ADC), which was later renamed Aid to Families with Dependent Children (AFDC) in 1962, was created to:

> Prevent the disruption of families on the ground of poverty alone and to enable the mother to stay at home and devote herself to housekeeping and the care of her children, releasing her from the inadequacies of the old type of poor relief and the uncertainties of private charity. The assurance of a definite amount of aid, not subject to change from week to week or month to month unless conditions in the family change, is one of the chief advantages of this form of assistance.[17]

The formulation of this critical piece of legislation is essential to understanding how welfare policy has been shaped. At this juncture, Congress had the opportunity to end the anti-Black legacy of Mother's Pensions and allow for aid to be viewed in the same universally objective manner as other social insurance policies. Groups such as the National Association for the Advancement of Colored People (NAACP) argued for a more race-neutral administration of ADC knowing the policy as written would be "like a sieve with the holes just big enough for the majority of Negroes to fall through,"[18] but they were silenced by national welfare groups such as the Children's Bureau who advocated for federal aid to be modeled after the racially exclusionary structure of Mother's Pensions. Ultimately, despite objections, Congress aligned with a strong contingency of Southern congressmen who wanted the power to withhold aid in an effort to maintain racial and economic subjugation. Southern congressmen achieved this by insisting upon decentralized regulation of the SSA and through the introduction of bills to exclude domestic and agricultural workers, the primary occupations of Black men and women.

Similar to the state-funded Mother's Pension programs, public support for federal aid was strong primarily because of the intended recipients of this aid. As legal scholar Angela Onwuachi-Willig states, "the American public accepted this early program as a necessary component of its campaign against poverty largely because of the 'deservingness' of its primary beneficiaries—again, pitiable white widows who needed help to properly perform their motherly duties."[19] Thus, when White women were the prominent recipients, aid was viewed more favorably by the public. Social worker and former President of the Children's Bureau, Grace Abbott, believed this widespread adoption was due to recognition that "it is in the public interest to conserve their child-caring functions."[20]

By the late 1940s, however, as more non-White recipients, particularly Black mothers, began to receive assistance, perceptions changed dramatically, and welfare came under attack. Just as criminality had become conflated with Black men, "welfare dependency" became conflated with Black women. As a result, local and state officials developed ever-changing eligibility standards that targeted Black mothers specifically. While some officials used more racially coded language, others were blatantly anti-Black. For example, a 1943 policy in Louisiana allowed assistance to be taken away during periods when Black women were expected to labor in cotton fields.[21] Other "employable mother" clauses routinely targeted Black women to maintain cheap domestic labor and servitude.[22] A social worker in a 1950s closed session stated,

> [T]he Negro mother has always worked in the past. The grandmother was there to look after the children. Now the mother has quit work. She stays at home and sits on the porch and rocks. Nobody wants to make the children suffer. What they want is for the mother to get out and work.[23]

Others began to perpetuate the idea that Black mothers were choosing to not work in order to receive welfare and would even have additional children as a means of receiving further aid. In 1951, the state welfare director in Georgia, referring specifically to Black mothers, stated, "some of them finding themselves tied down with one child are not averse to adding others as a business proposition."[24]

During the 1950s and 1960s, a multitude of factors led to an increase in the total number of welfare recipients and also widened the racial gap. White widows had become eligible for survivor's benefits under the SSA, but because widows of agricultural and domestic workers were ineligible, Black women were excluded from this aid. The Great Migration to northern and western states, however, gave Black families access to benefits not available in the South, resulting in further Black families accessing aid. Consequently, as the racial makeup of welfare recipients changed, ADC shifted from a right for deserving White mothers to means-tested welfare that needed to be earned by Black mothers. Caseworkers served as the very embodiment of state-sanctioned policing, establishing Black domestic spaces as "the ultimate scene of surveillance."[25] With Black recipients' morality and sexuality under scrutiny, mothers and their children were required to undergo "rituals of degradation" in exchange for aid,

> often forced to answer questions about their sexual behavior ("When did you last menstruate?"), open their closets to inspection ("Whose pants are those?"), and permit their children to be interrogated ("Do any men visit your mother?"). Unannounced raids, usually after midnight and without the benefit of a warrant, in which a recipient's home is searched for signs of "immoral" activities, have also been part of life on AFDC.[26]

Whereas Black mothers had previously been denied assistance, their entry into this system now afforded the state an opportunity to use the Black family as a site of social control. Thus, for the Black community, access to this system produced a new relationship with the state that became yet another reconfiguration of slave law.

The Louisiana Incident

On November 14, 1960, six-year-old Ruby Bridges became the first Black child to attend an all-White elementary school in New Orleans, Louisiana. Flanked by her parents and federal marshals, young Ruby walked through "jeers, hoots and yells of frantic, race-baiting white mobs."[27] A group of about forty White mothers organized boycotts and were yanking their own children out of school over the mere presence of a Black child. Police called the mothers the "cheerleaders," an alarmingly positive euphemism for a group of rageful vigilantes who even chased and assaulted the two White parents who did not participate in the anti-Black boycott. One "cheerleader" reportedly scoffed at a news reporter for referring to them as peaceful and asked, "What do we have to do, kill someone to get him to call us violent?"[28] Two days later, "rebellious white teenagers absented themselves from school forming roving mobs,"[29] attacking Black individuals, and stabbing one young Black boy.

This rageful backlash against a Black child simply gaining access to a White space not only sparked White supremacist violence at elementary schools and in city streets, but also in the Louisiana legislature. Despite the *Brown v. Board of Education* ruling in 1954, the state of Louisiana, spearheaded by segregationist Governor Jimmie Davis, had defiantly resisted school integration. During the height of the Civil Rights and Black Power movements, Governor Davis called multiple special legislative sessions during which he proposed a series of racially motivated bills, including education-related bills that prohibited "the furnishing of books, supplies, funds or assistance to or the recognition of schools which are integrated or in which both white and colored children are taught" and "empowered the governor to close any school under court order to desegregate."[30] Nine of these bills were designed to punish Black women's reproduction including imposing imprisonment for out-of-wedlock children and legally barring Black women from giving birth in charity hospitals across the state.[31] Sterilization bills were proposed for women who had subsequent children while receiving ADC. Louisiana was not alone in attempts to write eugenics into law as five other states proposed similar legislation. Although these bills did not officially pass in any state, sterilization programs targeting Black women were in operation until the 1970s. Governor Davis appallingly suggested that these mothers "engage in the business of illegitimacy in the same way as a cattleman raises beef."[32]

The legislature's combined focus on preventing school integration while punishing Black mothers, who had just recently gained access to aid previously afforded only to White mothers, made it clear that legislators were using their political power to retaliate against Black progress. Accounts from witnesses to these legislative sessions demonstrate that these laws were specifically aimed at controlling and punishing Black mothers. A White social worker expressed that these actions were understood to be a "tit for tat" while a Black community activist described the mood of legislators as "vindictive" and "clearly intent on targeting African Americans as a way to maintain power over them."[33]

Ultimately, many of these proposed acts were struck down and even deemed unconstitutional, but Acts 251 and 306, which "prohibited families from receiving payments from [ADC] if the mother gave birth out of wedlock, if the mother lived with a man, or if the caseworker considered the mother to be generally 'promiscuous' "[34] were signed into law on July 6, 1960. Over the next few months, roughly 22,500 children were expelled from the welfare rolls in Louisiana. Of this number, 98 percent were Black children.

Assistance could now be stripped away or denied if mothers did not meet certain moral standards. For example, if "the parent or other caretaker recipient of the child lived with a member of the opposite sex without a valid ceremonial marriage" or if the mother "had given birth to an illegitimate child at any time in the past after having been the payee of public assistance of any category at any time in the past, or the mother was found to be illegitimate pregnant," assistance was terminated immediately.[35] In the case of perceived promiscuity, the mother had to prove all illicit relationships had ceased for her eligibility to be reinstated.

The violence of this action drew local and international attention. An editorial in *The New York Times* read: "Louisiana has visited the sins of the fathers upon the children with a vengeance in its cruel law making a home where there is illegitimacy unsuitable for aid to dependent children."[36] News even spread to England, compelling a group of city council women to fly to New Orleans with food—and the intent to adopt the children, which was swiftly dismissed by their mothers.[37] A campaign called "Operation Feed the Children" was launched to provide food and housing. Although the Black male leaders of the Urban League of Greater New Orleans (ULGNO) are credited with starting the campaign, a group of Black mothers who held daily protests at the ULGNO offices had compelled the organization into action.[38]

Meanwhile, pressure from activists forced attention from the Department of Health, Education, and Welfare (HEW), the federal overseers of ADC. On October 1, 1960, the Commissioner of Social Security requested a hearing with the Louisiana Department of Public Welfare, where multiple groups, including the American Civil Liberties Union presented arguments on behalf of the children, stating, "Putting to the side of legal niceties concerning legislative motive, it would be fair to conclude—as has been general concluded publicly—that the Louisiana legislature adopted this measure as a punitive step to deter its Negro citizens from pursuing their goal of equality."[39]

On January 16, 1961, after considering the evidence presented at the hearing, W. L. Mitchell, Commissioner of Social Security, released a memo stating:

> There is reason to suspect that Louisiana's Act 251 was concerned more with controlling illegitimacy and disciplining parents than it was with assuring that children receiving public aid should be raised in suitable homes and wholesome surroundings. In any case, there is little doubt that the effect of the law and perhaps overzealous interpretation and implementation of

it brought immeasurable and unnecessary privation and suffering upon thousands of children who were completely innocent of any wrongdoing and whose condition could not possibly be improved by the denial of aid.[40]

The following day, Arthur Flemming, U.S. Secretary of Health, Education, and Welfare, released his decision on the hearing in what would become known as the "Flemming Rule." In his memorandum, Flemming noted that while other states' suitable home provisions were more "limited in scope," the Louisiana incident demonstrated the need for action. However, instead of challenging the notion of eligibility for services being linked to morality, Flemming argued that if homes were deemed unsuitable, rather than denying aid for those homes, children should be removed from those homes to ensure their protection. Specifically, he wrote:

> where for whatever reason the assistance agency determined that the mother or other relative has not mended her way . . . the result of the Aid to Dependent Children eligibility condition is to "protect" the child by withholding from him the funds necessary for his food and clothing, yet to leave him in the very home conditions found by the state assistance agency to be "unsuitable." *The state owes this protection to all children,* whether or not they are in economic need, but it can scarcely provide that protection even to children within the Aid to Dependent Children category by withholding financial support and even continued social service, yet permit the child to continue to stay in the same environment.

The Flemming Rule thus required that states could no longer deny eligibility for aid due to "unsuitability"; however, states could not simply ignore the needs of children in "unsuitable" homes. Rather, states were required to either provide services to make the home more suitable or remove the child from the home while services were provided. Importantly, there was no requirement to prove that any actual harm to the child was occurring—the home simply had to be deemed unsuitable by a state welfare worker, which allowed enormous discretion among what was nearly an entirely White workforce. Removal required a judicial determination; however, states only needed to demonstrate that remaining in the home was "contrary to the welfare of the child."[41] Further, the Flemming Rule provided, for the first time, federal reimbursement to states to assist in covering the costs of foster care if it was deemed that children needed to be removed from an unsuitable home.

Through this ruling, which was further codified through the Public Welfare Amendments to the Social Security Act in 1962, the federal government both encouraged and financially incentivized states to remove children from their homes for issues largely associated with poverty, or what would later become known as "neglect."

By 1961, 25 percent of children in foster care were Black, although they represented only 10 percent of the general child population. Some 81 percent of these children were in foster care solely because their parents were unmarried or they were deemed to be living in "broken homes."[42] Thus, we begin to see the shift from a system of "welfare" that was once viewed as a benevolent source of support for White families in poverty, to one that began to surveil, regulate, and punish Black families because of their poverty. This would only be exacerbated by the policy decisions that followed.

From Support to Surveillance and Separation

Concurrent with the shift in population of those receiving "welfare" services and the backlash directed toward Black mothers as a result, the concept of "child abuse" was just beginning to emerge in the public consciousness. Prior to the 1960s, apart from a few extreme incidents where children died or were horribly mistreated, in what was deemed at the time "cruelty to children," the public was largely unaware of what would later become known as "child abuse" or of the concept of "child protection." Most efforts that focused on the concept of "child protection" during this period grew from the work of the child-savers, who by this point were largely focused on the rapidly expanding juvenile legal system as a means of regulating the behaviors of youth engaging in "delinquent" activities, as well as "protecting" them from the influences in their families or communities that were contributing to these activities.

This changed in 1962 upon publication of C. Henry Kempe and colleagues' "The Battered-Child Syndrome."[43] Although a small number of studies had been conducted in the 1940s and 1950s by radiologists who identified bone fractures in children that they suspected had been inflicted by parents, they failed to gain much recognition.[44] However, the Kempe study, likely aided by the provocative title and publication in the prestigious *Journal of the American Medical Association* (JAMA), along with a sternly worded editorial that chastised the medical community for its failure to respond to these cases, brought the issue of severe physical harm of children into the public consciousness for the first time. *Newsweek* ran a headline in advance of the article's publication, titled, "When They're Angry . . . " in which the head of the Children's Bureau was quoted as stating, "Since 1959, we've been receiving an increasing number of reports from pediatricians and hospitals about physical abuse of children by their parents. We're now giving the problem of the battered child top priority."[45] The *Time Magazine* story following the article's publication took a much more alarmist approach, stating:

> To many doctors, the incident is becoming distressingly familiar. A child, usually under three, is brought to the office with multiple fractures—often including a fractured skull. The parents express appropriate concern, report the baby fell out of bed, or tumbled down the stairs, or was injured by a playmate. But X rays and experience lead the doctor to a different conclusion: the child has been beaten by his parents. He is suffering from what last week's A.M.A. Journal calls "the battered-child syndrome."[46]

The *Saturday Evening Post* ran a similarly attention-grabbing story, "Parents Who Beat Children: A Tragic Increase in Cases of Child Abuse is Prompting a Hunt for Ways to Detect Sick Adults Who Commit Such Crimes," claiming,

> In the United States generally, at least two children a day are savagely assaulted by their own parents. The most common form of parental abuse is beating. The second is burning . . . . Many are deliberately scalded with whatever happens to be bubbling on the stove . . . . The reports of the injuries read like the case book of a concentration-camp doctor.[47]

The resulting interest resulted in an "explosion" of coverage, both in popular news media and the medical literature, firmly establishing the newly identified issue of "child abuse" as a national concern.[48] In addition to this national interest, the Kempe article put forward two ideas that significantly impacted the policy decisions that would shape the response to "child abuse" over the next several years. First, Kempe clearly put forward the idea of individual pathology among parents, rather than any societal factors, as the cause of "child abuse," writing:

> In some of these published reports the parents, or at least the parent who inflicted the abuse, have been found to be of low intelligence. Often, they are

described as psychopathic or sociopathic characters. Alcoholism, sexual promiscuity, unstable marriages, and minor criminal activities are reportedly common amongst them. They are immature, impulsive, self-centered, hypertensive, and quick to react with poorly controlled aggression.[49]

Although he is quick to follow this by saying that abuse of children "is not confined to people with a psychopathic personality or of borderline socioeconomic status. It also occurs among people with good education and stable financial and social background,"[50] his descriptors of the abusive parent largely comport with long-standing stereotypes of poor Black parents rather than those of middle-class White parents, beginning the process of shaping how this issue would come to be understood over time.

Secondly, both the article and subsequent press clearly put forward the idea that a system of detection needed to be in place to protect children from this abuse. Note that at this time no organized system of "child protection" or "mandatory reporting" existed. Yet the Kempe article brought these issues to the forefront. In their editorial, the JAMA editors stated clearly:

> Because of the magnitude of the problem, consideration should be given to mandatory reporting of suspected cases of parental neglect and assault and of reevaluating state and local laws and regulations regarding the problem. In many instances these will be found to be too lax and to afford inadequate safeguards to the child. In addition, special protective services should be made available for all children.[51]

Similarly, in the *Newsweek* article accompanying the paper, Kempe is quoted as saying:

> One day last November, we had four battered children in our pediatrics ward. Two died in the hospital and one died at home four weeks later. For every child who enters the hospital this badly beaten, there must be hundreds treated by unsuspecting doctors. The battered child syndrome isn't a reportable disease, but it damn well ought to be.[52]

Here, in addition to calling for mandatory reporting, Kempe hypothesizes that for every child discovered with battered-child syndrome, there are "hundreds" more falling through the cracks undetected, furthering the urgency of a systematic mechanism for reporting and "protection."

The response to this was immediate. By 1963, the Children's Bureau published "model statutes" for states to consider as they were developing requirements for the reporting of child abuse.[53] This hugely influential document put forward three important aspects of potential "mandatory reporting" laws. First, in contrast to Kempe's very narrow recommendation that reports "be restricted to the objective findings which can be verified," the Children's Bureau put forth the much broader recommendation that reports be made whenever the reporter has "reasonable cause to suspect" that an injury to a child was not the result of an accident. Secondly, the Children's Bureau recommended an immunity from liability for a report made in good faith, which had often been suggested as the most significant barrier that prevented physicians from making reports.[54] Lastly, and perhaps most significantly, the recommendations included a "Penalty for Violation," stating, "Anyone knowingly and willfully violating the provisions of this Act shall be guilty of a misdemeanor."[55] Each of these recommendations strongly influenced what was to come by significantly broadening the scope of reporting and ensuring the "mandatory" aspect of reporting came with a consequence for failure to report.

In 1963, four states had mandatory reporting laws. By 1965, twenty-one states had enacted mandatory reporting, and by 1967 all fifty states had a mandatory reporting law.[56] Although initially most states limited the requirement of mandatory reporting to physicians or other healthcare providers, this shifted rapidly to states adding professional categories such as social workers and teachers, and ultimately to states adopting a "universal" reporting requirement, requiring any person with knowledge of suspected abuse to make a report. Fueled in part by the escalating panic over child abuse and media portrayals of horribly beaten children, the universal approach to reporting was believed to ensure "appropriate protection for the maximum number of children" by making the requirement to report "an unavoidable duty of all responsible persons with knowledge or suspicion of specific instances of child abuse."[57]

The period between 1963 and 1967 also saw a rapid expansion of what was considered "child abuse" and subject to a report. Although the initial recommendations from the Children's Bureau were limited to "serious physical injury," states such as New Mexico and South Dakota introduced the concept of "malnutrition" as requiring a report as early as 1965; a number of states expanded the reporting of injuries from "physical injury other than by accidental means" to "physical injury as a result of abuse *or neglect*,"[58] requiring the reporting of both intentional and accidental injuries that evidenced some form of parental inattention; and Nebraska, which was unsatisfied with the narrow definition of abuse put forward by the Children's Bureau, created its own definition that extended far beyond physical injuries, defining abuse as:

> Knowingly, intentionally, or negligently causing or permitting a minor child or an incompetent or disabled person to be: (a) placed in a situation that may endanger [the child's] life or health; (b) tortured, cruelly confined, or cruelly punished; (c) deprived of necessary food, clothing, shelter, or care; or (d) left unattended in a motor vehicle, if such minor child is six years of age or younger.[59]

This definition represented the first inclusion in mandatory reporting laws of what would later become known broadly as "neglect"—often defined as a failure to provide for basic needs including food, clothing, education, and shelter—and represented a significant deviation from the original intent of mandatory reporting laws, which focused narrowly on severe physical harm.

The impact of this rapid expansion of mandatory reporting laws, both in numbers and in scope, was immediate. In 1962, prior to most mandatory reporting laws being established, 662 cases of child abuse were reported across forty-eight states and the District of Columbia.[60] By 1967, when mandatory reporting laws were in effect in all fifty states, the number of reported cases had risen to 9,563. By 1968, one year later, the total number of reports had increased to nearly 11,000.[61] In total, between the years of 1962 and 1968, we see not only rapid expansions in the requirement to report "child abuse," but also who is required to report and what behaviors are deemed reportable under the rapidly widening umbrella of "child abuse."

Although it largely goes unrecognized in historical accounts of this expansion, the rapid rise of mandatory reporting during this period cannot be separated from the larger societal context of this time. Beginning with the *Brown v. Board of Education* decision in 1954, the modern civil rights era extended through 1968, culminating with the assassination of Dr. Martin Luther King, Jr. on April 4, 1968, and passage of the Civil Rights Act of 1968 one week later. In addition to the Louisiana Incident and the racist violence directed toward Ruby Bridges, this time in history included some of the most horrific acts of violence and intimidation directed toward Black Americans since the era of slavery, including the lynching of Emmett Till, the blocking of the Little Rock Nine from entering Central High School, the violence directed at the Freedom Riders throughout the South, the blocking of Black students from entering the University of Alabama by Governor George Wallace, the bombing of the 16th Street Baptist Church by the Ku Klux Klan, the assassination of Malcolm X, and the violence enacted on the Selma to Montgomery marchers including the murder of Jimmie Lee Jackson, who was shot to death by state troopers on Bloody Sunday. These acts of violence were undeniably in response to the progress being realized by Black Americans, most notably through the Civil Rights Act of 1964 and the Voting Rights Act of 1965. This violent backlash and the widely held racial animus during this time formed the backdrop to the rapid expansion of mandatory reporting laws and the subsequent explosion of reporting against Black families.

Of particular influence on the racial animus that existed during this time toward Black Americans, and particularly toward Black mothers, was the highly influential paper, *The Negro Family: The Case for National Action*, commonly referred to as the Moynihan Report after its author Daniel Patrick Moynihan, who served as Assistant Secretary of Labor under President Lyndon B. Johnson.[62] Published in March, 1965, at the height of activity to enact mandatory reporting laws and expand definitions of maltreatment, the core of the Moynihan Report argued that the "deterioration of the Negro family,"[63] which he attributed to the rise of families led by Black mothers, would be responsible for the decline of the entire Black population—a decline that could not be prevented by any legal advances such as those the Civil Rights Act hoped to achieve. In his view, this deterioration of the family was the "fundamental source of the weakness of the Negro community at the present time"[64] and the least understood aspect about the Black community among White Americans. In Moynihan's view, this lack of understanding of the real problem impacting Black Americans led to the false idea that these problems could be corrected through legislative changes. Thus, the purpose of this report was to demonstrate the deep-seated problems that existed within Black families, and to argue that real progress for Black Americans would only occur when these deep-seated problems were addressed.

In making this argument—one that undoubtedly had considerable influence on the mandatory reporting laws being enacted at the time—Moynihan began by firmly establishing the White family as the standard of stability and success, writing, "The white family has achieved a high degree of stability and is maintaining that stability. By contrast, the family structure of lower class Negroes is highly unstable, and in many urban centers is approaching complete breakdown."[65] He goes on to provide data to support a series of headlines demonstrating the deficiency of the Black family compared to their White counterparts—"Nearly a Quarter of Urban Negro Marriages Are Dissolved," "Nearly One-Quarter of Negro Births are Now Illegitimate," "Almost One-Fourth of Negro Families Are Headed by Females," and "The Breakdown of the Negro Family Has Led to a Startling Increase in Welfare Dependency."[66] Here, in addition to establishing Black families as inferior, Moynihan continues the growing narrative of Black families on welfare, stating, "The steady expansion of this welfare program [AFDC], as of public assistance programs in general, can be taken as a measure of the steady disintegration of the Negro family structure over the past generation in the United States."[67]

Perhaps most influential and enduring on how White Americans viewed Black families, Moynihan goes on to describe the "tangle of pathology" this "deterioration" of family structure creates, arguing that Black Americans have been "forced into a matriarchal structure which, because it is too out of line with the rest of the American society, seriously retards the progress of the group as a whole."[68] He describes the population of Black mothers as a "disturbed group" that ultimately "will be found to be the principal source of most of the aberrant, inadequate, or antisocial behavior that did not establish, but now serves to perpetuate the cycle of poverty and deprivation."[69] Regarding the children in these homes, Moynihan states, "most Negro youth are in *danger* of being caught up in the tangle of pathology that affects their world," and goes on to describe the various deficits in education, intelligence, and employment among Black children that he believes can only be attributed to the lack of a father presence.[70] He goes on to state, "The combined impact of poverty, failure, and isolation among Negro youth has had the predictable outcome in a disastrous delinquency and crime rate," and, "It is probable that at present, a majority of the crimes against the person, such as rape, murder, and aggravated assault are committed by Negroes."[71] Thus, Moynihan firmly establishes the idea that Black single mothers are responsible for raising Black children, particularly Black boys, in inner-city "ghettos," who will become the criminals and underclass of whom White Americans should be very afraid.

Moynihan concludes his report by specifically stating that the intent of the report was not to provide solutions, but rather to define a problem. The rationale for this, he states, is that there are those "within and without the Government, who do not feel the problem exists, at least in any serious degree."[72] Thus, the intent of the report was to clearly define the problem of "the deterioration of the Negro family" and the need for national action to address this. Although specific policy solutions are not provided, Moynihan closes this report with what was perhaps the most consequential factor for the rapid escalation of mandatory reporting laws that followed and the vast racial disparities in reporting that would soon emerge, stating, "At this point, the present tangle of pathology is capable of perpetuating itself without assistance from the white world."[73] Here Moynihan makes a clarion call to the White child-savers and the need for their intervention, for it is only through their intervention that Black children can be saved from the "tangle of pathology" their "disturbed" Black mothers have brought upon them.

From the earliest data available, it was clear that Black children were disproportionately impacted by mandatory reporting laws. In both 1967 and 1968, Black children and other children of color were reported for "child abuse" at a rate more than three times that of White children. Specifically, Black children represented nearly half of all reports—45.7 percent—by far the largest group of children reported, with White children representing only 38.8 percent of reports.[74] This despite the fact that White children vastly outnumbered Black children in the general population.

For many, the high incidence of reporting of Black children was not unexpected. David Gil, author of the first groundbreaking study of the characteristics of national child abuse reporting during 1967 and 1968, stated, "Such a higher incidence rate among nonwhites is not unexpected in view of the higher incidence among them of socioeconomic deprivation, fatherless homes, and large families, all of which were found in the present study to be strongly associated with child abuse."[75] Across this study, it was clear that poverty, unemployment, low education, single-parenting, and large household sizes were associated with increased rates of abuse, all factors that were more likely to be present in Black families. Yet Gil was very clear in how these factors related to maltreatment, stating plainly, "life in poverty . . . generates stressful experiences, which are likely to become precipitating factors of child abuse."[76] More specifically, in referencing the higher rates of reporting among Black families, he states, "it should be remembered that as a result of centuries of discrimination, non-white ethnic minority status tends to be associated in American society with low educational achievement and low income. The incidence rates of child abuse among these minority groups are likely to reflect this fact."[77]

Here, and throughout his study, Gil clearly argues that the association be-tween poverty and physical abuse are the result of external stressors inflicted upon Black families by the broader society rather than any individual char-acter deficits among Black parents. This was in direct contrast to the ideas put forward by Kempe and others in the medical field who clearly wanted the emerging understanding of child abuse to be seen as one of individual psy-chopathology, which they had the responsibility to "treat," rather than being viewed as a broader societal problem where the solutions fell outside their realm of influence.[78] The increasing body of evidence being collected at the time was, however, clearly beginning to suggest otherwise.

Yet Gil also clearly acknowledged that in addition to the stressors related to poverty that likely contributed to different rates of abuse, differences in reporting rates were also clearly the result of reporting bias, stating, "Some of the observed overrepresentation seems to be a function of discrimina-tory attitudes and practices on the part of reporting sources with respect to minority groups."[79] He further stated, "it may be valid to argue, on the basis of much evidence, that the poor and nonwhites are more likely to be reported for anything they do or fail to do, and that their overrepresenta-tion in cohorts of reported child abuse may be in part a function of this kind of reporting bias."[80] Thus, in addition to the social and environmental stressors that may create risk for certain types of abuse, bias on the part of mandatory reporters was also clearly a factor at play from the earliest days of mandatory reporting.

This also was not unexpected. From early on, critics warned of consequences to poor and minoritized families that would result from the rise in mandatory reporting laws due to both the vagueness inherent in them and the ways in which early descriptions of "abusive parents" were used to label those parents as "deviants." In his article, "The Social Construction of Child Abuse," Richard Gelles stated:

> There is one, as yet unrecognized, theme that runs throughout the study of child abuse, which has not been discussed but which pervades all the work and findings we have to date: child abuse is social deviance. Because child abuse is social deviance, all the cases that make up the data on in-cidence . . . are influenced by the *social process* by which individuals and groups are labeled and designated as deviants.[81]

In describing how this "social process" manifests, he states,

> [W]hen I speak of the social construction of abuse, I mean the process by which: (a) a definition of abuse is constructed; (b) certain judges or "gatekeepers" are selected for applying the definition; (c) the definition is applied by designating the labels "abuse" and "abuser" to particular individuals and families.[82]

Here Gelles identifies two important constructs—first, what is deemed abuse is largely subjective, and second, this determination is made by a "gatekeeper"—a person who observes a behavior or a situation and makes a decision that the behavior or situation meets their subjective idea for what constitutes "abuse." He goes on to describe this as follows:

> [D]eviance is not a property inherent in certain forms of behavior; it is a property conferred upon these forms by audiences which directly or indirectly witness the behavior in question. The conferring of a label requires an audience or labeler, and it requires that a label be successfully applied. The successful application of a label of deviance is dependent on circumstances of the situation and place, the social and personal biographies of the labelers and the "deviant," and the bureaucratically organized activities of agencies of social control.[83]

It is important to recall the societal context in which this "social construction of abuse" is occurring—the understanding of "child abuse" is relatively new, available information suggests this occurs largely among poor and minoritized families, and medical professionals have clearly stated that parents who abuse their children are both psychological and morally deficient. Recall the characteristics that Kempe used to describe the abusive parent—low intelligence, psychopathic, alcoholic, sexually promiscuous, unstable, criminal, immature, self-centered, and aggressive. In other words, for the "gatekeepers,"—White middle-class professionals—parents who abuse their children are fundamentally not like them—they are the "other." It is in this process of labeling that the disproportionate impact on poor and Black families becomes clear:

> In short, if the literature states, or the practitioner's experience has been, that a person who has certain personality traits is likely to abuse his children, and a person with those traits then shows up with an injured child, the practitioner would seem likely to label that person an abuser. Conversely, a

person who arrives with an injured child, but does not fit the stereotype of abuse, may be more likely to avoid the label.[84]

Thus, it is not that abuse was not happening in White, middle-class families—it is that White, middle-class families—and White, middle-class professionals—became the arbiters of who the label of "abuser" was applied to. Other scholars and medical professionals of the time were even more explicit in identifying how this would impact poor minoritized families. In reflecting on the impact of mandatory reporting laws and the "medicalization and legalization of child abuse," Drs. Eli Newberger and Richard Bourne stated:

> Poor and minority families' children will increasingly be the victims of this policy . . . for it is they who preferentially attract the labels "abuse" and "neglect." Affluent families' childhood injuries are more likely to be termed "accidents," where the conceptual model of cause and effect implicit in the name is of an isolated, random event rather than the result of parental fault.[85]

Scholars also commented on the intentions behind this, which were increasingly becoming more transparent. While those within the medical field wanted child abuse to be associated with pathology rather than societal concerns so they could retain a sense of ownership over the problem, those of higher socioeconomic status sought to target and remove a problematic behavior associated with the lower class. As sociologist Stephen Pfohl stated:

> Two characteristics emerge from an examination of these interests. They either have a professional stake in the problem or represent the civic concerns of certain upper-middle class factions. In either case the labellers were socially and politically removed from the abusers, who . . . were characterized as lower class and minority group members. The existence of a wide social distance between those who abuse and those who label, facilitates not only the likelihood of labelling but nullifies any organized resistance to the label by the "deviant" group itself . . . Labelling was generated by powerful medical interests and perpetuated by organized media, professional and uppermiddle class concerns. Its success was enlarged by the relative powerlessness and isolation of abusers, which prevented the possibility of organized resistance to the labelling.[86]

It is here that we see how the social construction of abuse manifested to en-sure that poor Black families were those who became most associated with this problem. Although evidence pointed to the fact that the incidence of abuse was significantly impacted by both poverty and societal racism, it was the families themselves who became the problem rather than these societal concerns through the process of labeling and the gatekeeping that deter-mined who was reported and who was not. Black parents were now firmly identified as the problem and the shift from a system that once provided sup-port to White families living in poverty to one that focused on surveillance and separation of Black families because of poverty was further solidified.

Two "Disparate Entities" Become One

The combined effects of the shift in "welfare" as support for White families to surveillance of Black families, the Flemming Rule's emphasis on family separation as a means of addressing "unsuitability," and the rapid growth of mandatory reporting laws that all occurred amidst the racist turmoil and vi-olence of the 1960s created the perfect storm for the "child welfare" system to begin its transformation from a system that once intentionally excluded Black families for the purpose of maintaining their oppression to one that now intentionally overincluded them to achieve the same purpose. As Black families were stereotyped, demonized, and used as pawns for political agendas, the number of Black children in foster care predictably began to rise in the early 1960s and steadily increased over the next several decades.[87]

The harms inflicted on Black families by the ever-expanding reach of the "child welfare" system were so obvious and egregious to the Black community that the National Association of Black Social Workers (NABSW) took the stage at the 1968 National Conference on Social Welfare and outlined a ten-point position statement. Their demands included the need for "white so-cial workers to involve themselves with solving the problem of white racism" and that the conference "publicly repudiate the current welfare system which serves as a tool of oppression of black people as well as the social workers providing services." They further proclaimed, "We, the Black Social Workers of America, will no longer support social welfare systems and/or programs designed to maintain the unequal participation of the Black community."[88]

Yet this did not deter the family policing system from continuing its trans-formation, which was grounded in the idea of "unequal participation of the

Black community." Rather, the state worked in direct opposition to activists by capitalizing on White opposition to Black progress and reinforcing entrenched stereotypes of Black families. By declaring a "War on Poverty" coinciding with a "War on Crime," the Johnson administration connected gendered and racist misnomers of poverty with crime. Ill-conceived and underfunded antipoverty programs juxtaposed with militaristic funding to fight a nonexistent crime wave were in fact a declaration of war that disproportionality harmed Black families. The structural failures of the "War on Poverty" could now be projected onto an "underclass" of people who should be able to overcome deeply entrenched structural barriers, navigate hyperpolicing of their communities, and simply pull themselves up by their bootstraps. In the 1960s, when Black families were a much smaller percentage of AFDC recipients, the media perpetuated this by increasingly using images of Black people in stories about welfare fraud while stories of the impacts of the recession on the deserving poor featured White people.[89] A poll in the mid-1970s found that 89 percent of Americans believed welfare requirements were not restrictive enough and 86 percent thought "too many people on welfare cheat by getting money they are not entitled to."[90] In congressional records from 1967, legislators made direct connections between recipients of AFDC and the 1965 Watts uprising, with one wondering "how many of those hoodlums . . . came out of homes in which the child did not know the identity of its father and the mother could not have cared less."[91]

It was within this narrative of Black families, and specifically Black mothers, that Congress began the process of considering what would become the Child Abuse Prevention and Treatment Act (CAPTA) of 1974. Spurred by continued awareness and growing concern over the perceived problem of "child abuse," CAPTA represented the first effort by the government to establish a federal requirement for mandatory reporting of child abuse, one that would unite existing state laws and establish a minimum and consistent reporting requirement across all fifty states. CAPTA also represented the key piece of legislation needed to fully transform what was once a system of support for White families in poverty to one that began to surveil and separate Black families because of their poverty. Although the inclusion of "neglect" was inconsistent in state reporting laws, CAPTA dangerously classified "child neglect" along with "child abuse" under the broader category of "child maltreatment," firmly establishing the idea that parents who are unable to meet their children's needs due to poverty were responsible for maltreatment and subject to intrusive state intervention. Although an abundance of evidence pointed to the connections between poverty and maltreatment, particularly forms of maltreatment that would become known as "neglect," those advocating for the passage of CAPTA intentionally obscured this reality. As Senator Walter Mondale, the lead sponsor of CAPTA, infamously said during the CAPTA hearings, "You may go into some of the finest communities from an economic standpoint and find child abuse as you would in the ghettos of this country . . . this is not a poverty problem; it is a national problem."[92] As attorney Don Lash later wrote about this, "The effect is to obscure the institutional racism in which poverty and its consequent problems for children are rooted, and to focus on the perceived failures and pathology of people caught up in the system."[93] This effect was by design.

By classifying neglect as "child maltreatment" and disassociating neglect from poverty, CAPTA made certain that the "disease" model of child abuse could proliferate thereby making neglect "classless" and blaming parents for systemic failures. In other words, if the root of the problem was portrayed as parental failure, more children, particularly Black children, could be removed and funneled into foster care. During the hearings, experts repeatedly cautioned that conflating the two "disparate entities" would put families in poverty at significant risk of being charged with abuse.[94] Professor David Gil directly warned of the surveillance and overreporting that would result, testifying that poor communities are "open to more scrutiny. Everything they do or fail to do is immediately reported and considered a major issue whereas the upper and middle classes get away with a variety of questionable acts and behaviors."[95]

These warnings were ignored and CAPTA was ultimately passed, grounded in the parental "pathology" frameworks of Kempe and Moynihan. Through the logic of CAPTA, families who are experiencing poverty are individually responsible for their condition and need to be "treated" through punitive interventions employed by the government—even if this means taking their children from them. Evading the realities of oppression and poverty "allowed policymakers to avoid addressing deeply entrenched structural, economic, and racial inequities affecting children's wellbeing."[96] The intended consequence of this—and the harm that has since been inflicted on Black families as a result—cannot be understated.

From this point forward, state mandatory reporting laws were absorbed into CAPTA with states required to have procedures in place for receiving and responding to allegations of abuse or neglect in exchange for federal funding. Further, states were required to define abuse and neglect in a way that was consistent with CAPTA, which vaguely defined both terms as "the physical or mental injury, sexual abuse, negligent treatment, or maltreatment of a child."[97] Any programs related to child abuse or neglect under Title IV of the Social Security Act, specifically AFDC, were required to comply with CAPTA's reporting and investigation measures as well as cooperate with law enforcement, courts, and state human service agencies. This coordinated effort further established the carceral web designed to surveil and ensnare Black families.

Under CAPTA, judicial proceedings were not required if parents voluntarily accepted services and were cooperative. That said, "voluntary" services are nonexistent under threats of family separation by a coercive system. Furthermore, Black parents' understandable lack of trust in the system is often perceived as uncooperative. For families who do become involved in judicial proceedings, CAPTA requires the child be appointed a guardian ad litem to represent the interests of children in foster care. Although the guardian ad litem is often an attorney, many states allow for the appointment of a Court Appointed Special Advocate (CASA) to serve in this role, or to serve alongside an attorney to represent the interests of children. The CASA model, now a national organization that lobbied to be included in the CAPTA funding stream, began as a "local experiment" in 1979.[98] With just thirty hours of training, CASA volunteers conduct their own investigation into the family and make recommendations to the judge. This use of CASA volunteers to represent the interests of children has been identified by many as a means by which racism is perpetuated in the family policing system, given that the large majority of CASA volunteers are middle-class White women who hold extraordinary power in determining what is in the best interests of poor Black children. Yet this model continues and now, with a cadre of both volunteers and professionals largely comprised of White, middle-class people, CAPTA has provided states with both investigatory funding and a powerful civilian arm to do its bidding.[99]

Thus we see a racist transformation completed. What began as a system for widowed White mothers to protect their children from poverty had become a system to surveil and punish Black families, particularly Black mothers, to "protect" their children from the poverty for which they were solely responsible. This was not what some describe as an "unintended consequence" of CAPTA. This was a clearly foreseeable result of the policy decisions that were made from the early 1900s through the 1970s culminating with the passage of CAPTA that cemented the role of the modern family policing system in maintaining White supremacy. CAPTA has since been amended and reauthorized by Congress multiple times, with few changes or even discussion that would reduce the harm to Black families it was intended to cause.

The Racism Is in the Discretion

By the end of the 1970s, following the passage of CAPTA, it was well documented that Black children had become the most overrepresented population in the family policing system, comprising more than 28 percent of children in foster care.[100] By the year 2000, the percentage of children in foster care who were Black had ballooned to 38 percent, a rate more than double their proportion of the population.[101] As we have and will continue to see, this is not evidence of a problem—this is evidence of the family policing system fulfilling its purpose. The family policing system was designed to maintain the oppression of Black children and families—and it excels at doing so.

Since the earliest iterations of the family policing system, policy has been used as the tool to ensure the system produces its intended outcomes—the oppression of Black Americans and the maintenance of White power. As this chapter has demonstrated, the ideal of a White, middle-class parenting standard against which all other families are judged has been embedded in modern "child welfare" policy since its earliest origins in the 1960s. Over the decades that followed, these policies have been developed alongside a racialized cultural narrative that vilified Black parenting, and specifically Black mothers—all for the purpose of reinforcing the idea that Black parents are not only harmful to their children but also a threat to society. Thus, the ideal of a White, middle-class parenting standard, combined with the racialized narratives of Black parenting that have been reinforced for decades, create a condition within the family policing system wherein Black families and Black parenting always appear not only deficient, but also unsafe.

These racialized narratives of Black parenting have a profound impact on decision-making due to the vast subjectivity that exists in family policing policy. Exacerbated by what has historically been and remains a largely White workforce, the vagueness of what constitutes "child maltreatment" and the lack of any specific criteria for what should result in family separation create a condition where the subjective values and beliefs of individual decision-makers about "good parents" versus "bad parents" and "safe" versus "unsafe" profoundly influence the decisions they make on what constitutes maltreatment and on when more punitive forms of intervention must be applied to ensure "protection."

This is most notably seen in the intentional vagueness of CAPTA. While CAPTA primarily functioned to establish mandatory reporting laws for all fifty states, it also established minimum federal definitions of maltreatment. However, CAPTA intentionally allowed states broad discretion to expand on those definitions, resulting in laws that vary widely by state and often reflect current social problems within those states. The result is an immensely vague set of laws that can be used at any time by those in power as a means of targeting a marginalized group for political gain. Take, for example, the expansion of definitions of maltreatment in Texas in 2022. On February 22, 2022, Texas Governor Greg Abbott wrote to the Commissioner of the Texas Department of Family and Protective Services:

> [T]he Office of the Attorney General (OAG) has now confirmed in the enclosed opinion that a number of so-called "sex change" procedures constitute child abuse under existing Texas law. Because the Texas Department of Family and Protective Services (DFPS) is responsible for protecting children from abuse, I hereby direct your agency to conduct a prompt and thorough investigation of any reported instances of these abusive procedures in the State of Texas.[102]

Thus, with the stroke of a pen, the governor of Texas declared that providing gender affirming care to children was "child abuse," directing mandatory reporters to report this, and requiring state officials to investigate and potentially separate families for providing this care.

For some, this directive brought new awareness to the harms of the family policing system and to the power of the state to weaponize mandatory reporting laws against certain families or communities. Although this was happening now to families in Texas with transgender youth, this has been happening to Black families for decades, such as when "crack babies" were removed en masse from Black parents upon birth in the 1990s despite the lack of any evidence these babies were at risk of harm.[103] The ability of the state to weaponize mandatory reporting laws is the reason these laws were written so vaguely. At any moment, the state can decide a particular behavior or way of existence is undesirable, and at any moment, that behavior or way of existence can be defined as maltreatment and subject to coercive state intervention.

Yet in the family policing system, what begins as discretion in mandatory reporting and definitions of "child maltreatment" extends throughout child welfare policy to allow this discretion to continue. For Black families, the cumulative effects of this discretion have been vast and immense. From the early 1960s and the discovery of "child abuse" and early reporting laws, to the passage of CAPTA, which enshrined poverty as "child neglect," to the Adoption and Safe Families Act of 1997, which incentivized the speedy termination of parental rights to free Black babies for adoption by White parents—each of these policies were both informed by and grounded in the racist stereotypes of Black parenting that have been present in society since the era of chattel slavery. From the "tangle of pathology" of the 1960s, to the "welfare queen" of the 1980s, to the false "epidemic" of babies born to crack-addicted Black mothers in the 1990s—these are the narratives those in power have constructed to maintain White supremacy and these are the narratives upon which the family policing system was built. And these are the narratives that persist through to today.

Notes

1. Gwendolyn Mink, "The Lady and the Tramp: Gender, Race, and the Origins of the American Welfare State," in *Women, the State, and Welfare*, edited by Linda Gordon (Madison: University of Wisconsin Press, 2012), p. 104.
2. Deborah E. Ward, *The White Welfare State: The Racialization of U.S. Welfare Policy* (Ann Arbor: University of Michigan Press, 2005), p. 40.
3. Mink, "The Lady and The Tramp," p. 110.
4. Ward, *The White Welfare State*, p. 30.
5. "Proceedings of the Conference on the Care of Dependent Children," Washington, DC, January 25–26, 1909, pp. 5–6, https://archive.org/details/proceedingsconf00s tatgoog/page/n8/mode/2up.
6. Theodore Roosevelt, *The Foes of Our Own Household* (New York: George H. Doran Company, 1917) p. 246.
7. Roosevelt, *The Foes of Our Own Household*, p. 258.
8. "Proceedings of the Conference on the Care of Dependent Children," p, 11.
9. "Proceedings of the Conference on the Care of Dependent Children," p. 10.
10. Ward, *The White Welfare State*, p. 36.

11. Emma Octavia Lundberg, "Public Aid to Mothers with Dependent Children: Extent and Fundamental Principles," (Washington, DC: U.S. Department of Labor, Children's Bureau, 1926), p. 2.
12. Ward, *The White Welfare State*, p. 47.
13. Winifred Bell, *Aid to Dependent Children* (New York: Columbia University Press, 1965), p. 5.
14. Mink, "The Lady and The Tramp," p. 110.
15. Bell, *Aid to Dependent Children*, p. 9.
16. Mink, "The Lady and The Tramp," p. 110.
17. "Social Security in America," Committee on Economic Security, Social Security Administration, accessed August 1, 2022, https://www.ssa.gov/history/reports/ces/cesbookc13.html.
18. Ward, *The White Welfare State*, p. 106.
19. Angela *Onwuachi-Willig*, "The Return of the Ring: Welfare Reform's Marriage Cure as the Revival of Post-Bellum Control," *California Law Review* 93, (December 2005): p. 1666.
20. Joanne L. Goodwin, "'Employable Mothers' and 'Suitable Work': A Re-Evaluation of Welfare and Wage-Earning for Women in the Twentieth-Century United States," *Journal of Social History* 29, no. 2 (1995): p. 255.
21. Ife Floyd, Ladonna Pavetti, Laura Meyer, Ali Safawi, Liz Schott, Evelyn Bellew, and Abigail Magnus, *TANF Policies Reflect Racist Legacy of Cash Assistance: Reimagined Program Should Center Black Mothers* (Center on Budget and Policy Priorities, August 2021), https://www.cbpp.org/research/family-income-support/tanf-policies-reflect-racist-legacy-of-cash-assistance.
22. Bell, *Aid to Dependent Children*, p. 63.
23. Bell, *Aid to Dependent Children*, p. 64.
24. Bell, *Aid to Dependent Children*, p. 67.
25. Saidiya Hartman, *Scenes of Subjection: Terror, Slavery, and Self-Making in 19th Century America* (New York: Oxford University Press, 1997), p. 160.
26. Frances Fox Piven and Richard Cloward, *Regulating the Poor: The Functions of Public Welfare*, 2nd ed. (New York: Vintage Books, 1993), p. 166.
27. John E. Rousseau, "In New Orleans School Desegregation: 6-Year-Old Negro Girls Mob Targets," *New Pittsburgh Courier (1959–1965)*, November 26, 1960, http://search.proquest.com.ezproxy.lib.uh.edu/newspapers/new-orleans-school-desegregation-6-year-old-negro/docview/371583614/se-2.
28. John G. Warner, "Mob Threatens 2 for Defying School Boycott: Women Scream at Her Routed for Profanity Guarded by Police Carries U.S. Flag," *The Washington Post, Times Herald (1959–1973)*, December 1, 1960, http://search.proquest.com.ezproxy.lib.uh.edu/historical-newspapers/mob-threatens-2-defying-school-boycott/docview/141299135/se-2.
29. John E. Rousseau, "In New Orleans School Desegregation: 6-Year-Old Negro Girls Mob Targets," *New Pittsburgh Courier (1959–1965)*, November 26, 1960, http://search.proquest.com.ezproxy.lib.uh.edu/newspapers/new-orleans-school-desegregation-6-year-old-negro/docview/371583614/se-2.

30. *Bush v. Orleans Parish School Board* 190 F. Supp. 861(1960).
31. Andrew Pope, "Making Motherhood a Felony: African American Women's Welfare Rights Activism in New Orleans and the End of Suitable Home Laws, 1959–1962," *Journal of American History* 105 (2018): pp 291–310, https://doi.org/10.1093/jahist/jay145.
32. Pope, "Making Motherhood a Felony," p. 291.
33. Taryn Lindhorst and Leslie Leighninger, "'Ending Welfare as We Know It' in 1960: Louisiana's Suitable Home Law," *Social Service Review* 77, no. 4 (2003): pp. 564–584.
34. Pope, "Making Motherhood a Felony," p. 291.
35. Editors, Social Service Review, "The 'Suitable-Home' Requirement," *Social Service Review* 35, no. 2 (June 1961): p. 204, https://www.jstor.org/stable/30017252.
36. Editors, Social Service Review, "Hungry Children in Louisiana," *Social Service Review* 34, no. 4 (December 1960): p. 444, https://www.jstor.org/stable/30016658.
37. Pope, "Making Motherhood a Felony."
38. Pope, "Making Motherhood a Felony."
39. Editors, Social Service Review, "The 'Suitable Home' Requirement," p. 206.
40. W. L. Mitchell, "Decision of the Commissioner of Social Security," *Social Service Review* 35, no. 2 (June 1961): p. 208, https://www.jstor.org/stable/30017253.
41. Public Law 87–31, May 8, 1961, p. 76, https://www.govinfo.gov/content/pkg/STATUTE-75/pdf/STATUTE-75-Pg75.pdf#page=1.
42. Helen R. Jeter, *Children, Problems, and Services in Child Welfare Programs* (U.S. Department of Health, Education, and Welfare, Children's Bureau, 1963), p. 4, https://babel.hathitrust.org/cgi/pt?id=uc1.32106001078572.
43. C. Henry Kempe, Frederic N. Silverman, Brandt F. Steele, William Droegemueller, and Henry K. Silver, "The Battered-Child Syndrome," *Journal of the American Medical Association* 181, no. 1 (July 7, 1962): pp. 17–24, doi:10.1001/jama.1962.03050270019004.
44. See for example John Caffey, "Multiple Fractures in the Long Bones of Infants Suffering from Chronic Subdural Hematoma," *American Journal of Roentgenology* 56, no. 2 (August 1946): pp. 163–173; and Frederick N. Silverman, "The Roentgen Manifestations of Unrecognized Skeletal Trauma in Infants," *American Journal of Roentgenology* 69, no. 3 (March 1953): pp. 413–426.
45. "When They're Angry . . . ," *Newsweek,* April 16, 1962, p. 74.
46. "Medicine: Battered-Child Syndrome," *Time,* July 20, 1962, p. 60, https://time.com/vault/issue/1962-07-20/page/78/.
47. Charles Flato, "Parents Who Beat Children: A Tragic Increase in Cases of Child Abuse is Prompting a Hunt for Ways to Detect Sick Adults Who Commit Such Crimes," *Saturday Evening Post,* October 6, 1962, p. 30, https://www.saturdayeveningpost.com/flipbooks/issues/19621006/.
48. Ian Hacking, "The Making and Molding of Child Abuse," *Critical Inquiry* 17, no. 2 (Winter 1991): pp. 253–288, https://www.jstor.org/stable/1343837.
49. Kempe et al., "The Battered-Child Syndrome," p. 18.
50. Kempe et al., "The Battered-Child Syndrome," p. 18.

51. JAMA Editorials, "The Battered-Child Syndrome," p. 42.

52. "When They're Angry . . . ," *Newsweek*, p. 74.

53. U.S. Department of Health and Human Services, Children's Bureau, *The Abused Child: Principles and Suggested Language for Legislation on Reporting of the Physically Abused Child* (Washington, DC: 1963), https://babel.hathitrust.org/cgi/pt?id=pur1.32754078884032.

54. For example, see Henry H. Foster, Jr., "Lawmen, Medicine Men and Good Samaritans," *American Bar Association Journal* 52, no. 3 (March 1966): p. 226, https://www.jstor.org/stable/25723541; and Monrad G. Paulson, "Child Abuse Reporting Laws: The Shape of the Legislation," *Columbia Law Review* 67, no. 1 (January 1967): pp. 3–4, https://www.jstor.org/stable/1121129.

55. U.S. Department of Health and Human Services, Children's Bureau, *The Abused Child*, p. 13.

56. For an exceptional account of the history of mandatory reporting laws, see Mical Raz, *Abusive Policies: How the American Child Welfare System Lost Its Way* (Chapel Hill: University of North Carolina Press, 2020); also see "Statutes: Saving Battered Children," *Time,* January 8, 1965, p. 43, https://time.com/vault/issue/1965-01-08/page/49/; Leonard G. Brown, III and Kevin Gallagher, "Mandatory Reporting of Abuse: A Historical Perspective on the Evolution of States' Current Mandatory Reporting Laws with a Review of the Laws in the Commonwealth of Pennsylvania," *Villanova Law Review Online: Tolle Lege* 59, no. 6 (2014): pp. 37–80, https://digitalcommons.law.villanova.edu/vlr/vol59/iss6/5/.

57. Vincent De Francis, "Child Abuse—The Legislative Response," *Denver Law Journal* 44, no. 1 (Winter 1967), p. 20, https://digitalcommons.du.edu/dlr/vol44/iss1/15/.

58. De Francis, "Child Abuse," p. 12.

59. Brown and Gallagher, "Mandatory Reporting of Abuse," p. 41.

60. Vincent De Francis, *Child Abuse—Preview of a Nationwide Survey* (American Humane Association, May 1963), https://babel.hathitrust.org/cgi/pt?id=mdp.39015004877752.

61. David G. Gil, *Violence Against Children: Physical Child Abuse in the United States* (Cambridge: Harvard University Press, 1970).

62. Daniel Patrick Moynihan, *The Negro Family: The Case For National Action* (Office of Policy Planning and Research, U.S. Department of Labor, March 1965), https://www.dol.gov/general/aboutdol/history/webid-moynihan.

63. Moynihan, *The Negro Family*, p. 5.

64. Moynihan, *The Negro Family*, p. 5.

65. Moynihan, *The Negro Family*, p. 5.

66. Moynihan, *The Negro Family*, pp. 6–12.

67. Moynihan, *The Negro Family*, p. 14.

68. Moynihan, *The Negro Family*, p. 29.

69. Moynihan, *The Negro Family*, pp. 29–30.

70. Moynihan, *The Negro Family*, p. 30.

71. Moynihan, *The Negro Family*, p. 38.

72. Moynihan, *The Negro Family*, p. 47.

73. Moynihan, *The Negro Family*, p. 47.

74. Gil, *Violence Against Children*.

75. Gil, *Violence Against Children*, p. 106.

76. Gil, *Violence Against Children*, p. 138.

77. David G. Gil, "Violence Against Children," *Journal of Marriage and Family* 33, no. 4 (November 1971): p. 645, https://www.jstor.org/stable/349436.

78. In addition to Kempe et al., "The Battered-Child Syndrome," see for example John J. Spinetta and David Rigler, "The Child-Abusing Parent: A Psychological Review," *Psychological Bulletin* 77, no. 4 (1972): pp. 296–304, https://doi.org/10.1037/h0032419.

79. Gil, *Violence Against Children*, p. 106.

80. Gil, *Violence Against Children*, p. 138.

81. Richard J. Gelles, "The Social Construction of Child Abuse," *American Journal of Orthopsychiatry* 45, no. 3 (April 1975): p. 364, https://doi.org/10.1111/j.1939-0025.1975.tb02547.x.

82. Gelles, "The Social Construction of Child Abuse," p. 365.

83. Gelles, "The Social Construction of Child Abuse," p. 366.

84. Gelles, "The Social Construction of Child Abuse," p. 368.

85. Eli H. Newberger and Richard Bourne, "The Medicalization and Legalization of Child Abuse" (lecture, Symposium on Violence in the Family, International Society on Family Law, Montreal, June 13, 1977).

86. Stephen J. Pfohl, "The 'Discovery' of Child Abuse," *Social Problems* 24, no. 3 (1976): pp. 320–321.

87. Jeter, *Children, Problems, and Services in Child Welfare Programs*; Ann W. Shyne and Anita G. Schroeder, *National Study of Social Services to Children and Their Families: Demographic Data* (U.S. Department of Health and Human Services, Administration for Children, Youth, and Families, June 1982), https://archive.org/details/ERIC_ED217983/; Alicia Summers, Steve Wood, and Jennifer Donovan, *Disproportionality Rates for Children of Color in Foster Care* (National Council of Juvenile and Family Court Judges, May 2013), https://www.ncjfcj.org/wp-content/uploads/2013/06/Disproportionality-Rates-for-Children-of-Color-in-Foster-Care-2013.pdf.

88. National Association of Black Social Workers, *Harambee: 30 Years of Unity—Our Roots Position Statement*, May 29, 1968, p. 10, https://cdn.ymaws.com/www.nabsw.org/resource/collection/E1582D77-E4CD-4104-996A-D42D08F9CA7D/NABSW_30_Years_of_Unity_-_Our_Roots_Position_Statement_1968.pdf.

89. Martin Gilens, "How the Poor Became Black," in *Race and the Politics of Welfare Reform*, edited by Sanford F. Schram, Joe Soss, and Richard C. Fording (Ann Arbor: University of Michigan Press, 2003).

90. Floyd et al., *TANF Policies Reflect Racist Legacy of Cash Assistance*, p. 20.

91. Lucy A. Williams, "Race, Rat Bites and Unfit Mothers: How Media Disclosure Informs Welfare Legislation Debate," *Fordham Urban Law Journal* 22, no. 4 (1995): p. 1182.

92. Senate Committee of Labor and Public Welfare, "Child Abuse Prevention Act, 1973. Hearings Before the Subcommittee on Children and Youth of the Committee on Labor and Public Welfare," (Washington, DC: Congress of the U.S., 1973), p. 17, https://files.eric.ed.gov/fulltext/ED081507.pdf.

93. Don Lash, *"When the Welfare People Come": Race and Class in the US Child Protection System* (Chicago: Haymarket Books, 2017), p. 43.

94. Senate Committee of Labor and Public Welfare, "Child Abuse Prevention Act, 1973," p. 364.

95. Senate Committee of Labor and Public Welfare, "Child Abuse Prevention Act, 1973," p. 18.

96. Angela Olivia Burton and Angeline Montauban, "Toward Community Control of Child Welfare Funding: Repeal the Child Abuse Prevention and Treatment Act and Delink Child Protection From Family Well-Being," *Columbia Journal of Race and Law* 11, no. 3 (July 2021): p. 667, https://journals.library.columbia.edu/index.php/cjrl/article/view/8747.

97. Child Abuse Prevention and Treatment Act, Public Law 93–247 (1974).

98. Amy Mulzer and Tara Urs, "However Kindly Intentioned: Structural Racism and Volunteer CASA Programs," *City University of New York Law Review* 20, no.1 (2016): pp. 37–38.

99. See Mulzer and Urs, "However Kindly Intentioned." Research shows CASA volunteers are 80 to 90 percent White and studies from the organization have shown CASA volunteers spend less time with Black children compared to White children.

100. Shyne and Schroeder, *National Study of Social Services to Children and Their Families: Demographic Data.*

101. Summers, Wood, and Donovan, *Disproportionality Rates for Children of Color in Foster Care.*

102. Greg Abbott, *Letter from Governor Greg Abbott to the Honorable Jamie Masters* (Governor, the State of Texas, February 22, 2022), https://gov.texas.gov/uploads/files/press/O-MastersJaime202202221358.pdf.

103. See for example, Susan Okie, "The Epidemic That Wasn't," *The New York Times,* January 6, 2009, https://www.nytimes.com/2009/01/27/health/27coca.html.

4

Manifestations of Surveillance, Regulation, and Punishment in the Afterlife of Slavery

The racialized, gendered, and economic classificatory systems that once justified human chattel slavery have continued to haunt Black families throughout the twenty-first century, infiltrating our social institutions and normalizing the disparate treatment of Black communities. These remnants of slavery have contributed to the maintenance of a resilient social order rooted in White supremacy, one that has enabled and justified mass incarceration, eugenic practices, histories of displacement, and the ongoing separation of Black families. Unsurprisingly, the family policing system has been at the crux of these violent acts against Black families and remains the primary catalyst for family separations at the hands of the state.

As Billingsly and Giovannoni noted over fifty years ago, the system was never created for Black children. Rather, since the abolition of slavery, the system has simply adapted its service model over time per a social barometer that aims to hold poor Black people at the bottom.[1] The twenty-first century version of the family policing system continues this role, largely policing those who are poor and Black, while adapting its practices to incorporate modern technological innovations and decision-making tools to reinforce the racist intents upon which it began. Rather than addressing the racism inherent in family policing, these new models of decision-making bolster and reinforce the underlying racist schema built deeply within the family policing system and its myriad institutional ties.

In today's family policing system, Black families continue to be disproportionately involved at every stage of family policing intervention. Beginning with the point of initial referral, Black children are more likely to be reported for suspected maltreatment than White children, more likely to be involved in investigations in which allegations of maltreatment are substantiated, and more likely to be forcibly separated from their families and placed in foster care. Once in foster care, Black children are less likely to be returned to their families and more likely to experience permanent

Confronting the Racist Legacy of the American Child Welfare System. Alan J. Dettlaff, Oxford University Press.
© Oxford University Press 2023. DOI: 10.1093/oso/9780197675267.003.0005

termination of parental rights.[2] In today's family policing system, nearly one in ten Black children born in the United States will be forcibly separated from their parents before their eighteenth birthday.[3] In some states, such as California, nearly one in eight Black children will be forcibly separated and placed in foster care.[4] The extent of this practice remains an echo of the family separations that were brutally inflicted on Black families during human chattel slavery and is nothing short of an ongoing practice of state sanctioned terror.

The Carceral Logic of the Family Policing System

This massive overinvolvement in the lives of Black families and the excessive use of family separations are the direct and intended consequences of the policy shifts that began in the 1960s, which transformed the "child welfare" system from one that focused on poverty relief for widowed White mothers to one that viewed poverty as an individual and moral failure—a failure that existed mostly among Black families and required punitive government intervention as a means of "treating" those failures. This was not an unintentional shift in strategy. As demonstrated in Chapter 3, this was a direct response to a time in history when Black Americans were gaining power, and White Americans were growing increasingly fearful of this power. Where poverty was once viewed as a plight of widowed White mothers who needed government assistance to stay home and take care of their children, poverty was now framed as a "tangle of pathology" deriving from single Black mothers who were raising their children to become the criminals White people feared.[5] Thus the shift in intention that transformed the "child welfare" system into the present-day family policing system was designed for the purpose of maintaining White supremacy by treating poverty as a pathological problem that could only be solved by punishment and correction— punishment and correction that is disproportionately inflicted on Black families.

Today, building on decades of policy development that reinforced the shift that began in the 1960s, the family policing system operates as a massive arm of the broader carceral state with significant and almost unlimited power to oppress Black families by not only seizing their children but also through the enormous consequences that result from these family separations. This power to destroy Black families is both wielded and allowed to exist through the carceral logic employed by the family policing system that punishes parents for their poverty and the racialized narratives of poverty that have demonized Black families, particularly Black mothers, over decades. Since the origins of the modern family policing system, both the carceral logic employed by the system and the racialization of poverty have been reinforced and bolstered through carceral ideologies that result in the state of family policing today.

In essence, the carceral logic of the family policing system establishes that families who are experiencing poverty are individually responsible for this poverty and need to be "treated" through punitive interventions employed by the government. This individualization of blame serves as a distraction from the broader societal problems that allow poverty to exist and from the racism that allows poverty to exist disproportionately among Black families. This logic was firmly established through the Child Abuse Prevention and Treatment Act (CAPTA) in 1974, which classified "child neglect" along with "child abuse" under the broader category of "child maltreatment"—thus cementing the idea that parents who are unable to meet their children's needs due to poverty were responsible for maltreatment and subject to state intervention.

Another effect of employing a carceral logic to individualize blame for poverty is that this rationalizes the use of punitive interventions as a means of "treating the problem." This is an important and necessary aspect of carceral logic because it impacts not only how the family policing system responds to families living in poverty, but it also shifts the broader societal understanding about why poverty exists and what should be done to address it. As Lash further states:

> The child welfare system helps to make the impoverishment and societal neglect of children tolerable to the larger population by promoting the idea that children are valued and protected. Perhaps of greater importance, the system situates blame for the danger and harm imposed on children on their families rather than on the material conditions of their existence.[6]

In other words, poverty—and the disproportionate number of Black families living in poverty—is accepted by the public because we know the "child welfare" system will protect them from this. With poverty clearly understood as the result of the failure of "bad" parents, we allow poverty to continue to exist without question because we believe their children will ultimately be protected. If this results in separating those children from their parents, this is the necessary and appropriate response to those parents' deficiencies.

Finally, carceral logic maintains and reinforces the idea that originated during chattel slavery that Black parents, particularly Black mothers, do not care about their children. Building from this original framing and extending the ideas established in the Moynihan Report, carceral logic frames Black mothers as threats to society—threats that do not care about their children, threats that allow their children to live in impoverished communities without making any effort to improve themselves, and threats that are ultimately responsible for crime and social dysfunction. Rather than the government having the responsibility to address the poverty it intentionally created within Black communities, Black parents have the sole responsibility to address the poverty they face, and if they cannot, the government must step in to protect their children from them. This intentional framing of poverty as solely an individual failure, and particularly a failure of Black parents, undergirds the model of the family policing system, which employs mechanisms of surveillance, regulation, and punishment to respond to families living in poverty—a construct that is now firmly established by the state as "child maltreatment."

Mechanisms of Surveillance

Although surveillance is a primary mechanism used by the family policing system today, surveillance of Black families is rooted in the history of enslavement in the United States and has been used for centuries to reify a racial hierarchy through the monitoring, control, and punishment of Black people. As stated by Simone Browne in *Dark Matters,* "Surveillance is nothing new to black folks. It is the fact of antiblackness."[7] As this statement suggests, surveillance is not a recent development, nor was it spurred by modern technological advancement. Rather, surveillance existed long before the twenty-first century and has always been embedded in anti-Blackness. For Black communities, surveillance has persisted generationally from "runaway slave" ads and eighteenth-century lantern laws to midnight welfare raids, to large databases, biometric technologies, geofence warrants, and drones. Surveillance occurred during the points of departure in which African people were captured, persisted through the moments of arrival onto Indigenous lands in North America, was maintained and fortified during enslavement, and continues today in the afterlife of slavery to uphold the racial hierarchy.[8] As such, Browne uses the term *racializing surveillance* to describe the technologies of "social control where surveillance practices, policies, and performances concern the production of norms pertaining to race and exercise a power to define what is in or out of place."[9]

Surveillance has been a key mechanism in tracking and monitoring "threats" to society, with threats being defined by our broader social context and those who remain in power. "Fugitive slaves" were labeled as threats because they threatened the stability of the plantation and the cycle of enslaved labor. Black children have been labeled "superpredators" and have been ascribed to a "tangle of pathology" wherein Black mothers were labeled as threats to society.[10] Black women have been deemed a threat to society in multiple ways, labeled "welfare queens," "jezebels," drug users, and other tropes used to justify state violence. Racializing surveillance continues to be a way to reify these various tropes that rely on biocentric categorizations, and which subsequently lead to the ongoing capture and control of Black individuals. This capture and control influences Black people's mobilities and livelihood within society today.

Surveillance has always relied on the use of data and databases—both of which have often necessitated the flattening or minimizing of Black life.[11] Slave schedules reduced Black individuals to numbers and symbols, for the sole use of enslavers and the slave trade.[12] This information included the name of enslavers; the quantity of enslaved people on a plantation; the age, sex, and color of the enslaved; the fugitive status of the enslaved; the number of enslaved people manumitted; and if the enslaved were "deaf & dumb, blind, insane, or idiotic."[13] Runaway slave ads were written from a White gaze and included a description of enslaved people by their physical appearance, the amount of money associated with the return of an enslaved person, and geographic information about where they were last seen.[14] Runaway slave ads and slave schedules were ways to practice surveillance, tracking and monitoring Black life for the purpose of upholding and maintaining White supremacy.

Twenty-first-century technological advances that are developed from large datasets mimic the same violent flattening effect that slave schedules incited, often depicting Black people as numbers that fill a list and frequently from the White gaze for the purpose of control. Black individuals have been required to submit personal information to the government to ensure they were not committing welfare fraud, have been placed into predictive policing algorithms that determine who will commit future crimes, and more recently have had their children taken away due to predictive algorithms that classify them as a "high" safety risk. These technologically assisted decision-making tools and processes claim to be neutral and often are touted as remedies to flawed human decision-making. As suggested by Browne, however, these technological remedies are anything but neutral. Technological techniques and objects such as data sets and algorithms are a projection of social, political, and economic relations that have been normalized in our society.[15] Algorithms and data sets have been used to track "threats" to "public health" or "public safety." In other words, these technologies promise to be more efficient in catching people in the act of committing crimes, crimes often associated with poor people of color. As suggested by the concept of *racializing surveillance*, predictive algorithms are not built in an ideological bubble but are fueled by the same societal context in which human decision-making occurs.

As addressed in Chapter 3, during the early 1960s, amidst waves of civil rights protests in the South, welfare offices were engaging in midnight raids in the homes of Aid to Dependent Children (ADC) recipients to enforce "man in the house" rules and to punish the sexuality of single mothers. Through the 1970s and into the 1980s, following the passage of CAPTA, increasing societal distrust in welfare recipients began to emerge. This distrust was paired with the assumption that welfare recipients were Black, and this rhetoric of distrust led to quality control measures imposed by the government. Along with an increase in reporting requirements for welfare recipients, the federal government started tracking more data, including the error rates in food stamp and welfare provisions, as well as applicants' Social Security numbers. This period marked the first widespread use of data exchange among governments and the computer tracking of the poor.[16] Soon, the trope of the "welfare queen" began to proliferate, winning Ronald Reagan a presidency and spurring a period of "tough on crime" policies and punitive laws. These laws most significantly impacted Black children who were given mandatory sentences and automatic adult court transfers, and Black families who continued to suffer through home invasions better known as welfare fraud investigations. The rhetoric of criminality and laziness, as well as the association of Black people with "threat," continued to increase punitive welfare fraud control through the 1990s. As part of welfare fraud control, many states implemented family cap regulations for Temporary Assistance for Needy Families (TANF) recipients and required them to provide biometric imaging.[17] Numerous other examples throughout history illustrate the ways that technology has consistently been used as a tool to advance the interests of the powerful through regulation and control. Technology has aided policies that "effectively deny the existence—the personhood and the economic needs—of children born to mothers who are poor and usually single. They punish mothers for non-normative, meaning nonmarital, sex and child-bearing."[18] These policies and practices reveal that anti-Blackness is foundational to new technological innovations, even when they are advertised as neutral.

The data collected by violent surveillance regimes such as midnight welfare raids and racist welfare control policies are still used today, specifically by the family policing system. In fact, the family policing system has used various forms of surveillance for years, breaching the civil liberties and rights of families for generations under the facade of "child protection." The data collected from multiple carceral institutions have led to a "social tagging system" that works to label individuals rather than protect them.[19] The family policing system not only recycles and amplifies several of these past data points that were once gathered in violence, it also perpetuates similar intrusive data collection processes to make a similarly violent decision—the decision of whether certain Black families deserve to keep their children. These data collection processes include the ways that family policing agents visit homes unannounced to identify what they perceive as harms and irregularities. More often than not, parents are not informed of their rights when a family policing agent arrives at their home to investigate and are not given access to legal representation. Surveillance also includes the ways that agents can bypass certain parental consent processes by interviewing children while they are in school, as well as the ways hospital staff perform nonconsensual drug tests on Black pregnant mothers and then report this to family policing systems.[20]

Despite knowing the harms of technological decision-making processes, as well as the histories of midnight raids and violent data collection processes, the government, researchers, and philanthropic organizations have continued to encourage the surveillance of families. As a result, there has been a steady increase in the family policing system's use of these technologies over the past decade. For example, the Family First Prevention Services Act (FFPSA) of 2018 requires a range of technological data collection processes. The FFPSA requires states to discuss their monitoring and oversight of children receiving services, explicitly naming the use of risk assessments. Further the FFPSA requires states to use an "electronic interstate case-processing system for the exchange of data and documents to expedite the placements of children in foster, guardianship, or adoptive homes across state lines," as well as data integration with law enforcement and judicial agencies.[21]

Along with the federal government, philanthropic and academic institutions have also encouraged the use of technologically assisted decision-making tools. In 2018, Casey Family Programs held a convening of judges, policymakers, and doctors to explore a framework for a "21st Century Child Welfare System" that would "transform" the existing system into a "family well-being system."[22] At the convening, stakeholders identified "technical excellence" as an essential component of a twenty-first-century system, with a goal to "enhance decision making through tools such as predictive analytics."[23] Further, real-time data sharing became a core theme of the convening, with stakeholders encouraging "the use of high-quality cross-systems data collection and sharing, predictive analytics and the use of real-time data to inform decision making."[24]

With the federal government and philanthropic organizations encouraging the use of predictive analytics, an ACLU report shows that as of 2021 at least twenty-six states and the District of Columbia had considered using predictive tools, with eleven already using them.[25] Yet some automated tools have been successfully halted due to criticism over the outcomes they produce—outcomes that disproportionately target Black families. For example, Los Angeles County piloted a tool called the Approach to Understanding Risk Assessment (AURA) that aimed to track child fatalities and "critical incidents" by using prior child abuse referrals, involvement with law enforcement, mental health records, and substance use history to create a "risk score." Growing concern occurred when AURA identified 3,829 false positive incidents where no critical event occurred 95.6 percent of the time in a presumed "high risk" situation.[26] AURA was halted by Los Angeles County soon after. Oregon recently discontinued use of its artificial intelligence tool due to backlash from advocates and family members following an investigation into a similar tool used in Pennsylvania that was shown to produce racist outcomes.[27] This tool, the Allegheny Family Screening Tool (AFST) has continuously been critiqued due in part to its pattern of disproportionately flagging Black children for "mandatory" neglect investigations,[28] but also because it contributes to the creation of a "digital poorhouse" through the "iterative process of classifying and predicting the futures of Black, Indigenous, and poor people."[29]

As stated by Abdurahman, this "actuarial approach to human decision making" reproduced "a mythology of Black inferiority in part by codifying a transposition of demographic traits that correlate to poor social outcomes as the cause of poor social outcomes."[30] The encouragement of continued surveillance of Black families, especially poor Black families, within the family policing system denotes the continuation of violence that occurred during their enslavement. The implications of the surveillance that occurs within this system follow Black families for generations. By marking Black families through the data collection process or through the use of automated decision-making tools, families are captured in a penal regime that impacts their future abilities to have children and live unwatched by the government. It impacts Black families' abilities to get future housing assistance or employment. Central registries such as the Child Abuse Central Index (CACI) in Los Angeles County maintain a database of substantiated cases of child maltreatment so the information can "aid law enforcement investigations, prosecutions, and provide notification of new child abuse investigation reports involving the same suspect/victims."[31] In this system, even inconclusive investigations where caseworkers are unable to determine if child maltreatment occurred are still "retained for ten years unless there is an investigation of subsequent allegations of child abuse or severe neglect against the same child."[32] As a result, data spanning generations is continually used against Black family members, ensuring they remain followed into the future due to new technological and data-enhanced systems—thus ensuring they remain perpetually impacted by racist violence.

Regulating Families

The vast use of surveillance targeted on Black families and communities originates from the racist ideology that Black families must be regulated or made to fit into the norms created by the dominant culture. As Chapter 3 demonstrated, the ideal of a White, middle-class parenting standard has been uplifted in family policing policy since its earliest origins when "child welfare" services shifted from a focus on poverty relief to one of "child protection." This shift necessitated the development of federal standards that established a minimum set of acts or behaviors that constitute abuse or neglect, upon which states have vast discretion to expand. As Chapter 3 also notes, these state definitions of child maltreatment have, over time, been largely influenced by racialized narratives surrounding poverty and parenting, as well as White policymakers' beliefs about appropriate parenting that reflect a White, middle-class lens.

Thus, family policing policy establishes the standard for parenting behaviors to which parents are expected to conform. Family policing policy then allows for judgments to be made against this standard through the vagueness and discretion that is built into this policy. This is perhaps best exemplified by the "best interests of the child" standard, the foundational principle that governs family policing decision-making, which has been repeatedly challenged due to its ambiguity. Legal scholar Tanya Asim Cooper said of the best interest standard, "Its lack of definitive guidance allows foster care professionals and even judges to substitute their own judgment about what is in a child's best interest and allows unintended biases to permeate decision-making."[33] Even the Supreme Court has acknowledged the potential for subjectivity, stating the best interest standard "is imprecise and open to the subjective values of the judge."[34] Thus, all decision-making made by family policing agents is filtered through both the White, middle-class standards embedded within family policing policy and the subjective values of the decision-maker, all for the purpose of regulating families' behavior to conform to the norms of the dominant culture.

At its core, regulation is demonstrated through acts of compliance. This need for compliance or "performance" of certain tasks relates back to the carceral logic that situates the blame for poverty and the conditions that result solely on parents. Rather than addressing the material needs that often bring families to the attention of the family policing system, parents are expected to comply with a complex series of "services" that reinforce the ideology that they are responsible for their circumstances. As Lash states,

> In a typical case, a parent doesn't need childcare; she needs parenting classes. She doesn't need affordable housing or a living wage or adequate income for quality food; she needs budgeting help and nutrition training. If she disagrees with the treatment plan, she's in denial and needs counseling, and if she *vehemently* disagrees, she may need anger management classes. If there's something she really does need, like addiction treatment, it may not be available without a long wait, and it may be in a program that can't accommodate parents. Her reward if she does everything right is to be described as "compliant," giving her a better chance of getting her kids back.[35]

This emphasis on compliance is largely due to the reality that the "services" provided by family policing systems are fundamentally not able or designed to meet what families need. If a family lacks housing, the family policing system is not designed to provide this housing or address the broader societal conditions that contribute to a lack of affordable housing; yet the system can mandate that a parent attend a money management class and then document their attendance in this class as a measure of "progress"—all while maintaining the expectation that the parent find appropriate housing for themselves and their children on their own. Similarly, if parents are unable to maintain consistent employment, the family policing system will send these parents to job skills training classes and document their participation in these classes as a means of demonstrating how "serious" they are about obtaining employment and having their children returned to them—while doing nothing to address the broader societal conditions that lead to a lack of employment opportunities. Yet compliance and performance of these tasks becomes the sole measure by which parents are deemed worthy of either keeping their children or having their children returned to them.[36]

Thus, compliance in mandated activities becomes the substitute for how the family policing system measures not only parents' commitment to their children, but also the extent to which they have "taken responsibility" for the factors that brought them to the attention of the system. This logic dictates that if parents truly care about their children, they will do everything they can to comply with the expectations demanded of them. If for any reason they are unable to meet these expectations, they are deemed "noncompliant" or "uncooperative," a judgment that is made to imply both a lack of commitment and a lack of willingness to address the circumstances that led to their involvement in the system. This often escalates a case to the next stage of punitive intervention—family separation or termination of parental rights.

Yet this expectation for compliance is imposed on families with no understanding or empathy for the myriad reasons why compliance may be impossible. Families are routinely mandated to participate in services with no consideration given to issues of accessibility, availability of transportation, or job responsibilities, reinforcing the White middle-class parenting standard upon which family policing is based.[37] The barriers to meeting the expectations of the family policing system are structural and are exacerbated for families living in poverty—families who are disproportionately Black. Thus, although these expectations may be reasonable for a White middle-class parent who has access to transportation and may be able to take time away from her job to participate in classes, they are not reasonable for a poor Black parent struggling to prove to the system that she can provide for her children, because taking a day off from work to participate in classes can have considerable financial consequences due to a loss of wages as well as possibly result in termination of employment if these days off become unacceptable to an employer.

Here is where the design of the family policing system, and the intention behind this design, become clear. Building from the carceral logic that the conditions that brought families to the attention of the family policing system must be "treated" rather than remedied, the emphasis on compliance as the only means to demonstrate progress toward addressing these conditions ensures that the most marginalized parents in society—largely poor Black parents—will suffer the most severe consequences when compliance is not met. Thus, compliance becomes the mechanism by which the family policing system justifies disproportionate rates of family separations among poor Black families, while reinforcing the narrative that the fault for these separations lies solely with Black parents due to their lack of compliance. This also reinforces the societal ambivalence that allows the destruction of Black families to continue. Rather than being seen as victims of a government system designed to maintain their oppression, the family policing system perpetuates the idea that Black parents are simply unable to care for their children—even when a host of "services" are provided—thus any level of state intervention is not only warranted, but necessary.

Compliance by Punishment

The surveillance and regulatory mechanisms of the family policing system work to uphold Eurocentric standards that stem from the larger societal context within the United States. These standards are focused primarily on the actions and behaviors of individual parents, rather than the broader societal failures caused by systemic racism and other forms of marginalization. As stated before, this individualized focus impacts mostly poor Black families who are caught within the carceral ecosystem and who are expected to comply with the cultural norms and demands that are perpetuated by the family policing system and family policing agents. To enforce this compliance and the broader mechanism of social control, the system relies on the use of punitive processes. By adhering to a retributive justice framework, the system ensures that there is always a punitive or carceral consequence for families and even agents who fail to meet the system's subjective and required expectations. Though family policing advocates may argue that these punishments are not meant to harm families but are rather instituted for the "protection" of children, many impacted community members report that these punishments have had long-lasting consequences, are mentally and physically devastating, and are reminiscent of the treatment that was endured by Black families during slavery.[38]

Mariame Kaba describes punishment as "inflicting suffering on others in response to an experience of harm/violence/wrongdoing."[39] Definitions of "harm," and the related concept of "risk," are socially constructed, and thus are often associated with poor Black communities in the United States.[40] These subjective definitions seep into our social institutions, which, in turn, police and regulate specific communities. In particular, the family policing system often uses stereotypes and assumptions to criminalize poor families and families of color, considering certain behaviors such as "non-compliance," houselessness, and substance use as irreparably harmful. These classifications send a message to society that certain parents are harmful or unsafe, and that children are best protected through separation. In many instances separating Black children from their families is seen by the system as an urgent necessity rather than a subjective choice. As previously stated, the ideologies that fuel this criminalization and the punishment of families are not a product of modernity. Rather, carceral logics are used to uphold racialized and gendered classifications that *maintain and reinforce* what was started during human chattel slavery. Tactics such as surveillance and family separation that are used by the family policing system today are therefore not modern practices but are deeply rooted in historical processes that have become normalized and ingrained into our current context.

During chattel slavery, family separation was not merely an economic transaction of human commodity—it was also a way to ensure that White enslavers could control and dominate capital, labor, and the reproduction of Black people. Moreover, although it is often said that enslavers dehumanized enslaved people by inflicting violence and stripping them of autonomy and rights, they also weaponized the *humanity* of enslaved people and their families to force compliance at the plantation through severe forms of punishment. Henry Bibb recounted the grief associated with experiencing this as a enslaved person, stating,

[B]ut I could never look upon the dear child without being filled with sorrow and fearful apprehensions, of being separated by slaveholders, because she was a slave, regarded as property. And unfortunately for me, I am the father of a slave, a word too obnoxious to be spoken by a fugitive slave. It calls fresh to my mind the separation of husband and wife; of stripping, tying up and flogging; of tearing children from their parents, and selling them on the auction block....But oh! When I remember that my daughter, my only child, is still there, destined to share the fate of all these calamites, it is too much to bear.[41]

Mary Prince, a formerly enslaved person, also recounted in her narrative:

I could stand the floggings no longer; that I was weary of my life, and therefore I had run away to my mother; but mothers could only weep and mourn over their children, they could not save them from cruel masters—from the whip, the rope, and the cowskin. He told me to hold my tongue and go about my work, or he would find a way to settle me . . . I was not permitted to see my mother or father, or poor sister and brothers, to say good bye, though going away to a strange land, and might never see them again. Oh the Buckra people who kept slaves think that black people are like cattle, without natural affection. But my heart tells me it is far otherwise.[42]

Enslavers believed that enslaved people were incapable of feeling a deep emotional connection with their family members, thus they frequently denied families the ability to say goodbye to one another before separation. Paradoxically however, many enslavers also used family separation and the assumed bond between parent and child to coerce enslaved people into "behaving" according to their wishes. Enslaver Thomas Maskell stated in brief, "I govern them the same way your late brother did, without the whip by stating to them that I should sell them if they do not conduct themselves as I wish."[43] By using the threat of separation, enslavers were able to coerce Black individuals into complying with their demands such that the current social order was perpetually being reconstituted. Family separation was and continues to be the master's tool, a weapon used to regulate and control White people's own economic stability, their social standing, and their general quality of life.[44]

Today, family separation—including the threat of separation—continues to be used to punish and control Black communities across the

United States. Though there have been minimum efforts to reduce the harm that family separation causes, no family policing system will commit to eradicating the harmful practice of separation, even though it would halt the cycle of terror and punishment that Black families have endured generationally. Further, instead of eradicating harmful practices such as family separation, the system has insidiously found new ways to make punishment more expansive and long-lasting. Those impacted by the system rarely describe punishment as solely being associated with family separation. Rather, discussions of punishment often include experiences of increased surveillance and deep loss.[45] When families fail to meet the demands of the system, such as not answering the phone or not attending a required class, they are faced with not only a complete loss of autonomy over decision-making power, but also further punishment through increased surveillance such as random visits. Often an individual's "failure to comply" is noted in court documents that are sent to the judges who preside over dependency cases, or they are inputted into risk assessment protocols that increase the risk score of families—leading to subsequent family separation.[46]

The punishment regime used by the family policing system not only works to punish families but is also used to punish caseworkers and community members for "failure to comply." This is embedded within family policing policy, specifically CAPTA, which imposes severe penalties for noncompliance, including arrest, incarceration, and fines, on any individual who fails to report their suspicions of child abuse or neglect. Due to the fear of punishment, individuals often report cases that are not necessarily a high safety risk. Similar to the ideologies that justified chattel slavery, the family policing system uses carceral logic and practices to diminish community power by deputizing community members to turn against their own neighbors, breaking down community bonds and separating families across generations. Historian Walter Johnson said of the era of chattel slavery, "like a disease that attacks the body though its own immune system, slaveholders used the enslaved families and communities that usually insulated slaves from racism and brutality as an instrument of coercion, to discipline their slaves."[47] This remains the tactic used by the family policing system today. The system does more than separate families as punishment—like a disease it infiltrates and changes the entire fabric of communities by diminishing community power both materially and politically.

The Path Forward

As prior chapters have demonstrated, since the abolition of human chattel slavery, White Americans have sought mechanisms to recreate systems of forced labor and the perpetuation of an exploitable labor class. From the Black codes to Jim Crow Laws, from the criminal punishment system to the family policing system, these policies and systems have worked in tandem to achieve this. Through its mechanisms of surveillance, regulation, and punishment—mechanisms nearly identical in function and outcomes to those of policing and prisons—the family policing system has been designed to systematically punish Black families for their poverty, and through the consequences of this punishment, the system ensures Black families remain in poverty. Thus, while the police and prisons maintain a system of forced labor within their prison walls, the family policing system operates more insidiously—by ensuring Black families never escape poverty and will always be forced into labor simply to survive, perpetually remaining the underclass that capitalist accumulation depends upon. And just as slavery used family separations to maintain compliance with a system that caused immeasurable harm, today's family policing system uses family separations for the same end. Family separations, and the persistent threat of separations, both achieve the goals of the family policing system—the regulation of Black families' behavior and the maintenance of poverty—while also acting to ensure Black families do not resist the system too strongly, due to the ever-present threat of family separation.

Yet where is the resistance from outside the system? As Chapter 1 demonstrated, the visceral understanding of the horror of family separations became the catalyst that moved the country toward abolition. What prevents this understanding from re-entering the public consciousness today? Has the family policing system been so effective in propagating the myth of benevolence that we are blind to the harm it produces? Or is it the pervasive anti-Blackness that exists in society that allows so many to turn a blind eye to the harm being produced? In *Shattered Bonds*, over twenty years ago, Dorothy Roberts notably stated, "The color of America's child welfare system is the reason Americans have tolerated its destructiveness." The anti-Black racism at the heart of this observation remains the most significant barrier to ending the harms perpetuated by the family policing system. Yet there have been times in our history where we have collectively wanted something better, where we have collectively understood that the harms that result from anti-Blackness could no longer be tolerated. There have been times in our history where these harms have become untenable, and there have been times in our history where we have taken action to end these harms. That time has come again.

Notes

1. Andrew Billingsley and Jeanne M. Giovannoni, *Children of the Storm: Black Children and American Child Welfare* (New York: Harcourt, Brace, Jovanovich, 1972).

2. For summaries of racial disproportionality and disparities, see Alan J. Dettlaff and Reiko Boyd, "Racial Disproportionality and Disparities in the Child Welfare System: Why Do They Exist, and What Can Be Done to Address Them?" *Annals of the American Academy of Political and Social Science* 692 (November 2020): pp. 253–274, https://doi.org/10.1177/0002716220980329; and John Fluke, Brenda Jones Harden, Molly Jenkins, and Ashleigh Ruehrdanz, *Disparities and Disproportionality in Child Welfare: Analysis of the Research* (Annie E. Casey Foundation, December 2011), https://www.aecf.org/resources/disparities-and-disproportionality-in-child-welfare.

3. Frank Edwards, Sara Wakefield, Kieran Healy, and Christopher Wildeman, "Contact with Child Protective Services is Pervasive but Unequally Distributed by Race and Ethnicity in Large US Counties," *Proceedings of the National Academy of Sciences of the United States of America* 118, no. 30 (July 2021), https://doi.org/10.1073/pnas.210 6272118; Youngmin Yi, Frank R. Edwards, and Christopher Wildeman, "Cumulative Presence of Confirmed Maltreatment and Foster Care Placement for US Children by Race/Ethnicity, 2011–2016," *American Journal of Public Health* 110, no. 5 (May 2020): pp. 704–709, doi:10.2105/AJPH.2019.305554.

4. Emily Putnam-Hornstein, Eunhye Ahn, John Prindle, Joseph Magruder, Daniel Webster, and Christopher Wildeman, "Cumulative Rates of Child Protection Involvement and Terminations of Parental Rights in a California Birth Cohort, 1999–2017," *American Journal of Public Health* 111, no. 6 (June 2021): pp. 1157–1163, https://doi.org/10.2105/AJPH.2021.306214.

5. Daniel Patrick Moynihan, *The Negro Family: The Case For National Action* (Office of Policy Planning and Research, U.S. Department of Labor, March 1965), https://www.dol.gov/general/aboutdol/history/webid-moynihan.

6. Don Lash, *"When the Welfare People Come": Race and Class in the US Child Protection System* (Chicago: Haymarket Books, 2017), p. 9.

7. Simone Browne, *Dark Matters: On the Surveillance of Blackness* (Durham, NC: Duke University Press, 2015), p. 10.

8. Saidiya Hartman uses the term "afterlife of slavery" to denote a condition where "black lives are still imperiled and devalued by a racial calculus and a political arithmetic that were entrenched centuries ago," in *Lose your mother: A journey along the Atlantic slave route* (New York: Farrar, Straus and Giroux, 2007), p. 6.

9. Browne, *Dark Matters*, p. 16.

10. John J. Dilulio, Jr. "My Black Crime Problem, and Ours," *City Journal,* Spring 1996, https://www.city-journal.org/html/my-black-crime-problem-and-ours-11773.html; Daniel Patrick Moynihan, *The Negro Family: The Case For National Action* (Office of Policy Planning and Research, U.S. Department of Labor, March 1965), p. 30, https://www.dol.gov/general/aboutdol/history/webid-moynihan.

11. Katherine McKittrick, *Dear Science and Other Stories* (Durham, NC: Duke University Press, 2021).

12. For examples and additional resources, see Toni Carrier, "United States 1860 Census Slave Schedules," International African American Museum, Center for Family History, accessed October 29, 2022, https://cfh.iaamuseum.org/united-states-1860-census-slave-schedules/.

13. Jeff Forret, "'Deaf & Dumb, Blind, Insane, or Idiotic': The Census, Slaves, and Disability in the Late Antebellum South," *The Journal of Southern History* 82, no. 3 (August 2016): pp. 503–548, https://www.jstor.org/stable/43918666.

14. Arlene Balkansky, "Runaway! Fugitive Slave Ads in Newspapers," Library of Congress, October 1, 2019, https://blogs.loc.gov/headlinesandheroes/2019/10/runaway-fugitive-slave-ads-in-newspapers/.

15. Safiya Umoja Noble, *Algorithms of Oppression: How Search Engines Reinforce Racism* (New York: NYU Press, 2018).

16. Kaaryn S. Gustafson, *Cheating Welfare: Public Assistance and the Criminalization of Poverty* (New York: NYU Press, 2011).

17. Gustafson, *Cheating Welfare.*

18. Gustafson, *Cheating Welfare,* p. 62.

19. Sue Penna, "The Children Act 2004: Child Protection and Social Surveillance," *Journal of Social Welfare and Family Law* 27, no. 2 (2005): p. 148, https://doi.org/10.1080/09649060500168150.

20. Victoria Copeland, "It's the Only System We've Got: Exploring Emergency Response Decision-Making in Child Welfare," *Columbia Journal of Race and Law* 11, no. 3 (October 2021): pp. 43–74, https://doi.org/10.52214/cjrl.v11i3.8740.

21. Family First Prevention Services Act of 2017, H.R. 253, 115th Cong. https://www.congress.gov/bill/115th-congress/house-bill/253/text.

22. "21st Century Child Welfare System Draft Framework," Casey Family Programs, March 19, 2019, https://aphsa.org//CCFWB/NCLHSA/LiA.aspx.

23. "21st Century System: Convening Summary and Next Steps," Casey Family Programs, May 2018, p. 3, https://aphsa.org//CCFWB/NCLHSA/LiA.aspx.

24. "21st Century System," Casey Family Programs, p. 5.

25. Anjana Samat, Aaron Horowitz, Sophie Beiers, and Kath Xu, *Family Surveillance by Algorithm: The Rapidly Spreading Tools Few Have Heard Of* (American Civil Liberties Union, September 2021), https://www.aclu.org/news/womens-rights/family-surveillance-by-algorithm-the-rapidly-spreading-tools-few-have-heard-of.

26. Daniel Heimpel, "Uncharted Waters: Data Analytics and Child Protection in Los Angeles," *The Imprint,* July 20, 2015, https://imprintnews.org/featured/uncharted-waters-data-analytics-and-child-protection-in-los-angeles/10867.

27. "Oregon Is Dropping an Artificial Intelligence Tool Used in Child Welfare System," National Public Radio, June 2, 2020, https://www.npr.org/2022/06/02/1102661376/ oregon-drops-artificial-intelligence-child-abuse-cases.

28. Sally Ho and Garance Burke, "An Algorithm that Screens for Child Neglect Raises Concerns," *Associated Press News*, April 229, 2022, https://apnews.com/article/child-welfare-algorithm-investigation-9497ee937e0053ad4144a86c68241ef1

29. J. Khadijah Abdurahman, "Calculating the Souls of Black Folk: Predictive Analytics in the New York City Administration for Children's Services," *Columbia Journal of Race and Law* 11, no. 4 (July 2021): p. 83, https://doi.org/10.52214/cjrl.v11i4.8741.

30. Abdurahman, "Calculating the Souls of Black Folk," p. 84.

31. Article I: Administration of the Child Abuse Central Index, California Department of Justice, Division of California Justice Information Services, Child Protection Program, accessed August 2, 2022, https://oag.ca.gov/sites/all/files/agweb/pdfs/chi ldabuse/OAL_approval_final_text.pdf.

32. Article I: Administration of the Child Abuse Central Index, California Department of Justice.

33. Tanya Asim Cooper, "Commentary: Race Is Evidence of Parenting in America: Another Civil Rights Story," in *Civil Rights in American Law, History, and Politics,* edited by Austin Sarat (New York: Cambridge University Press, 2014), p. 107.

34. *Lassiter vs. Department of Social Services* 452 US 18 (1981).

35. Lash, *When the Welfare People Come*, pp. 43–44.

36. For a thorough discussion of how compliance is used in ways that further exacerbate the harms of family policing intervention, see Tina Lee, *Catching A Case: Inequality and Fear in New York City's Child Welfare System* (New Brunswick, NJ: Rutgers University Press, 2016).

37. Wanja Ogongi and Community Legal Services, *Barriers to Successful Reunification of Children with their Families After Foster Care* (Stoneleigh Foundation, August 2012), https://stoneleighfoundation.org/wp-content/uploads/2018/02/Ogongi.Moving-the-Dial.pdf.

38. Victoria Copeland, "Dismantling the Carceral Ecosystem: Investigating the Role of Child Protection and Family Policing in Los Angeles" (PhD dissertation, University of California Los Angeles, May 2022).

39. Mariame Kaba, *Against Punishment* (Project NIA & Interrupting Criminalization, May 2021), p. 3, https://issuu.com/projectnia/docs/against-punishment__1_.

40. See Gustafson, *Cheating Welfare*; Brandon Hasbrouck, "Abolishing Racist Policing with the Thirteenth Amendment," *UCLA Law Review* 67 (2020): pp. 1108–1129, https://scholarlycommons.law.wlu.edu/wlufac/631/; and Moynihan, *The Negro Family*.

41. Henry Bibb, *Narrative of the Life and Adventures of Henry Bibb, an American Slave* (New York: Published by the Author, 1849), p. 44.

42. Mary Prince, *The History of Mary Prince, a West Indian Slave* (London: F. Westley and A. H. Davis, Stationers' Hall Court, 1831), p. 9.

43. Walter Johnson, *Soul by Soul: Life Inside the Antebellum Slave Market* (Cambridge, MA: Harvard University Press, 1999), p. 23.

44. Audre Lorde, "The Master's Tools Will Never Dismantle the Master's House," *Sister Outsider: Essays and Speeches* (Berkeley, CA: Crossing Press, 1984); Clint Smith, *How the Word Is Passed: A Reckoning with the History of Slavery Across America* (New York: Little Brown, 2021).

45. J. Khadijah Abdurahman, "Birthing Predictions of Premature Death," *Logic Magazine*, August 22, 2022, https://logicmag.io/home/birthing-predictions-of-premature-death/; Copeland, "Dismantling the Carceral Ecosystem."

46. See for example, "December 20, 2005 Amendment to Board Agenda Item #44: Skid Row Outreach Strategies," County of Los Angeles Department of Child and Family Services, December 20, 2005, http://file.lacounty.gov/SDSInter/bos/bc/043186_060308_Amendment_to_Board_Agenda_Item_%2344_Skid_Row_Outreach_Str ategies.PDF

47. Johnson, *Soul by Soul*, p. 23.

5

The Intended Consequences

The harms of the family policing system are unknown to most. This is by design. For decades, the family policing system has shrouded itself in a myth of benevolence—a myth that it exists to help the most vulnerable children in society; and although it has some flaws, it is a fundamentally essential system due to the help and protection it provides. This myth perpetuates the dissonance that allows for national outrage over the separations that occurred at the southern border in 2018, while hundreds of thousands of children are separated by family policing agents each year in the United States. As Dorothy Roberts notably points out in *Torn Apart,* "local CPS agents take as many children from their parents every week as were separated under the entire Trump 'zero tolerance' policy."[1] Although the outrage that occurred in the aftermath of "zero tolerance" was wholly warranted and served to end the harmful separations that were occurring, this is the outrage that is needed to end the separations occurring every day in neighborhoods across the country. Yet the myth of benevolence has prevented this from occurring.

In many ways, this myth is perpetuated by media accounts of severely abused children and the family policing system's response when these rare incidents of abuse occur. Consider this recent headline: "Texas teens escape real-life house of horrors: Documents detail torture 16-year-old twins endured." After describing the alleged abuse occurring in this home, the story concludes by saying, "The children are now in CPS custody."[2] For many, headlines such as this create the idea that these are the types of cases to which the family policing system routinely responds. Yet incidents such as this are extremely rare and account for just a fraction of cases investigated by the family policing system. As noted previously, the system is almost entirely focused on investigating families for poverty-related concerns under the guise of "neglect." Yet as a result of this misperception, the myth of benevolence persists, and the real harms inflicted by the system itself remain unknown.

Yet these harms are not unknown to the family policing system. Decades of research have documented the severe harms that result to children, families, and communities from both family separation and placement in foster care.

Confronting the Racist Legacy of the American Child Welfare System. Alan J. Dettlaff, Oxford University Press.
© Oxford University Press 2023. DOI: 10.1093/oso/9780197675267.003.0006

Family policing agents witness this harm each time they forcibly take a child from their mother's arms. They see this harm again when children scream and cry when they are forced to leave the one-hour weekly visits they are allowed with their mother. And they see this harm again and again when the children in their "care" are abused, mistreated, and thrown out of their foster homes. The family policing system is built to harm and oppress marginalized children and it excels at doing so.

Consequences to Children

When children are forcibly separated from their parents the harms that result are vast and immense. Consider the context of how family separations occur by imagining for a moment you are a child being separated from their parents. A family policing agent arrives unannounced at your home accompanied by an armed police officer. You may have previously seen the agent during an interview process, but the agent is mostly a stranger. The stranger informs your mother that they are "removing" you from your home and placing you in foster care. It is your mother who is forced to convey this news to you; she is angry and crying but tries to reassure you that you'll be OK. The stranger instructs you to drop everything and go with them and the police officer. You are also screaming and crying, panicking that you are being taken away from your mother and have no control over anything that's happening. You are told to get in the stranger's car. You are not told why you are being taken; the stranger may say something vague about ensuring your safety. You also are not told when or if you will ever return home. If you ask about this, the stranger will say they don't know. You are taken to a strange home, in a strange neighborhood, with other parents and children you've never seen before. These parents and children do not look like you. You don't know how long you will have to stay there and when you ask about this, you're not given an answer. You're not able to call or talk to your mother. You wake up crying every morning not knowing where you are, what's going to happen to you, or if you'll ever see your mother again.

This is the pain and horror of family separation. And this is the pain and horror caused to hundreds of thousands of children every year by the family policing system. The harms of this pain and horror last a lifetime. Much of what we know about the harms of forcible family separation comes from research done on children who are forcibly separated from their parents due to parental incarceration,[3] and more recently on children forcibly separated from their parents due to immigration enforcement and detention.[4] Despite these being very different circumstances for separation, the consequences to children are nearly identical and include anxiety, depression, difficulty sleeping, behavioral problems including isolation and aggression, learning disabilities, developmental delays, poor educational outcomes including low grades, poor attendance, suspensions and expulsions, and the development of toxic stress, which can lead to significant health problems in later life, including cancer, diabetes, and autoimmune diseases.

Studies with children who have been forcibly separated from their parents by the family police confirm the pain and trauma they endure. Although the body of research specific to the experience of family separation by the family policing system is small compared to that of parental incarceration and immigration enforcement—likely due to the myth of benevolence the system has perpetuated—these studies consistently document children's feelings of trauma, loss, fear, anger, and helplessness, as well as stress, shock, and confusion.[5] In one qualitative account of children who have been forcibly separated, one child described this as, "It's like you're being kidnapped, and no one wants to tell you [nothing]."[6] It is important to note here the overwhelming feelings of confusion that children consistently report after being separated from their parents by the family police. Further countering the notion of an essential system that is responding to children at risk of serious harm, in study after study children consistently report they do not even understand why they have been taken from their parents. Even after spending some time in foster care, most children remain unaware of why they are there. Yet the trauma this separation produces is life changing. Another child described this experience as follows:

> I felt like my life was tooken away, I felt like I didn't have no freedom, no independence, it was, to be completely honest with you really, it was one of the worst experiences in my life, going on 21 years that I've been on this Earth that was definitely one of the worst experience in my life, right there . . . You know, it was terrible. You know, I, I lost my strength, I lost my life, I lost myself. It was, it was, it was hell man.[7]

Following the thousands of family separations that occurred during the period of the Trump administration's zero-tolerance policy and the public outrage that ensued, multiple psychologists and other medical professionals, including the American Psychological Association, came forward to decry the practice of forcible family separations. Citing decades of research on family separations that occur under any circumstance, these medical professionals consistently attested to the harm and trauma that result. Dr. Erin Dunn, a social and psychiatric epidemiologist at Massachusetts General Hospital's Center for Genomic Medicine, stated, "The scientific evidence against separating children from families is crystal clear. No one in the scientific community would dispute it—it's not like other topics where there is more debate among scientists. We all know it is bad for children to be separated from caregivers. Given the scientific evidence, it is malicious and amounts to child abuse."[8] In describing how children experience separation, one report based on conversations with medical professionals stated:

> Their heart rate goes up. Their body releases a flood of stress hormones such as cortisol and adrenaline. Those stress hormones can start killing off dendrites—the little branches in brain cells that transmit messages. In time, the stress can start killing off neurons and—especially in young children— wreaking dramatic and long-term damage, both psychologically and to the physical structure of the brain.[9]

A petition signed by 7,700 mental health professionals and 142 organizations stated, "To pretend that separated children do not grow up with the shrapnel of this traumatic experience embedded in their minds is to disregard everything we know about child development, the brain, and trauma."[10] The evidence documenting the harm of forcible family separation is so clear, Dr. Charles Nelson, a pediatrics professor at Harvard Medical School, concluded, "There's so much research on this that if people paid attention at all to the science, they would never do this."[11]

Once again, there remains a disconnect in our public consciousness. The family policing system forcibly separates over 200,000 children every year from their parents, yet these separations go largely unnoticed. There is no public outcry. Physicians and mental health professionals do not speak out against this as they did the forcible separations that occurred at the Southern border. Yet the harm and trauma children experience when they are forcibly separated by the family policing system are the same. As hundreds of physicians attested in calling for separations at the border to end, decades of scientific research have documented these harms. Yet the myth of benevolence created by the family policing system and perpetuated by its supporters has removed this from our collective understanding.

Following family separation, children's experiences in foster care continue to be harmful and traumatic. In addition to not understanding why they were taken from their parents, children receive little to no information on when or if they will ever be returned home. While in foster care, children continue to be moved multiple times, also with little explanation. Studies demonstrate that the frequency of moves can result in as many as fifteen moves during the first eighteen months of placement.[12] One large-scale study of over six hundred youth who spent time in foster care found the average number of placement changes to be 6.5, with one-third of youth moving more than eight times; youth also changed schools as many as ten times while in foster care.[13] Although some moves may result from serious concerns, studies show that moves are often done at the whim of foster parents who simply do not like something about the children they agreed to house. One study showed that toddlers were moved because of tantrums, while teenagers were moved for refusing to do chores. One child in this study was moved twice because their foster parents did not approve of their sexual orientation.[14]

Children in foster care are also particularly vulnerable to physical and sexual abuse at the hands of their foster providers, whether those providers are foster parents or institutional staff. Multiple studies across decades have shown that rates of physical and sexual abuse among children in foster care are two to four times greater than rates of physical and sexual abuse in the general population.[15] In the same study mentioned earlier of youth who had spent time in foster care, one-third of those youth reported being maltreated by their foster parents.[16] In another large study of youth who had spent time in group home settings, reports of physical and sexual abuse at the hands of staff members were frequent. One youth reported, "I was hit. I was punched in the face. One time I was knocked unconscious, one staff grabbed my arm, I was trying to get it out, he full on judo hit me and knocked me out. I had a bunch of staff restrain me."[17] In describing the rampant sexual abuse that occurs in institutional care, another youth stated, "I think the number one thing I would change is the amount of sexual assault that happens . . . In residential facilities, staff are molesting female residents."[18] Another youth reported being sexually trafficked by her group home staff, stating, "The group home staff was my pimp."[19]

Although this may seem like an extreme, isolated incident, it is not. Recent reports have demonstrated that youth in group home settings are frequently trafficked for sex by the staff of those facilities, with investigations into this practice occurring in multiple states.[20] The system that justifies its existence on the need to protect children from harm is a direct cause of that harm for tens of thousands of children every year.

Likely due to the trauma children experience from family separation and foster care, children in foster care are more likely to use substances, have a substance use disorder, and have significantly higher rates of mental health concerns when compared to children in the general population. Research shows that the rate of drug dependence for children in foster care is more than twice the rate of dependence in the general population and rates of alcohol dependence are more than three times the rate in the general population.[21] Children in foster care with mental health concerns range anywhere from two to fifteen times the rate of children in the general population, with some studies showing as many as two-thirds of children in foster care having a mental health diagnosis.[22] Finally, children in foster care are more than three times as likely to attempt suicide than children not in foster care,[23] a staggering figure demonstrating the depth of trauma and pain children in foster care experience.

Although the harm and trauma children experience during foster care are enormous, it is the outcomes children experience as adults, after they exit foster care, where the consequences of this harm and trauma are realized. Multiple studies across decades have shown that children who spend time in foster care are at significant risk of a host of adverse outcomes as adults. One of the largest studies of former foster youth—including over 1,600 youth across the country who had spent at least one year in foster care—found that these youth experienced post-traumatic stress disorder (PTSD) at a rate nearly five times that of the general population, a rate that exceeded that of United States war veterans. Former foster youth also experienced panic disorders at a rate three times that of the general population, seven times the rate of drug dependence, and nearly two times the rate of alcohol dependence. One in five youth were homeless after leaving foster care, college attendance was lower than in the general population, and former foster youth were significantly less likely to be employed than comparable adults in the general population.[24] A study of over six hundred former foster youth in the Northwest revealed similar findings—when compared to adults in the general population, youth who had spent time in foster care were significantly more likely to be diagnosed with PTSD or major depression, less likely to be employed, less likely to have health insurance, and more likely to be homeless. Notably, only 2.7 percent of these former foster youth had earned a bachelor's degree by their twenty-fifth birthday.[25]

Study after study show similar findings. Children who spend time in foster care are consistently more likely to experience unemployment or low earnings, less likely to graduate high school, more likely to rely on income assistance programs, more likely to have significant mental health and substance use disorders, and significantly more likely to be incarcerated. One recent study of over six thousand people incarcerated across twelve states found that one in four had spent the majority of their childhood in foster care. One person interviewed for this study who was now incarcerated and on death row said, "The state that neglected me as a kid and allowed me to age out of its support is the same state that wants to kill me."[26] In another study examining over 1,400 young adults experiencing homelessness, nearly 40 percent reported spending time in foster care as children.[27] Although not all studies examining outcomes of former foster youth included comparisons based on race, those that did consistently found that Black youth experienced far poorer outcomes than White youth—in particular, Black former foster youth were significantly more likely to be unemployed,[28] more likely to be receiving public assistance,[29] less likely to have a high school diploma,[30] more likely to have experienced homelessness,[31] and more likely to be incarcerated than White former foster youth.[32]

Here it is important to note that children who enter foster care may have experienced other forms of trauma prior to entering foster care that could account for some of their outcomes later in life. However, a number of studies have compared youth who experienced foster care with youth who experienced similar forms of maltreatment but remained in their homes—essentially isolating the effects of family separation and foster care—and found similarly poor outcomes for youth who entered foster care. A series of causal studies done by MIT economist Joseph Doyle found that children who experienced foster care were twice as likely to experience teen motherhood, three times as likely to be incarcerated as adults, and had employment and earning rates 40 percent lower than similarly situated children who never entered foster care.[33] Other causal studies have produced similar findings—when compared to youth with similar backgrounds and experiences, youth who experience foster care experience lower levels of educational attainment and higher rates of poverty, homelessness, early parenthood, referral to drug or alcohol treatment, and incarceration.[34]

It is also important to note that the consequences that result from foster care can be experienced by all children who are forcibly separated from their families. Family separation and foster care are harmful to all children. The risk of experiencing these outcomes is, however, significantly exacerbated for Black children due to both the disproportionate rates this is inflicted on them and the entrenched disadvantage and inequities that exist in the United States due to decades of social policies that have been designed to ensure this persists. As a result, Black children in the United States are already at risk of experiencing poor outcomes over the course of their lives including poverty, poor health, low educational attainment, homelessness, and incarceration.[35] For Black children who then experience the added trauma of family separation and placement in foster care—practices known to result in these same conditions—the family policing system all but assures these conditions will be realized.

Because of this, it is necessary to consider what forced family separation means for Black children in a racist society. Due to decades of structural racism, Black youth are more likely to reside in community contexts characterized by inequitable educational systems, concentrated poverty, systemic disinvestment, police brutality, and economic blight. Their communities are resource deprived and used as a strike against them in risk assessments made by family policing agents. As such, the inequities that exist in the family policing system exacerbate what is already an unequal playing field and feed a cycle of inequality that makes it even more likely that Black children and families will experience a host of negative conditions that directly compromise their health and well-being. Disproportionate separation and placement in foster care perpetuates the negative outcomes, adverse experiences, and disparaging contexts to which Black children are already disproportionately subjected.

Thus, in fully considering the experiences of Black children, family separation and placement in foster care cannot be considered a race-neutral event. For Black children, in addition to changes in their primary home setting, being placed in foster care is often associated with changes in several key arenas such as schools, community settings, and social networks. Because of structural inequity that is embedded across neighborhood contexts, foster homes and services are often concentrated outside of youths' communities of origin. As a result, Black children more often face the predicament of navigating unfamiliar social, cultural, and structural landscapes. They are also increasingly surveilled through constant interactions with social workers, service providers, group home staff, judges, attorneys, and medical professionals within contexts of interviews, court hearings, assessments, examinations, therapeutic interventions, and home visits. Although some interactions with professionals may be experienced as helpful or culturally responsive, Black children may also experience racial microaggressions and direct racial prejudice in interactions across these settings.

As a result, it is important to consider the developmental contexts that occur within childhood to fully understand the harms and consequences that result when Black children are forcibly separated from their families. The backdrop to any single Black child's experience in foster care occurs in a racist society with structurally racist institutions that generate and sustain the inequitable distribution of resources and access to opportunity. Due to this context, and to the deep disparities that occur across these institutions, family separation and foster care come with distinct consequences and risks for Black children.

As infants, Black children experience disparities in the most consequential health indicators measured at birth, including low birth weight and pre-term delivery. Disparities in birth outcomes carry serious health implications because, in addition to increased mortality risk during infancy, survivors of low birth weight and preterm delivery face increased likelihood of experiencing problems across the life span. These include impaired growth, risk of emotional and developmental deficits, lower cognitive and academic achievement, hypertension, diabetes, higher rates of respiratory illness and cardiovascular disease, and psychiatric illness in adulthood.[36] As a result, for Black children placed in foster care during infancy, typical challenges such as placement changes and disruption in continuity of care may lead to additional far-reaching consequences.

In early and middle childhood, Black children face increased likelihood of experiencing inequities in systems of education. In addition to gaps in school quality and available resources, Black children are subject to disproportionate rates of school discipline. Studies demonstrate that Black students are disproportionately dealt the harshest exclusionary penalties including expulsions and out-of-school suspensions.[37] Black children represent 18 percent of the nation's pre-school population, yet they comprise 48 percent of those receiving more than one out-of-school suspension.[38] Even more troubling, compared to White students, Black students are 2.3 times more likely to receive a referral to law enforcement or be subject to a school-related arrest.[39] Each of these challenges may be exacerbated for Black children in foster care. For example, experiences of disparate school discipline result in additional threats to foster care placements that are already unstable. Further, foster care placement can directly contribute to educational instability when it is necessary for children to change schools because of their placement. Multiple subsequent changes in placement can disrupt school enrollment, create barriers to consistent attendance, and hinder academic performance. Each of these issues can contribute to cycles of inequality that further marginalize Black children.

During adolescence, in addition to continued inequities embedded in educational contexts, Black adolescents also experience pervasive overrepresentation and disparate outcomes in the juvenile legal system. Although Black, White, and Latinx youth commit acts deemed "delinquent" at comparable rates, Black youth are more likely to be arrested for misdemeanor and felony crimes.[40] Beyond arrests, racial disparities continue at every point of contact across the juvenile legal system, with Black youth being more likely than other youth to be referred to juvenile court, sent to secure confinement, and sent to adult criminal court and state prisons.[41] For youth in foster care, research shows that Black youth are significantly more likely than other youth to "crossover" into the juvenile legal system.[42] Beyond juvenile system involvement, disparities in reunification and permanency outcomes contribute to Black youth spending extended periods of their adolescence in foster care, an arrangement known to be less amenable to typical adolescent growing pains and experimentation.

Thus, in addition to the direct harms that family separation and placement in foster care inflict on Black children, family policing intervention interacts with other systems that exacerbate and add further harms unique to Black children. At each developmental stage, Black children are both directly and indirectly harmed through family policing intervention due to the broader racial context in which family separations occur. Thus, the family policing system acts independently to disproportionately harm Black children. These harms are then exacerbated and extended through the racism that exists in the broader society and across government institutions.

Consequences to Parents

Although the consequences to children that result from the family policing system have been well-documented, the consequences that result for parents have been examined less. This is due in part to the myth of family policing intervention that frames parents as "abusers" who deserve to have their children taken from them. However, just as it is the reality of the family policing system that less than one-fifth of children who are seized from their parents have experienced any form of physical or sexual abuse, it is also the reality that less than one-fifth of *parents* whose children are forcibly taken from them are responsible for any physical or sexual harm to their children. Rather, the vast majority of parents who experience the harshest form of punishment that can be inflicted on them by the state are parents living in poverty, struggling to do everything they can to meet the needs of their children, who are then blamed and labeled as "neglectful" by the state when their efforts fail to meet the White, middle-class standard the state has judged them against. Yet, this is the purpose of the family policing system—to maintain the oppression of poor Black families by punishing them for their poverty. This punishment comes in the form of both forcible family separation and the consequences that result.

Studies that have examined mothers' mental health following the forced separation of their children have shown severe consequences including the development of post-traumatic stress syndrome, as well as other mental health issues including depression and anxiety.[43] Mothers also describe debilitating feelings of loss and grief following the separation of their children, with these feelings impacting every aspect of their daily lives. Multiple studies have shown that mothers whose children are forcibly separated from them turn to prescription drugs and alcohol to manage the pain of losing their child.[44] The pain of this loss can be so severe, a recent study found that mothers who experience forced separation of a child by the family police were more likely to experience unintentional, nonfatal overdoses compared to mothers who had never experienced this loss.[45] Another study showed that mothers who lost a child due to forced separation were more likely to experience suicide attempts and death by suicide compared to mothers who had family police involvement but did not experience forced separation.[46]

Along with severe trauma and loss, mothers also experience significant stigma associated with forcible family separation, a stigma that often does not accompany other forms of loss. Mothers report that this sense of stigma has broad impacts on their sense of purpose and ambitions, as well as the relationships they form with others.[47] This sense of stigma can be so severe, studies have shown that mothers who lose a child to the family police have higher rates of depression, substance use, and use of psychotropic medications than mothers who experience the death of a child, likely due to a loss of social support and a lack of social acknowledgment of the grief they experience.[48]

Exacerbating the mental health consequences mothers experience, forcible family separation can have significant financial consequences for parents who are already experiencing financial hardship. Following family separation, parents are presented with a "service plan," detailing the classes, tests, and other requirements with which they are expected to comply if they hope to be considered for what the state refers to as "re-unification." The costs associated with these requirements include taking significant time off from work for appointments that are largely only held during working hours, as well as significant travel time which often must be done via public transportation. This comes with no consideration or empathy from family policing agents who expect mothers to comply with all service demands without regard for issues of accessibility, transportation, or job responsibilities. It is important to note that these demands are all made within a system of surveillance and punishment that penalizes parents for any form of "non-compliance." In this regard, "compliance" and "non-compliance" are judgments passed on parents solely related to participation in services, not whether services are effective in meeting their needs. As a result, mothers commonly experience loss of employment in order to comply with service demands.[49]

Adding to the costs of compliance, parents experience direct financial consequences including the costs to participate in certain services or to obtain regular drug tests. Parents also lose eligibility for certain resources when their children are taken from them, including access to certain housing programs, for which they need to be eligible to have their children returned. Thus, parents lose eligibility to certain resources when their children are forcibly separated from them—then the state requires them to access the resources for which they are no longer eligible to have their children returned. States may also order that parents pay child support to offset the costs of foster care.[50] If this does not happen while children are in foster care, states can bill parents for the cost of foster care following reunification—bills that can exceed tens of thousands of dollars.[51] To underscore the intentionally vicious circle this creates—states forcibly separate children from their parents for reasons largely related to poverty, then if parents somehow meet the intense demands put on them by the system, they are presented with a bill for the care of their children while they were in foster care, further driving them into poverty—the very reason that led to their children being taken from them. This is the logic of family policing.

It is not an accident or an unintended consequence that this happens disproportionately to poor Black parents, particularly to poor Black single mothers. Decades of policy development, dating back to the Black codes that followed abolition of slavery, have created the conditions of oppression and disadvantage that disproportionately impact Black parents, and decades of family policing policy dating back to the passage of the Civil Rights Act have created the conditions that ensure Black parents face the most severe consequences of family policing intervention. These consequences are not only vast and severe—causing significant harm to parents' physical and mental health, as well as significant financial consequences—they serve the purpose of creating the conditions that drive Black parents' continual involvement in the system through the surveillance and policing that occurs in poor Black communities. Thus, the family policing system creates the conditions of disadvantage that disproportionately impact Black families across generations—these conditions then fuel Black families' continual involvement in the system.

Consequences to Communities

The consequences that result from the family policing system at the community level have similarly been understudied because examining the broader sociopolitical impacts of family policing intervention at the community level presents many challenges. It is at the community level, however, that the consequences of family policing have their greatest cumulative impact. These consequences are also the means by which the family policing system fulfills its true intent—the continued subjugation of Black Americans and the advancement of White supremacy.

The consequences of the family policing system at the community level were first illuminated by Dorothy Roberts in *Shattered Bonds*, in which she outlined the harmful effects that the disproportionate separation of individual Black children from individual Black families has on Black people as a collective and as a community. In this groundbreaking work, Roberts argues that the disproportionate separation of Black children by the family policing system, which is coupled with the surveillance of Black families in Black communities, has a harmful effect on both the community identity and community power shared among Black people. When Black families are disproportionately torn apart within Black communities, the harms experienced by individual children and parents—poverty, unemployment, substance use, mental health disorders—are extended across entire communities, exacerbating the structural disadvantages these communities already face and further weakening their collective ability to overcome these disadvantages.[52] Thus, the collective power that Black communities could harvest to challenge decades of oppressive government systems and structures is systematically quashed by intensive surveillance, regulation, and punishment by those government systems, including the family policing system.

The consequences of intensive family policing in Black communities were further explored in Roberts' subsequent study of Black women in Chicago, which documented the harmful consequences of family policing involvement on family and community relationships. Participants in this study described the vast reach and fear of this system that permeated throughout their community to the point where every resident had either personally been impacted by family policing intervention or knew someone who had been impacted by this intervention. This intense level of surveillance and intervention in families' lives resulted in an overwhelming feeling of oppression that impacted all aspects of family and community engagement. This included a significant impact on mothers' perceptions of parental authority, as widespread fear of the family policing system impacted their ability to make decisions about how to discipline their children. Mothers also described significant harm to their social relationships due to fears that personal disputes would lead to calls to the family police, resulting in a lack of trust among neighbors. Overall, the vast impact of family policing within Black communities served to significantly weaken family and community ties, dismantling social networks, and turning Black families against each other.[53]

It is through this weakening of community relationships and weakening of collective political power that the family policing system achieves its true purpose. Massive state overreach into families' lives combined with the devastating consequences that result from disproportionate family separations within Black communities maintains the conditions of oppression that White supremacy relies on and weakens Black families' and communities' ability to overcome this oppression. Further, the specific racial terror inflicted on Black communities through the ever-present threat of family separation prohibits Black communities from uniting and revolting against the harm inflicted on them. Just as the threat of family separations instilled fear and regulated the behavior of enslaved Black Americans during the era of chattel slavery, the collective fear and terror that has been instilled across Black communities by the family policing system across decades achieves its purpose by maintaining their subjugation.

The True Intents of the Family Policing System

The family policing system and its supporters will tell you the consequences described in this chapter are unintended consequences. They are not. These are the consequences that occur within a system of White supremacy that has been designed to ensure this result. It is also important to understand that these consequences are known by all actors within the family policing system. Each of the consequences outlined in this chapter have been known to the family policing system for decades, and despite this awareness, each of these consequences continues to occur. Since its earliest origins, actors within the family policing system have known of the disproportionate harm inflicted on Black children and families, and decade after decade, these actors have chosen to allow these harms to continue. The abundance of knowledge that has been available regarding these harms over these decades is evidence of the system's intent. If the intent had been different, the harm would have stopped. Rather, this evidence forms the basis for understanding the true intents of the family policing system. By knowingly subjecting an already oppressed population to an intervention known to result in significant harm, the family policing system ensures this oppression is maintained. Since its earliest origins, the family policing system was designed for this purpose, and this is the purpose that remains today.

Notes

1. Dorothy Roberts, *Torn Apart: How the Child Welfare System Destroys Black Families— and How Abolition Can Build a Safer World* (New York: Basic Books, 2022), p. 49.
2. "Texas Twins Escape Handcuffs After They Were Allegedly Abused by Mother, Police Say," ABC7 Eyewitness News, Houston, October 22, 2022, https://abc7.com/twins-texas-child-abuse-escape/12361828/.

3. Kristin Turney and Rebecca Goodsell, "Parental Incarceration and Children's Wellbeing," *The Future of Children* 28, no. 1 (Spring 2018): pp. 147–164, https://www.jstor.org/stable/10.2307/26641551; Christopher Wildeman, Alyssa W. Goldman, and Kristen Turney, "Parental Incarceration and Child Health in the United States," *Epidemiologic Reviews* 40, no. 1 (2018): pp. 146–156, https://doi.org/10.1093/epirev/mxx013.

4. Kristina Lovato, Corina Lopez, Leyla Karimli, and Laura S. Abrams, "The Impact of Deportation-Related Family Separations on the Well-Being of Latinx Children and Youth: A Review of the Literature," *Children and Youth Services Review* 95 (December 2018): pp. 109–116, https://doi.org/10.1016/j.childyouth.2018.10.011; Laura C. N. Wood, "Impact of Punitive Immigration Policies, Parent-Child Separation and Child Detention on the Mental Health and Development of Children," *BMJ Paediatrics Open* 2: e000338 (2018), doi:10.1136/bmjpo-2018-000338.

5. Rosalind D. Folman, "'I Was Tooken': How Children Experience Removal from Their Parents Preliminary to Placement into Foster Care," *Adoption Quarterly* 2, no.2 (1998): p. 735, http://dx.doi.org/10.1300/J145v02n02_02; Monique B. Mitchell, "'No One Acknowledged My Loss and Hurt': Non-death Loss, Grief, and Trauma in Foster Care," *Child and Adolescent Social Work Journal* 35, no. 1 (February 2018): pp. 1–9, doi:10.1007/s10560-017-0502-8.

6. Monique B. Mitchell and Leon Kuczynski, "Does Anyone Know What Is Going On? Examining Children's Lived Experience of the Transition Into Foster Care," *Children and Youth Services Review* 32 (2010): p. 440, http://dx.doi.org/10.1016/j.childyouth.2009.10.023.

7. Mitchell, "No One Acknowledged My Loss and Hurt," p. 3.

8. Allison Eck, "Psychological Damage Inflicted by Parent-Child Separation is Deep, Long-Lasting," *NOVA Next,* June 20, 2018, https://www.pbs.org/wgbh/nova/article/psychological-damage-inflicted-by-parent-child-separation-is-deep-long-lasting/.

9. William Wan, "What Separation from Parents Does to Children: 'The Effect Is Catastrophic,'" *The Washington Post,* June 18, 2018, https://www.washingtonpost.com/national/health-science/what-separation-from-parents-does-to-children-the-effect-is-catastrophic/2018/06/18/c00c30ec-732c-11e8-805c-4b67019fcfe4_story.html.

10. Wan, "What Separation from Parents Does to Children."

11. Wan, "What Separation from Parents Does to Children."

12. Rae R. Newton, Alan J. Litrownik, and John A. Landsverk, "Children and Youth in Foster Care: Disentangling the Relationship Between Problem Behaviors and Number of Placements," *Child Abuse & Neglect* 24, no. 10 (October 2000): pp. 1363–1374.

13. Peter J. Pecora, Ronald C. Kessler, Jason Williams, Kirk O'Brien, A. Chris Downs, Diana English, James White, Eva Hiripi, Catherine Roller White, Tamera Wiggins, and Kate Holmes, *Improving Family Foster Care: Findings from the Northwest Foster Care Alumni Survey* (Casey Family Programs, March 2005), https://www.casey.org/northwest-alumni-study/.

14. Nancy Rolock, Eun Koh, Ted Cross, and Jennifer Eblen Manning, *Multiple Move Study: Understanding Reasons for Foster Care Instability* (Child and Family Research

Center, University of Illinois at Urbana-Champaign, November 2009), https://cfrc.illinois.edu/pubs./rp_20091101_MultipleMoveStudyUnderstandingReasonsForFosterCareInstability.pdf.

15. Mary I. Benedict, Susan Zuravin, Diane Brandt, and Helen Abbey, "Types and Frequency of Child Maltreatment by Family Foster Care Providers in an Urban Population," *Child Abuse & Neglect* 18, no. 7 (July 1994): pp. 577–585, doi:10.1016/0145-2134(94)90084-1; Nina Biehal, "Maltreatment in Foster Care: A Review of the Evidence," *Child Abuse Review* 23 (2014): pp. 48–60, doi:10.1002/car.2249; J. William Spencer and Dean D. Knudsen, "Out-of-Home Maltreatment: An Analysis of Risk in Various Settings for Children," *Children and Youth Services Review* 14 (1992): pp. 485–492, doi:10.1016/0190-7409(92)90002-D.

16. Pecora et al., *Improving Family Foster Care.*

17. Sarah Fathallah and Sarah Sullivan, *Away From Home: Youth Experiences of Institutional Placements in Foster Care* (Think of Us, July 2021), https://www.thinkof-us.org/awayfromhome, p. 40.

18. Fathallah and Sullivan, *Away From Home*, p. 41.

19. Fathallah and Sullivan, *Away From Home*, p. 41.

20. Luz Moreno-Lozano, "'There is Not a Good Answer': Texas Foster Care Under Fire After Refuge Sex Trafficking Allegations," *Austin American-Statesman,* March 18, 2022, https://www.statesman.com/story/news/2022/03/18/texas-foster-care-under-fire-after-refuge-sex-trafficking-allegations-bastrop-county/7075522001/; Sherman Smith, "'Twisted Cruelty': Foster Girls Crushed by Abuse at Newton Group Home," *The Topeka Capital-Journal,* June 1, 2020, https://www.cjonline.com/story/news/politics/state/2020/06/02/rsquotwisted-crueltyrsquo-foster-girls-crushed-by-abuse-at-newton-group-home/114926130/.

21. Peter J. Pecora, Catherine Roller White, Lovie J. Jackson, and Tamera Wiggins, "Mental Health of Current and Former Recipients of Foster Care: A Review of Recent Studies in the USA," *Child & Family Social Work* 14 (2009): pp. 132–146, doi:10.1111/j.1365-2206.2009.00618.x.

22. Pecora et al., "Mental Health of Current and Former Recipients of Foster Care."

23. Rhiannon Evans, James White, Ruth Turley, Thomas Slater, Helen Morgan, Heather Strange, and Jonathan Scourfield, "Comparison of Suicidal Ideation, Suicide Attempt and Suicide in Children and Young People in Care and Non-Care Populations: Systematic Review and Meta-Analysis of Prevalence," *Children and Youth Services Review* 82 (2017): pp. 122–129.

24. Peter J. Pecora, Jason Williams, Ronald C. Kessler, A. Chris Downs, Kirk O'Brien, Eva Hiripi, and Sarah Morello, *Assessing the Effects of Foster Care: Early Results from the Casey National Alumni Study* (Casey Family Programs, December 2003), https://www.casey.org/national-alumni-study/.

25. Pecora et al., *Improving Family Foster Care.*

26. Laura Bauer and Judy L. Thomas, "Throwaway Kids: We Are Sending More Foster Kids to Prison Than College," *The Wichita Eagle* (December 15, 2019), https://www.kansas.com/news/politicsgovernment/article238206754.html.

27. Sarah C. Narendorf, Daphne M. Brydon, Diana Santa Maria, Kimberly Bender, Kristin M. Ferguson, Hsun-Ta Hsu, Anamika Barman-Adhikari, Jama Shelton, and Robin Petering, "System Involvement Among Young Adults Experiencing Homelessness: Characteristics of Four System-Involved Subgroups and Relationship to Risk Outcomes," *Children and Youth Services Review* 108 (2020), https://doi.org/10.1016/j.childyouth.2019.104609.

28. Amy Dworsky and Elissa Gitlow, "Employment Outcomes of Young Parents Who Age Out of Foster Care," *Children and Youth Services Review* 72 (2017): pp. 133–140, http://dx.doi.org/10.1016/j.childyouth.2016.09.032; Jennifer L. Cook and Mark E. Courtney, "Employment Outcomes of Former Foster Youth as Young Adults: The Importance of Human, Personal, and Social Capital," *Children and Youth Services Review* 33 (2011): pp. 1855–1865, doi:10.1016/j.childyouth.2011.05.004; Toni Watt and Seoyoun Kim, "Race/Ethnicity and Foster Youth Outcomes: An Examination of Disproportionality Using the National Youth in Transition Database," *Children and Youth Services Review* 102 (2019): pp. 251–258, https://doi.org/10.1016/j.childyouth.2019.05.017.

29. Amy Dworsky, Catherine Roller White, Kirk O'Brien, Peter Pecora, Mark Courtney, Ronald Kessler, Nancy Sampson, and Irving Hwang, "Racial and Ethnic Differences in the Outcomes of Former Foster Youth," *Children and Youth Services Review* 32 (2010): pp. 902–912, doi:10.1016/j.childyouth.2010.03.001.

30. Dworsky et al., "Racial and Ethnic Differences in the Outcomes of Former Foster Youth."

31. Dworsky et al., "Racial and Ethnic Differences in the Outcomes of Former Foster Youth."

32. Watt and Kim, "Race/Ethnicity and Foster Youth Outcomes."

33. Joseph J. Doyle, Jr., "Child Protection and Child Outcomes: Measuring the Effects of Foster Care," *American Economic Review* 97, no. 5 (December 2007): pp. 1583–1610, doi:10.1257/aer.97.5.1583; Joseph J. Doyle, Jr., "Child Protection and Adult Crime: Using Investigator Assignment to Estimate Causal Effects of Foster Care," *Journal of Political Economy* 116, no. 4 (2008): pp. 746–770, https://doi.org/10.1086/590216; Joseph J. Doyle, Jr., "Causal Effects of Foster Care: An Instrumental-Variables Approach," *Children and Youth Services Review* 35 (2013): pp. 1143–1151, doi:10.1016/j.childyouth.2011.03.014; Joseph J. Doyle, Jr. and Anna Aizer, "Economics of Child Protection: Maltreatment, Foster Care & Intimate-Partner Violence," *Annual Review of Economics* 10 (August 2018): pp. 87–108, https://doi.org/10.1146/annurev-economics-080217-053237.

34. Sylvana M. Côté, Massimiliano Orri, Mikko Marttila, and Tiina Ristikari, "Out-of-Home Placement in Early Childhood and Psychiatric Diagnoses and Criminal Convictions in Young Adulthood: A Population-Based Propensity Score-Matched Study," *The Lancet Child & Adolescent Health* 2, no. 9 (September 2018): pp. 647–653, http://dx.doi.org/10.1016/S2352-4642(18)30207-4; Sue D. Hobbs, Daniel Bederian-Gardner, Christin M. Ogle, Sarah Bakanosky, Rachel Narr, and Gail S. Goodman, "Foster Youth and At-Risk Non-Foster Youth: A Propensity Score and Structural Equation Modeling Analysis," *Children and Youth Services Review* 126

(2021), https://doi.org/10.1016/j.childyouth.2021.106034; William P. Warburton, Rebecca N. Warburton, Arthur Sweetman, and Clyde Hertzman, "The Impact of Placing Adolescent Males Into Foster Care on Education, Income Assistance, and Convictions," *Canadian Journal of Economics* 47, no. 1 (February 2014): pp. 35–69, https://doi.org/10.1111/caje.12064.

35. For examples of studies that demonstrate that impact of societal racism on outcomes for Black Americans, see Elan C. Hope, Lori S. Hoggard, and Alvin Thomas, "Emerging Into Adulthood in the Face of Racial Discrimination: Physiological, Psychological, and Sociopolitical Consequences for African American Youth," *Translational Issues in Psychological Science* 1, no. 4 (2015): pp. 342–351, http://dx.doi.org/10.1037/tps0000041; and David R. Williams, Harold W. Neighbors, and James S. Jackson, "Racial/Ethnic Discrimination and Health: Findings from Community Studies," *American Journal of Public Health* 93, no. 2 (February 2003): pp. 200–208, https://doi.org/10.2105/AJPH.93.2.200.

36. Richard E. Behrman and Adrienne Stith, Eds., *Preterm Birth: Causes, Consequences, and Prevention* (Washington, DC: The National Academies Press, 2007).

37. Daniel J. Losen, Tia Martinez, and Jon Gillespie, *Suspended Education in California* (The Center for Civil Rights Remedies at the Civil Rights Project, April 10, 2012), https://civilrightsproject.ucla.edu/resources/projects/center-for-civil-rights-remedies/school-to-prison-folder/summary-reports/suspended-education-in-california.

38. "Civil Rights Data Collection: Data Snapshot (School Discipline)," U.S. Department of Education Office for Civil Rights, March 21, 2014, https://ocrdata.ed.gov/assets/downloads/CRDC-School-Discipline-Snapshot.pdf.

39. "2013–2014 Civil Rights Data Collection: A First Look," U.S. Department of Education Office for Civil Rights, October 28, 2016, https://www2.ed.gov/about/offices/list/ocr/docs/2013-14-first-look.pdf.

40. Howard N. Snyder and Melissa Sickmund, *Juvenile Offenders and Victims: 2006 National Report* (National Center for Juvenile Justice, March 2006), https://www.ojjdp.gov/ojstatbb/nr2006/downloads/nr2006.pdf.

41. Marcy Mistrett and Mariana Espinoza, *Youth In Adult Courts, Jails, and Prisons* (The Sentencing Project, December 16, 2021), https://www.sentencingproject.org/publications/youth-in-adult-courts-jails-and-prisons/; Josh Rovner, *Black Disparities in Youth Incarceration* (The Sentencing Project, July 15, 2021), https://www.sentencingproject.org/publications/black-disparities-youth-incarceration/.

42. Karen M. Kolivoski, Sara Goodkind, and Jeffrey J. Shook, "Social Justice for Crossover Youth: The Intersection of the Child Welfare and Juvenile Justice Systems," *Social Work* 62, no. 4 (October 2017): pp. 313–321, https://doi.org/10.1093/sw/swx034.

43. Wendy L. Haight, James E. Black, Sarah Mangelsdorf, Grace Giorgio, Lakshmi Tata, Sarah J. Schoppe, and Margaret Szewczyk, "Making Visits Better: The Perspectives of Parents, Foster Parents, and Child Welfare Workers," *Child Welfare* 81, no. 2 (March/April 2002): pp. 173–202, https://www.jstor.org/stable/45390056; Kathleen S. Kenny, Clare Barrington, and Sherri L. Green, "'I Felt for a Long Time Like Everything Beautiful In Me Had Been Taken Out': Women's Suffering, Remembering, and Survival Following the Loss of Child Custody," *International Journal of Drug Policy* 26, no. 11

(November 2015): pp. 1158–1166, https://doi.org/10.1016/j.drugpo.2015.05.024; Kendra L. Nixon, H. L. Radtke, and Leslie M. Tutty, "'Every Day It Takes a Piece of You Away': Experiences of Grief and Loss Among Abused Mothers Involved with Child Protective Services," *Journal of Public Child Welfare* 7, no. 2 (2013): pp. 172–193, https://doi.org/10.1080/15548732.2012.715268; Laura Dreuth Zeman, "Etiology of Loss Among Parents Falsely Accused of Abuse or Neglect," *Journal of Loss and Trauma* 10, no. 1 (2005): pp. 19–31, doi:10.1080/15325020490890624.

44. Kenny et al., "I Felt for a Long Time Like Everything Beautiful In Me Had Been Taken Out"; Nixon et al., "Every Day It Takes a Piece of You Away."

45. Meaghan Thumath, David Humphreys, Jane Barlow, Putu Duff, Melissa Braschel, Brittany Bingham, Sophie Pierre, and Kate Shannon, "Overdose Among Mothers: The Association Between Child Removal and Unintentional Drug Overdose in a Longitudinal Cohort of Marginalised Women in Canada," *International Journal of Drug Policy* 91 (May 2021), doi: 10.1016/j.drugpo.2020.102977.

46. Elizabeth Wall-Wieler, Leslie L. Roos, Marni Brownell, Nathan Nickel, Dan Chateau, and Deepa Singal, "Suicide Attempts and Completions Among Mothers Whose Children Were Taken into Care by Child Protective Services: A Cohort Study Using Linkable Administrative Data," *Canadian Journal of Psychiatry* 63, no. 3 (March 2018): pp. 170–177, doi:10.1177/0706743717741058.

47. Kenny et al., "I Felt for a Long Time Like Everything Beautiful In Me Had Been Taken Out."

48. Elizabeth Wall-Wieler, Leslie L. Roos, James Bolton, Marni Brownell, Nathan Nickel, and Dan Chateau, "Maternal Mental Health after Custody Loss and Death of a Child: A Retrospective Cohort Study Using Linkable Administrative Data," *Canadian Journal of Psychiatry* 63, no. 5 (2018): pp. 322–328, doi:10.1177/0706743717738494.

49. Wanja Ogongi and Community Legal Services, *Barriers to Successful Reunification of Children with their Families After Foster Care* (Stoneleigh Foundation, August 2012), https://stoneleighfoundation.org/wp-content/uploads/2018/02/Ogongi.Moving-the-Dial.pdf.

50. Maria Cancian, Steven T. Cook, Mai Seki, and Lynn Wimer, "Making Parents Pay: The Unintended Consequences of Charging Parents for Foster Care," *Children and Youth Services Review* 72 (2017): pp. 100–110, http://dx.doi.org/10.1016/j.childyouth.2016.10.018.

51. Joseph Shapiro, Teresa Wiltz, and Jessica Piper, "States Send Kids to Foster Care and Their Parents the Bill—Often One Too Big to Pay," *National Public Radio*, December 27, 2021, https://www.npr.org/2021/12/27/1049811327/states-send-kids-to-foster-care-and-their-parents-the-bill-often-one-too-big-to-.

52. Dorothy Roberts, *Shattered Bonds: The Color of Child Welfare* (New York: Basic Civitas Books, 2001).

53. Dorothy Roberts, "The Racial Geography of Child Welfare: Toward a New Research Paradigm," *Child Welfare* 87, no. 2 (2008): pp. 125–150, https://cap.law.harvard.edu/wp-content/uploads/2015/07/robertsrd.pdf.

6

Reforms Are Designed to Fail

As prior chapters have demonstrated, today's family policing system was designed with the specific aim of creating the conditions that maintain the oppression of Black Americans for the purpose of maintaining White supremacy. The disproportionate involvement of Black children and families in the family policing system and the harms that result were not only the clearly foreseeable consequences of the policies that have been shaped and reaffirmed over decades, they were the intended outcomes of family policing intervention since its earliest origins. This stark level of overinvolvement of Black families and the vast disparities that exist in outcomes between Black children compared to White children have been known by the system for decades, and as prior chapters have demonstrated, have been present since the earliest days of the modern family policing system. As Chapter 5 demonstrated, study after study has shown the pervasive harm and trauma that result from these disparities. This harm and trauma have not only impacted generations of Black children and their parents, but family policing intervention has also devastated Black communities across generations.

Despite the overwhelming evidence that exists, the family policing system has largely been able to avoid mass critique due to the myth of benevolence and a widely misunderstood belief that the family policing system exists to help society's most vulnerable children. This belief persists in large part due to media depictions of extremely rare cases of severe maltreatment in which family policing agents respond and intervene to protect children from this harm. But beyond media depictions, the system itself perpetuates this myth, beginning with the names by which the system is commonly known—the "child welfare" system or "child protective services"—implying the system exists to ensure children's "welfare" and "protection" while intentionally obscuring the harm that results to the children and families who experience its intervention. Even when some of these harms are known, the myth that this system is needed, and the myth that

Confronting the Racist Legacy of the American Child Welfare System. Alan J. Dettlaff, Oxford University Press.
© Oxford University Press 2023. DOI: 10.1093/oso/9780197675267.003.0007

forcibly separating children from their parents is an appropriate response to protect them from harm, is so pervasive it allows the system to justify its continued existence.

The family policing system also justifies its continuing existence through an endless cycle of reforms in which the system has been engaging since it began. Within the highest level of the system, family policing administrators acknowledge the challenges the system faces and the areas in which it has fallen short. Within this acknowledgement, they maintain they are needed to protect children from severe harm, while messaging to the public and to legislators that they are actively engaged in reforms to address the problems they and others have identified. Even in cases where extreme corruption or abuse to children within their custody have come to light and resulted in lawsuits or consent decrees, the solution has been to develop a reform plan and report back to a judge or legislature the improvements that have been made in response to these reforms. And in every case, even when there is only evidence of minimal improvement, these improvements are accepted because of the myth of indispensability and assurances by the system that it will continue to improve.

Over the last several decades, one of the issues most subject to calls for reform has been the ongoing and significant racial disparities that have existed since the system began. Growing awareness of this throughout the 1980s and 1990s led to increasing calls by legislators and children's advocates for states to develop responses to address these disparities, leading several state legislatures beginning in the mid-2000s to pass broad legislation mandating system responses.[1] In addition, national philanthropic efforts pledged millions of dollars to assist in these endeavors .[2] Yet in many cases, only minimal changes were realized, while other efforts were entirely discontinued after the national focus shifted to other areas of concern.[3] Thus, despite decades of alleged reforms, and constant messaging to the public and to legislators that the system is actively working to address this problem, significant disparities persist and the harm and oppression of Black children and families continues. Ultimately, the system and its supporters know these reforms will not change the outcomes the system is intended to produce. Yet, the veneer of these reforms conveys the message that the system is aware of its concerns while also pacifying those who have raised them, allowing the harmful architecture of the system to continue.

A History of Failed Reforms

In 1972, Billingsley and Giovannoni wrote in *Children of the Storm* that child welfare services fail Black children. They argued that child welfare services fail Black children because of racism, and the services developed by the system were never developed for Black children; rather they were developed "by white people for white children, and are maintained and controlled by white people." They assessed existing efforts to reform the child welfare system as "incomplete and abortive."[4] Thus for over fifty years, reforms have been attempted and reforms have proven themselves unsuccessful in accomplishing their stated goals.

While over these last fifty years reform efforts have varied tactically, they have chased similar goals to achieve racial equity within the system broadly, improve outcomes for children and families, reduce the occurrence of racial disproportionality, and reduce (or eliminate) racial disparities that children and families face throughout their involvement in the system. However, despite the reforms implemented since the system originated, and despite specific reforms undertaken by individual family policing agencies, the family policing system as a whole continues to prove itself both unable and unwilling to provide support to children and families that is free from racism, harm, and oppression. This is because, as prior chapters have demonstrated, racism, harm, and oppression are the very constructs on which the family policing system is built.

Prevention-oriented reforms. Historically, family policing reforms have often attempted to shift funds or resources into preventative services as a strategy toward reducing family separations. At least 10 percent of children who are forcibly separated from their families are returned home within thirty days, indicating that whatever "dangers" were identified that caused the separation did not pose long-lasting threats.[5] Thus reforms have been made that attempt to shift services toward prevention with an emphasis on avoiding family separations altogether. These reforms typically prioritize families who are found to be at low or moderate risk for child maltreatment but could perhaps benefit from certain services (i.e., parenting classes, substance use treatment, mental health services, etc.) as a means of preventing family separation or other more punitive interventions. The logic behind these reforms frames the family policing system as a benign helping agency, which, with the right investments and focus, can offer children and families the support and services they need to be safe and remain together.

As one strategy toward a more prevention-oriented approach, many agencies have developed alternative or differential response pathways. In these models, instead of initiating an investigation when a report alleging maltreatment is received, differential response pathways link families who are assessed as having low or moderate risks to services with the goal of keeping children in their homes and preventing entry into foster care.[6] Alternative response systems differ from traditional investigations in that they often do not make a formal determination of child maltreatment and parents are not reported to child abuse registries. Alternative responses are said to support a more family-centered approach, one that engages families, prioritizes keeping children in their homes, and allows for more flexible decision-making.[7]

Alternative responses also attempt to minimize the role that discretion plays in exacerbating the racism that undergirds the family policing system. That is, alternative responses maintain that if family policing agents make better decisions about which families are at risk for abuse or neglect, only families in need of harsher responses from family policing will receive them. However, research examining the impact of alternative response on racial disparities in the family policing system demonstrates that racism also impacts which families are assigned the alternative pathways in the first place, with Black families being less likely to be assigned to these alternative pathways.[8] In addition, positioning alternative or differential response systems as an answer to racism within the family policing system assumes that interactions with family policing are neutral. The opposite is true. Alternative response systems can only exist in a society where surveillance and carceral logic control the lives of families and communities.

In order for families to be assigned to alternative responses, they have to be reported to the family policing system. When families are reported to the family policing system, they are reported by individuals who are both empowered by the existence of state apparatuses that control families and the belief that certain families are better off if they submit to the control of state apparatuses. Most families are reported to family policing hotlines by professionals— educators, doctors, police, and social services personnel. This means that people whom families rely on for services, support, and help are empowered by the state to play a part in their surveillance. Research on preventative services—the services often offered through alternative response—shows that those reporting families to family policing hotlines are influenced to do so in part because they know that family policing agencies hold a coercive threat over families to force them to engage in services—the threat to take their children away from them.[9]

Similar to alternative responses that emphasize prevention, the Family First Prevention Services Act (FFPSA) is a national reform to the family policing system that shifts the way that federal funds for family policing services can be used. FFPSA allows funds to be used for preventative services that allow children who are at "imminent risk of entering foster care" to remain at home as long as they are monitored through an FFPSA specific case plan. The services provided through FFPSA must be identified as "evidence-based" and can only be provided for up to twelve months.[10] Like alternative responses, FFPSA attempts to limit the number of children that enter foster care by providing different avenues for families to receive services. Both alternative response systems and FFPSA follow the logic that some families—as long as they comply with preapproved services and monitoring—can stay together. Both of these reforms, however, also place families under the watchful eye of a system plagued by coercion and racism.

Any contact with the family policing system takes away families' agency to make decisions about themselves, subjects families to further surveillance, and places the power to decide families' fates within the hands of the state. Whether families are assigned to traditional pathways, alternative pathways, or FFPSA case plans does not change the fact that once families are in contact with family policing systems, the system holds the power to enact irreparable harm. Families know this and so do family policing agents. The idea that alternative response pathways or preventative services can soften the harshness of the family policing system and reduce racial disparities is incorrect. These reforms fundamentally rely on state surveillance and coercion—mechanisms that can only exist within a racist society in the first place.

Decision-making reforms. While alternative response systems and other prevention-oriented reforms attempt to change *what* decisions are made about families, family policing reforms have also targeted *how* decisions are made about families as a means of reducing racism. Reforms that target *how* family policing agents make decisions include the use of algorithms or "structured decision-making," and practices that employ aspects of "blind removals."

Structured decision-making (SDM) systems are used by family policing agents to determine and assign risk to families for child maltreatment. A key element of SDM is the risk assessment, which employs actuarial science (or an algorithm) to analyze thousands of prior child maltreatment investigations to determine which risk factors best predict the likelihood of future abuse or neglect—often referred to as predictive analytics.[11] A number of states and jurisdictions across the country, from California to Florida to Pennsylvania, use predictive analytics to make determinations and decisions about families. Algorithmic determinations can decide which families are subject to an investigation, what pathways families are assigned to, and which children need to be forcibly separated from their homes. Algorithms were introduced to family policing to rid out bias; the logic behind these reforms suggests that if science, rather than humans, makes decisions about families, those decisions cannot be attributed to individual family policing agents' biases. Algorithms have also been positioned as more accurate than human decision-making because of the science that undergirds them.[12]

Yet despite being labeled as "evidence-based," research consistently shows that algorithms both produce and exacerbate racial disparities. For example, within the criminal punishment system, research has shown that risk assessments used to determine criminality were more likely to falsely flag Black defendants as future criminals, while White defendants were consistently mislabeled as being at lower risk for future criminality.[13] Within the family policing system, research on the Allegheny Family Screening Tool, a predictive risk modeling tool used in Allegheny County, Pennsylvania, found that the tool assessed almost 33 percent of Black children as needing a mandatory investigation compared to only 21 percent of White children. This research also found that the algorithms used by Allegheny County made even more racially disparate decisions than individual family policing agents.[14] Thus, attempts to standardize how decisions are made about families do not reduce racism—they reinforce racism.

Given the racism within predictive analytics and other algorithmic practices, it is no wonder that alternative response assignments that rely on an assessment of risk by algorithms are less likely to be given to Black families—the very tools used by the system to assess risk inherently believe that Black families are at greater risk than White families solely because of their race. Moreover, these tools rely on logics that "compare families to standard or objective norms of well-being to assess their risk level,"[15] reinforcing the racism of the White parenting standard that family policing is based on while subjecting disproportionate numbers of Black families to the surveillance and control of the family policing system.

Blind removals are another decision-making reform effort developed with a goal similar to that of algorithms and SDM—to remove bias from what can be catastrophic decisions about families. Blind removals involve removing all demographic information about a family from their case record before a panel of supervisors decides whether a child should be separated from their parents. In Nassau County, New York, where blind removals were first piloted, initial data demonstrated that the percentage of Black children who were removed from their homes by the family policing system decreased from 57 percent to 21 percent after blind removals were implemented.[16] The accuracy of this data, however, was later debunked, and subsequent studies have demonstrated that blind removals have limited ability to reduce racial disproportionality.[17] Yet despite this, numerous family policing systems continue to express interest in or continue to implement blind removal practices, including Los Angeles and Baltimore counties.[18]

The growing use of blind removals provides a perfect example of the logic of family policing reforms. Despite evidence that this reform is entirely ineffective in reducing racial disproportionality, family policing systems continue to adopt this practice because to an unaware public, the logic of blind removals makes sense—if racially biased decision-making is the problem, simply remove information about race to eliminate bias. Whether the reform is effective is not of interest to the system. Despite knowing this reform will not work, the simple logic and appeal of the reform allows the system's administration to assure the public, as well as legislators, that they are implementing practices to address the challenges they face.

Blind removals also provide an example of the faulty logic behind family policing reforms, because even if they were effective, blind removals fundamentally fail to address the harm caused by family separation in the first place. Although blind removals might lend the family policing system greater credibility by enabling it to claim it was working to reduce racially biased decision-making, the process does nothing to end the harm and trauma that accompanies an investigation and family separation. Ultimately, blind removals leave family separation firmly intact while doing nothing to eliminate the carceral logic of invading families' homes, surveilling and regulating their behavior, and forcibly separating children from their parents.

Training and workforce reforms. Reformers have also attempted to address how family policing agents are trained and the makeup of the family policing workforce as a means of remedying the racism that exists within family policing. Reforms that have focused on training the family policing workforce have addressed an array of topics including implicit bias, cultural competency, and antiracism. These trainings may address how parenting

styles differ across cultures or how to slow down decision-making to miti-
gate unconscious biases that might impact how agents interact with families
of a different race. They also might learn about the history of racism in the
United States and how structural racism has created racial disparities that
bring Black families into the family policing system at higher rates. Yet regardless of the subject matter of these trainings, the undergirding logic of
training as a reform relies on the presupposition that if family policing agents
know how to address their own biases and can grasp an understanding of the
larger economic and social context that families face, they might make better,
more accurate decisions.

The efficacy of these trainings, however, continues to be dubious.[19] Their
inefficacy is due at least in part to a misunderstanding of how deeply racism
is embedded within the family policing system. Individual actors within
the system do have the ability to significantly impact families through their
decision-making. However, because family policing interventions are fundamentally harmful and rooted in anti-Blackness and White supremacy, even
tremendous shifts in individual behavior and biases cannot structurally reform a system predicated on oppression. Offering more training as an answer
to racism within the system fallaciously assumes that the daily actions of the
system—surveillance and family separation—can be done in ways that are
not racist and harmful.

Better training also assumes that the family policing system is organized
to solve problems that families face. Yet when children are deemed "unsafe"
in their homes due to issues stemming from poverty, the system provides
no financial support to address these issues. Rather, family policing intervention often drives families further into poverty as parents are referred to
programs that require them to miss work, lose wages, and obtain transportation they may not have access to, all while undergoing the emotional toll
of being under family policing surveillance. Better training for family policing agents does nothing to address this fundamental disconnect. Training
efforts, therefore, provide family policing systems cover while creating negli-
gible benefits for children, families, and communities. Ultimately, training as
a reform represents a misalignment between the problem and the solution.
If racism is systemic, then individual actors cannot loosen the grip of racism
within the system. If poverty overwhelmingly leads families into the system,
then solutions that fail to locate capitalism and capitalist exploitation as the
driver of poverty and financial precarity fall short of providing any concrete
material change to families and communities.

Beyond trainings, hiring a more diverse workforce is a tactic that reformers have proposed to "fix" many racist institutions, including the family policing system. For example, in response to police violence—whether lethal or the more mundane violence of everyday police surveillance in communities— reformers often suggest that a more diverse workforce can solve police violence. Yet much evidence suggests this is far from true. For example, in Washington, DC, Black police officers make up 50 percent of the police force while only 35 percent are White.[20] Despite this, in 2021 the Metropolitan Police Department was sued for keeping a blacklist of reporters and community members, an officer was indicted for murder of a 20-year-old Black man, and a lieutenant was accused of conspiring with the Proud Boys, a White supremacist organization.[21] Thus, despite significant diversity, the capital's police force routinely engages in anti-Black violence. This is because the diversity of a workforce cannot change racist outcomes if the intent of an institution is guided by the carceral logic of surveillance and punishment. Similarly, ensuring that family policing agents come from more diverse backgrounds does nothing to ensure racism will not occur because racism is embedded within the system itself.

Increasing workforce diversity overestimates the power of individuals to transform a system's functioning. Just as training family policing agents on implicit bias does not change the fact that their function requires them to surveil the behavior of mostly poor Black families, increasing the diversity among these agents does nothing to change this inherent function.

Ultimately, increasing diversity simply provides oppressive systems with the optics of progress while failing to change the underlying oppressive structures. Changing the makeup of the family policing workforce does not change the system's oppressive power to surveil, police, and separate families.

Why Reforms Will Never Work

For over fifty years, reforms to the family policing system have been proven ineffective at accomplishing their stated goals. Despite the millions of dollars spent on reforming family policing, Black children continue to be disproportionately separated from their families and communities, and Black children and families continue to be disproportionately harmed by these separations. Outside the family policing system, hundreds of thousands of Black families live under constant threat that their children will be taken from them. As prior chapters have shown, the disproportionate impact of this system on Black children, families, and communities is well-known. And as prior chapters have demonstrated, the harm that results from this disproportionate involvement is not simply an unintended consequence, but rather the fulfillment of the specific purpose upon which the family policing system was built—the maintenance of White supremacy and the continued oppression of Black children, families, and communities.

Thus, reforms to the family policing system will never succeed because these reforms ask the family policing system to do the impossible—to perform family policing and forcible separations in ways that are less racist and less harmful. Reforms ask the family policing system to become a nicer, friendlier system while ignoring the underlying architecture that was built to uphold a social order that maintains racism and White supremacy. Reforms of the family policing system, therefore—fundamentally and intentionally—both misdiagnose and disagree with the problems they seek to address. Reforms rely on mechanisms that seek to change how and to what degree children, families, and communities are oppressed and harmed, but they do not seek to end oppression and harm. Reforms are also inherently racist because they maintain that families need to be surveilled, regulated, and punished—just to a slightly lesser degree. In other words, as prison abolitionists have often said when asked about various reform efforts that attempt to improve the experience of being incarcerated, "Kinder, gentler cages are still cages."[22]

This is why "racial equity" cannot be an acceptable goal for the family policing system. Since the summer of 2020, as awareness grew of the racism and violence inflicted on Black Americans at the hands of the police, and scholars and activists began to draw parallels to the family policing system, "racial equity" emerged as the new goal that the system believes it can point to as a means of avoiding further critique. In August 2021, Aysha Schomburg, Associate Commissioner of the Children's Bureau, wrote to all "child welfare leaders" acknowledging the system's history of inequity and committing to "advancing equity through our work at the federal level and through our work with states, territories, tribes, and all other grantees."[23] This commitment to racial equity was affirmed in a subsequent blog post by Associate Commissioner Schomburg in which she declared, "Equity is a right."[24]

In theory, the logic of racial equity as a goal is understandable. If "racial disproportionality" is a problem because Black children are overrepresented among children in foster care, then the solution to this problem would be "proportional representation," or "racial equity." But once again, this logic both misdiagnoses and disagrees with the problem. By establishing racial disproportionality as the problem that can be solved by achieving "racial equity," the system establishes the idea that if it were to eliminate racial disproportionality, the problem would be solved and there would be no further need for reform. Yet, the harm and oppression inflicted on Black children and families by the family policing system are not problems that can be solved by simply adjusting the levels by which this harm and oppression are inflicted. Although reforms intended to achieve "equity" may result in less harm, and make the system appear more palatable, the underlying harm and oppression that results to Black children and families through family separations is maintained. Simply producing "equity" in a system responsible for harm and oppression intentionally misleads both the system and the public to believe the system can be sufficiently reformed while maintaining its underlying mechanisms of harm and oppression. Equitable harm is still harm. And equitably distributing harm will still disproportionately impact Black children and families through the conditions of oppression family policing intervention is designed to produce. The goal of "racial equity" is simply the system's latest iteration of committing to reform as a means of pacifying an increasingly concerned public, while fully knowing this attempt at reform will do nothing to address the underlying harm the system was designed to produce.

Why Reforms Persist

Carceral systems' existence is often justified by the notion that they *provide* society with something. Namely, they provide society with protection by separating "harmful" groups of people from the rest of society. They are worth the billions of dollars spent maintaining them because they are seen as a necessary element of society. Prisons are said to protect society from criminals, while mandated treatment facilities and psychiatric institutions separate those who are deemed to be mentally unwell from the rest of "high-functioning" society. Similarly, the family policing system not only separates children from "dangerous" or "neglectful" parents but also separates "good parents" from "bad parents." Bad parents must be surveilled, added to registries, mandated to attend parenting classes, and so on. Their categorization as a bad parent follows them, separating them from the parents who are not dangerous and neglectful.

Carceral systems are reinforced by the various policing and surveillance technologies they employ and because most of society deems them necessary for the protection they provide. Yet, the people existing within the hold of carceral systems are always disproportionately poor, Black, Native, Latinx, disabled, or queer. For years, narratives have been constructed about the people the carceral system ensnares to justify their place in them. Black parents do not care about their children; Black men are dangerous; disabled people are disposable. Once entangled within the carceral system, people experience a web of poverty and debt; the impact of system involvement is never ending and has long lasting repercussions for the future. Carceral systems exist to maintain and reinforce the existing social order in the United States—a social order built on racial capitalism grounded in racial hierarchy and oppression. Challenging the existence of carceral systems both challenges the notion that certain people need to be handled by oppression, surveillance, and punishment, and challenges the social order of the United States itself.

Dylan Rodriguez names reform as a logic rather than an outcome. He defines reform as "an approach to institutional change that sustains existing social, economic, political, and/or legal systems."[25] It is for this reason that despite the documented abuse of children that occurs within the family policing system, reform continues to emerge as the primary solution for creating institutional change within that system. And, despite the failures of reforms to end racial disproportionality and disparities, reforms persist as the answer to these problems. Ensuring that the family policing system remains in place guarantees that the existing social order in the United States is maintained. To truly address why harm occurs in communities, why children are hungry, and why families are houseless, the existing social order in the United States would have to be disrupted. That is, substantially addressing the root cause of why harm occurs to children and in communities would also require the end of racial capitalism and all oppressive systems.

Instead, the logic of reform maintains oppression and existing social order by blaming parents for the structural harm their children face and separating their children from them. Reform's project is to justify the need for the carceral system. There is an entire body of work dedicated to this cause. Individual family policing reformers claim that poverty creates negative behaviors that must be corrected through family policing. Rather than understanding the existence of the family policing system to be symptomatic of larger harms within society, reformers claim that family policing must exist to address the disproportionate need certain communities face. This logic of reform allows the family policing system to be seen as a benevolent system, one that provides children and society with something. The system's harms are then obscured, and the money spent on the system becomes necessary so the system can continue providing protection and safety. Despite the failure of reform to accomplish any of its goals, reformers continue working to rebuild systems, denying that the system itself is racist or flawed because carceral systems help society disappear undesirable communities.

Reform persists because it maintains the existing social order, while abolition is the antithesis to reform. Whereas reform suggests change can only come from the state and existing legal systems, abolition creates "irreconcilable confrontation with oppressive institutions and systems."[26] Since the origins of the United States, violence and oppression have been essential to the state's existence. From settler colonialism to chattel slavery, the project of the United States has been maintained through the oppression of Black and Indigenous communities. Yet, this oppression creates undesirable social outcomes. Houselessness, poverty, violence, and other social problems are a result of the capitalist accumulation that maintains the United States. Although it is within the state's power to eliminate these outcomes, the state instead relies on the existence of carceral systems to both disappear the social problems created by capitalism and to maintain racial hierarchy and oppression.

Critiques of Abolitionist Efforts

As this chapter has demonstrated, while it is clear that reforms not only will never work, they also are explicitly designed to fail. Reformers insist, however, that although flawed, the system is essential, and because of this indispensability, continued reforms are the only way to tackle the challenges the system may face. Reformers have also strongly critiqued abolitionist efforts, which they perceive as a fundamentally unsound strategy given the "protection" the system must provide. These critiques largely concern the issue of "evidence," stating that existing "evidence" does not support abolition, and that abolitionist movements use data inappropriately or incorrectly to support their arguments.[27] Throughout this book, we have presented research and data in making a call for abolition, and we believe this body of research clearly supports this call. We also question the narrow view of "evidence" used in forming some of these critiques. Much of the research cited in these critiques focuses on a narrow selection of quantitative studies based on large administrative data sets that attempt to demonstrate that family policing intervention is not grounded in racism and harm, while ignoring or discounting the large body of qualitative studies that provide firsthand accounts of this racism and harm. These critiques also ignore the daily testimonies of the children and parents who have been most harmed by family policing intervention and live every day with the consequences of these harms. These testimonies are "evidence," and we believe this evidence supports our call for abolition.

Reformers also fundamentally, and perhaps intentionally, misunderstand abolitionist arguments by claiming that abolition will only result in children being harmed. Abolitionists do not envision a world where children are unsafe and live in homes and communities where they will not thrive. Abolitionists envision the opposite. Abolitionists envision a society where all children and families have everything they need to be safe and thrive *within their homes and communities*. Abolitionists envision a society where a government system that forcibly separates children from their parents would never be brought into existence because the idea is so repellant. Abolitionists envision a society where we use our resources to support the safety and well-being of children living in their families and communities, with these communities working intensely, investing heavily, and collaborating creatively to ensure children are safe and families stay together.

Critiques of abolition that focus solely on the potential for harm also ignore the reality that the family policing system does not keep children safe from harm. As prior chapters have demonstrated, multiple studies across decades have documented the extent to which children are harmed in foster care, often at rates that far exceed the harm that occurs in families and communities.[28] Critiques that focus solely on the potential for harm serve to distract from the reality of family policing intervention. And they intend to stop us from imagining. Critiques that limit themselves to "What About?" scenarios maintain our focus on the myth of a needed system and prevent us from imagining that we can create something better. These critiques perpetuate the idea that although flawed, the current system is all we have.

Abolition requires that we aspire to something more.

Abolition is a vision of hope that we can end harmful, racist institutions and collectively build life-affirming resources, supports, and relationships.

We can have robust systems of accountability to prevent harm, we can address harm in nonviolent ways when it occurs, we can support and heal all members of a family system, and we can restore connections in families and communities. We cannot continue to implement the same reforms again and again and expect different outcomes. We cannot continue to invest countless resources in a harmful, racist system and expect that system to produce anything other than harmful, racist outcomes. It is time to collectively aspire for more.

Notes

1. See for example reform plans developed by Michigan Department of Human Services, Michigan Advisory Committee on the Overrepresentation of Children of Color in Child Welfare, *Equity: Moving Toward Better Outcomes for All of Michigan's Children* (Lansing: March 2006), https://vdocuments.net/equity-moving-toward-better-outcomes-for-all-of-toward-better-outcomes-for.html; and Texas Health and Human Services Commission, Department of Family and Protective Services, *Disproportionality in Child Protective Services: Policy Evaluation and Remediation Plan* (Austin: July 2006), http://www.dfps.state.tx.us/Child_Protection/Disproportionality/documents/2006-07-01_Disproportionality.pdf.

2. See for example Oronde A. Miller, *Breakthrough Series Collaborative: Reducing Racial Disproportionality and Disparate Outcomes for Children and Families of Color in the Child Welfare System* (Casey Family Programs, July 2009), http://www.centerforchildwelfare.org/kb/dispr/Reducing%20Disproportionality%20-Casey.pdf.

3. For example, following a legislative mandate in 2005, the state of Texas engaged in significant efforts to reduce racial disproportionality. This led to the formation of a statewide office established in 2010, the Center for Elimination of Disproportionality and Disparities, dedicated to reducing racial disparities across systems. This was defunded by the Texas legislature in 2017. For a history, see https://www.txbcfoundation.org/cedd. Similarly, in 2005 Casey Family Programs launched a "2020 Vision" designed to reduce the number of children in foster care by 50 percent by 2020. This included specific efforts for eliminating racial disproportionality and disparities. This was later significantly reduced and the goal to reduce the number of children in foster care by 50 percent by 2020 did not continue. For additional information, see https://www.gahsc.org/nm/2009/ppcasey2020vision.pdf.

4. Andrew Billingsley and Jeanne M. Giovannoni, *Children of the Storm: Black Children and American Child Welfare* (New York: Harcourt, Brace, Jovanovich, 1972), p. 4.

5. Vivek S. Sankaran and Christopher Church, "Easy Come, Easy Go: The Plight of Children Who Spend Less than Thirty Days in Foster Care," *University of Pennsylvania Journal of Law and Social Change* 19, no. 3 (November 2016): pp. 207–237, https://scholarship.law.upenn.edu/jlasc/vol19/iss3/2/.

6. Child Welfare Information Gateway, *Differential Response: A Primer for Child Welfare Professionals* (U.S. Department of Health and Human Services, Children's Bureau, October 2020), https://www.childwelfare.gov/pubpdfs/differential_response.pdf.

7. Tana Connell, "Accessing Alternative Response Pathways: A Multi-Level Examination of Family and Community Factors on Race Equity," *Child Abuse & Neglect* 108 (October 2020), https://doi.org/10.1016/j.chiabu.2020.104640.

8. Mi Jin Choi, Jangmin Kim, Ayla Roper, Catherine LaBrenz, and Reiko Boyd, "Racial Disparities in Assignment to Alternative Response," *Children and Youth Services Review* 125 (June 2021), https://doi.org/10.1016/j.childyouth.2021.105988; Connell, "Accessing Alternative Response Pathways."

9. Kelley Fong, "Getting Eyes in the Home: Child Protective Services Investigations and State Surveillance of Family Life," *American Sociological Review* 85, no. 4 (2020): pp. 610–638, https://doi.org/10.1177/0003122420938460.

10. "Title IV-E Prevention Program," U.S. Department of Health and Human Services, Children's Bureau, September 3, 2021, https://www.acf.hhs.gov/cb/title-iv-e-prevention-program.

11. Christopher Teixeira and Matthew Boyas, *Predictive Analytics in Child Welfare: An Assessment of Current Efforts, Challenges and Opportunities* (U.S. Department of Health and Human Services, Office of the Assistant Secretary for Planning and Evaluation, October 2017), https://aspe.hhs.gov/reports/predictive-analytics-child-welfare-assessment-current-efforts-challenges-opportunities.

12. Christopher E. Church and Amanda J. Fairchild, "In Search of a Silver Bullet: Child Welfare's Embrace of Predictive Analytics," *Juvenile & Family Court Journal* 68, no. 1 (March 2017): pp. 67–81, https://doi.org/10.1111/jfcj.12086.

13. Julia Angwin, Jeff Larson, Surya Mattu, and Lauren Kirchner, "Machine Bias," *ProPublica,* May 23, 2016, https://www.propublica.org/article/machine-bias-risk-assessments-in-criminal-sentencing.

14. Logan Stapleton, Hao-Fei Cheng, Anna Kawakami, Venkatesh Sivaraman, Yanghuidi Cheng, Diana Qing, Adam Perer, Kenneth Holstein, Zhiwei Steven Wu, and Haiyi Zhu, "Extended Analysis of 'How Child Welfare Workers Reduce Racial Disparities in Algorithmic Decisions,'" *CHI Conference on Human Factors in Computing Systems* (May 2022), https://doi.org/10.48550/arXiv.2204.13872.

15. Victoria Copeland and Maya Pendleton, *Surveillance of Black Families in the Family Policing System* (upEND Movement, June 2022), https://upendmovement.org/surveillance/.

16. Jessica Pryce, "To Transform Child Welfare, Take Race Out of the Equation" (TED Talk, August 21, 2018), https://www.ted.com/talks/jessica_pryce_to_transform_child_welfare_take_race_out_of_the_equation/.

17. Jeremy Loudenback, "Color Blind Ambition," *The Imprint,* April 1, 2021, https://imprintnews.org/los-angeles/color-blind-ambition-removals/52958.

18. Loudenback, "Color Blind Ambition"; Sara Tiano, "Los Angeles Leaders Vote to Try 'Colorblind' Foster Care Decisions," *The Imprint,* July 13, 2021, https://imprintnews.org/law-policy/los-angeles-leaders-vote-to-try-colorblind-foster-care-decisions/56897.

19. Michele D. Hanna, "Child Welfare System Issues As Explanatory Factors for Racial Disproportionality and Disparities," in *Racial Disproportionality and Disparities in the Child Welfare System,* edited by Alan J. Dettlaff (Springer, 2021), pp. 177–197, https://link.springer.com/chapter/10.1007/978-3-030-54314-3_10.

20. "We Are Strengthened by Our Diversity," Metropolitan Police Department, accessed September 10, 2022, https://mpdc.dc.gov/page/statistics.

21. Tamika Spellman, "A Safer D.C. Starts With a Smaller Police Department," *The Washington Post,* April 28, 2022, https://www.washingtonpost.com/opinions/2022/04/28/safer-dc-starts-with-smaller-police-department/.

22. Jessica Moulite, "'Kinder, Gentler Cages Are Still Cages': How Prison Abolitionists are Working Towards a Less Carceral Future," *The Root,* March 19, 2021, https://www.theroot.com/kinder-gentler-cages-are-still-cages-how-prison-aboli-1846505239.

23. Aysha E. Schomburg, *Letter From Aysha E. Schomburg on Equity in Child Welfare* (U.S. Department of Health and Human Services, Administration for Children and Families, Children's Bureau, August 10, 2021), https://www.acf.hhs.gov/cb/news/letter-aysha-e-schomburg-equity-child-welfare.

24. Aysha E. Schomburg, "Equity Is a Right," *Children's Bureau Express* 22, no. 8 (September 2021), https://cbexpress.acf.hhs.gov/article/2021/september/equity-is-a-right/963844031b92c150517620efe54bcba3.

25. Dylan Rodríguez, "Police Reform as Counterinsurgency: How Reformist Approaches to Police Violence Expand Police Power and Legitimate the Next Phase of Domestic Warfare," in *Abolition for the People: The Movement for a Future Without Policing and Prisons,* edited by Colin Kaepernick, p. 154.

26. Dylan Rodríguez, "Policing Reform as Counterinsurgency," p. 158.

27. See for example, Richard P. Barth, Jill Duerr Berrick, Antonio R. Garcia, Brett Drake, Melissa Jonson-Reid, John R. Gyourko, and Johanna K. P. Greeson, "Research to Consider While Effectively Re-Designing Child Welfare Services," *Research on Social Work Practice* 32, no. 5 (July 2022): pp. 483–498, https://doi.org/10.1177/1049731521 1050000. See also critiques of this article included in *Research on Social Work Practice* 32, no. 5 (July 2022), https://journals.sagepub.com/toc/rswa/32/5.

28. Mary I. Benedict, Susan Zuravin, Diane Brandt, and Helen Abbey, "Types and Frequency of Child Maltreatment by Family Foster Care Providers in an Urban Population," *Child Abuse & Neglect* 18, no. 7 (July 1994): pp. 577–585, doi:10.1016/0145-2134(94)90084-1; Nina Biehal, "Maltreatment in Foster Care: A Review of the Evidence," *Child Abuse Review* 23 (2014): pp. 48–60, doi:10.1002/car.2249; J. William Spencer and Dean D. Knudsen, "Out-of-Home Maltreatment: An Analysis of Risk in Various Settings for Children," *Children and Youth Services Review* 14 (1992): pp. 485–492, doi:10.1016/0190-7409(92)90002-D.

7

Abolition

A Radical, Evolving Movement Toward Liberation

The theory and praxis of abolition have deep historical roots that inform thinking and strategy today and continue to evolve. Too often, the idea of abolition is wrongly simplified to mean "dismantle" or "destroy" an institution or system and the deeper, richer meaning of abolition is erased. Although abolition directly intends to end harmful, racist systems, its focus is on building a new liberated society. It is not an outlandish utopian vision, but rather abolition is a process that requires constant critique of all forms of oppression, adapts and changes strategies over time, and ultimately builds new and better relationships for one another. Importantly, abolition is not a specific, detailed plan. Abolition has always been more expansive than one strategy, one program, one system—it demands freedom for all communities from oppression and violence. Abolition creates spaces for new ways of relationality and the freedom to dream. Opponents of abolition point to the need for a concrete, specific plan—but abolition is not a specific destination. These demands center a White supremacy culture that believes a small group of people can fix the larger history and current reality of oppression of Black people with a few well-designed interventions.[1] This thinking drives a demand for a concrete plan, while also narrowing a broad conversation and diverting from the larger structural and economic changes that are required. Abolitionists reject this and "champion a range of approaches to work toward a liberated future."[2]

Abolition is based on over two hundred years of tradition and thinking. It is not an ephemeral strategy, but rather is deeply informed by the study of history and the radical imagination and rebellion of our ancestors. This chapter is not a definitive history of abolition, as there are many others that accomplish this[3]—rather we provide an analysis of how the roots of abolition carry forward and evolve into today's efforts to abolish the family policing system. These roots offer the wisdom, inspiration, and hope that can bring about liberation and freedom for all.

Confronting the Racist Legacy of the American Child Welfare System. Alan J. Dettlaff, Oxford University Press.
© Oxford University Press 2023. DOI: 10.1093/oso/9780197675267.003.0008

From Where Our Dreams Began

In the United States, the origins of abolition derived from the need to address the horror and inhumanity of the enslavement of people of African descent. Abolition then as now comes out of recognition that existing conditions are untenable, and improvements within the confines of the existing system or institution are not possible. Abolition is not a response to missteps or minor infractions, but a response to the indefensible, relentless, and inhumane act of state-perpetuated violence and terror. As early abolitionist William Lloyd Garrison said in describing the need for and urgency of abolition:

> I am aware, that many object to the severity of my language; but is there not cause for severity? I *will be* as harsh as truth, and as uncompromising as justice. On this subject, I do not wish to think, or speak, or write, with moderation. No! no! Tell a man whose house is on fire, to give a moderate alarm; tell him to moderately rescue his wife from the hands of the ravisher; tell the mother to gradually extricate her babe from the fire into which it has fallen; but urge me not to use moderation in a cause like the present. I am in earnest—I will not equivocate—I will not excuse—I will not retreat a single inch—and I will be heard.[4]

Early abolitionists recognized that despite state efforts to limit the actions of extremely violent enslavers, the institution of slavery remained cruel and merciless for Black people, and thus beyond reform. To sustain slavery, enslavers, slave patrollers, and others relied on state-sanctioned and persistent violence and punishment of Black people as well as the complicit silence of non-enslaver Whites, many of whom had a financial interest in slavery.[5] The very design of the institution of slavery required brutality—it was not exceptional nor unusual.

Ultimately, the movement to abolish chattel slavery emerged from the people experiencing oppression. Historian Manisha Sinha in her book, *The Slave's Cause: A History of Abolition,* recognizes that "The actions of slave rebels and runaways, black writers and community leaders, did not lie outside of but shaped abolition and its goals. As most abolitionists understood, the story of abolition must begin with the struggles of the enslaved."[6] These "struggles" were in fact horrifying and often deadly. Frederick Douglass understood the power of relaying these struggles and forcing those in power to see the contradiction of enslavement of Black people and the rights of those

White men newly freed from British rule. In his famous speech, which later became known as "What to the Slave Is the Fourth of July?," he stated:

> What, to the American slave, is your 4th of July? I answer; a day that reveals to him, more than all other days in the year, the gross injustice and cruelty to which he is the constant victim. To him, your celebration is a sham; your boasted liberty, an unholy license; your national greatness, swelling vanity; your sounds of rejoicing are empty and heartless; your denunciations of tyrants, brass fronted impudence; your shouts of liberty and equality, hollow mockery; your prayers and hymns, your sermons and thanksgivings, with all your religious parade, and solemnity, are, to him, mere bombast, fraud, deception, impiety, and hypocrisy—a thin veil to cover up crimes which would disgrace a nation of savages. There is not a nation on the earth guilty of practices, more shocking and bloody, than are the people of these United States, at this very hour.[7]

Douglass in his advocacy did not soften the brutality of slavery to please White audiences. As Chapter 1 details, it was a critical strategy of abolitionists to support storytelling by enslaved and formerly enslaved people to describe the horrors of slavery. These efforts resulted in wide-scale public sympathy and recognition of the inhumanity of slavery and critically resulted in the rapid growth in abolitionists and support of the abolitionist movement. Abolitionist newspapers published drawings and stories documenting the atrocities of slavery, particularly gaining traction around the intentional and devastating cruelty of family separation. The arts also exposed the inhumanity of slavery through poetry and theater performances. As Sinha documented, "The free as well as the enslaved voiced their denunciation of slavery in letters, pamphlets, poems, hymns, slave narratives, eulogies, sermons, and orations."[8] As early as the 1700s, decades before Douglass' and others' powerful speeches, Phyllis Wheatley, the first known Black American and enslaved poet, wrote her thoughts on freedom in a poem dedicated to the secretary of state for North America:

> I, young in life, by seeming cruel fate
> Was snatched from Afric's fancy'd happy seat:
> What pangs excruciating must molest,
> What sorrow labour in my parent's breast?
> Steel'd was that soul and by no misery mov'd

That from a father seiz'd his babe belov'd:
Such, such my case. And can I then but pray
Others may never feel tyrannic sway?[9]

Abolitionists also did not stop with naming the horror and calling for the end of slavery—they also pushed for a society where liberation was realized for all. In 1863, near the end of the Civil War, Frederick Douglass insisted that the work of abolition would not be complete with the end of slavery. In a speech to the American Anti-Slavery Society titled, "Our Work Is Not Done," he stated:

> I am one of those who believe that we should consent to no peace which shall not be an Abolition peace. I am, moreover, one of those who believe that the work of the American Anti-Slavery Society will not have been completed until the black men of the South, and the black men of the North, shall have been admitted, fully and completely, into the body politic of America. I look upon slavery as going the way of all the earth. It is the mission of the war to put it down. But a mightier work than the abolition of slavery now looms up before the Abolitionist. This Society was organized, if I remember rightly, for two distinct objects; one was the emancipation of the slave, and the other the elevation of the colored people. When we have taken the chains off the slave, as I believe we shall do, we shall find a harder resistance to the second purpose of this great association than we have found even upon slavery itself.[10]

Here Douglass clearly stated that the work of abolition would not be complete with solely the end of slavery but would continue to work toward elevation and equality of the formerly enslaved; he also notably predicted that this work would encounter even greater resistance.

Subsequently, the idea of abolition extending beyond the end of slavery was further advanced by W. E. B. DuBois, who conceptualized the term "abolition democracy" in his 1935 work, "Black Reconstruction in America 1860–1880." In defining abolition democracy, DuBois described this as a theory of America "based on freedom, intelligence and power for all men." In contrast, the other theory of America was "industry for private profit directed by an autocracy determined at any price to amass wealth and power."[11] Thus, abolition democracy was an idea for the United States where Black Americans were not only no longer enslaved, but they had the social, economic, and political capital—including education, land, and the right to vote—to be considered equal members of society. Realizing this theory of America would require the creation of new institutions, new structures, and new social relationships as the means of achieving the true goal of abolition—a racially just society. As Angela Davis elaborated, "DuBois argued that the abolition of slavery was accomplished only in the negative sense. In order to achieve the *comprehensive* abolition of slavery— after the institution was rendered illegal and black people were released from their chains—new institutions should have been created to incorporate black people into the social order."[12] Legal scholar Allegra McLeod explained this idea further, stating:

> According to DuBois, to be meaningful, abolition required more than the simple eradication of slavery; abolition ought to have been a positive project as opposed to a merely negative one. DuBois wrote that simply declaring an end to a tradition of violent forced labor was insufficient to abolish slavery. Abolition instead required the creation of new democratic forms in which the institutions and ideas previously implicated in slavery would be remade to incorporate those persons formerly enslaved and to enable a different future for all members of the polity. To be meaningful, the abolition of slavery required fundamentally reconstructing social, economic and political arrangements.[13]

Thus, we see that the intention of abolition, from its earliest origins, has never been solely about collapsing institutions—it has always been about the generative act of creating, of building a new society founded on the principles of freedom and liberation. A racially just society free from oppression cannot be achieved solely by a negative action—it must also include the positive actions that bring about the new structures that maintain freedom from oppression.

From the earliest origins of the abolition movement, abolitionists were not only activists—they were revolutionaries, they were obstructionists, and they were radical agitators. They were everyday people who understood their current conditions were untenable and that another world was possible. Abolitionists were networked transatlantically and shared ideas, strategies, and tactics—in fact, the work of the original abolitionists in the United States was inspired by centuries of radical abolitionist thought that began in Western Europe and its colonies as early as the 1300s. It was be-cause of this radical thinking that early abolitionists were viewed as a threat and characterized as zealots and lunatics. They were accused of overstating the horrors of slavery and of manipulating Black people for their own benefit.[14] Early historians often demonized abolitionists as "fanatical, unreasonable, and extreme," with some going as far as to equate them to "terrorists."[15]

Thus, abolition is, and has always been, a radical movement in response to extreme oppression and exploitation of people and their labor. It threatens those who hold power and wealth. Backlash against abolitionists and their organizations was violent, severe, and swift. Backlash ranged from individual harassment and violence to policy and legislative changes further punishing Black Americans. As prior chapters have described, the White resistance that immediately followed emancipation led to the Black Codes, mass incarcer-ation of Black adults, convict leasing, and forced apprenticeships of Black children—all for the purpose of ensuring the idea of America envisioned by abolition would never be realized. As Nikole Hannah-Jones writes in *The 1619 Project*:

> The many gains of Reconstruction were met with widespread and coor-dinated white resistance, including unthinkable violence against the for-merly enslaved, wide-scale voter suppression, electoral fraud, and even, in extreme cases, the violent overthrow of democratically elected biracial governments. Faced with this violent recalcitrance, the federal govern-ment once again settled on Black people as the problem and decided that for unity's sake, it would leave the white South to its own devices. In 1877, President Rutherford B. Hayes . . . agreed to pull the remaining federal troops from the South. With the troops gone, white Southerners quickly went about eradicating the gains of Reconstruction.[16]

Following the end of Reconstruction, prisons became the primary mech-anism for maintaining the oppression of Black Americans, a legacy that began with the Black Codes and was maintained by the Thirteenth Amendment, which created a reconfiguration of slavery that imprisoned Black Americans and exploited them for their labor through convict leasing arrangements. During the period of 1874 to 1877, the population of people imprisoned in Alabama tripled. Ninety percent of those incarcerated were Black. During the same period, the population of those imprisoned in Mississippi grew by nearly 300 percent, while the prison population in Georgia also more than tripled. In total, by the end of the 1870s, 95 percent of the prison population in the South was Black.[17] This system of rapid criminalization and incarceration, largely for issues that were not formerly crimes, such as homelessness and unemployment, reversed any forward progress Black Americans had made during Reconstruction and reverted them once again to a subjugated and enslaved source of labor for their White former enslavers.

Upon revisiting the South after many years away, and witnessing the conditions of the formerly enslaved, Frederick Douglass lamented all that had been lost since Reconstruction and the hopes of abolition that remained unrealized. In a speech delivered on the twenty-sixth anniversary of emancipation, in April 1888, he stated:

> I admit that the Negro, and especially the plantation Negro, the tiller of the soil, has made little progress from barbarism to civilization, and that he is in a deplorable condition since his emancipation. That he is worse off, in many respects, than when he was a slave, I am compelled to admit, but I contend that the fault is not his, but that of his heartless accusers. He is the victim of a cunningly devised swindle, one which paralyzes his energies, suppresses his ambition, and blasts all his hopes; and though he is nominally free he is actually a slave. I here and now denounce his so-called emancipation as a stupendous fraud—a fraud upon him, a fraud upon the world.[18]

Thus, while backlash and the power of White supremacy squashed the true dreams of freedom and equality envisioned by the original abolitionists, those dreams and the original intentions of the movement continued to influence future generations of racial justice leaders and organizers. These early abolitionists "were the intellectual and political precursors of twentieth-century anti-colonial and civil rights activists, debating the nature of society and politics, the relationship between racial inequality and democracy, nation and empire, labor and capital, gender and citizenship."[19] While the thinking, work, and impact of these early abolitionists did not significantly arise again until nearly a century later, the original intentions and aspirations of their work—a racially just society and a dream of liberation—remain a dream unfulfilled and the motivation for the movement once again.

To Where Our Dreams Emerged—the Modern
Abolition Movement

The modern abolition movement has focused largely on abolition of prisons and policing; however, the thinking and practice upon which this current movement is built are similar to and informed by the rich history that preceded it. Since at least the 1960s, advocates, scholars, and those impacted by incarceration have protested against prisons, decrying not only their inhumane conditions, but also protesting against punishment as an appropriate or helpful intervention.[20] Over the last fifty years, the number of people incarcerated in the United States has grown outrageously from 200,000 to nearly 1.5 million, an increase of over 600 percent, disproportionately incarcerating poor and Black people.[21] As of 2019, Black Americans were incarcerated at a rate nearly five times that of White Americans. And although the enormous disparities that existed in the South immediately following Reconstruction have diminished, in twelve states today—Alabama, Delaware, Georgia, Illinois, Louisiana, Maryland, Michigan, Mississippi, New Jersey, North Carolina, South Carolina, and Virginia—more than half the prison population is Black.[22]

Although activism and organizing against prisons began as early as the 1960s, legal scholar Dorothy Roberts notes, "Some activists mark the launch of the current prison abolition movement as occurring at an international conference and strategy session, *Critical Resistance: Beyond the Prison Industrial Complex*, held at the University of California, Berkeley, in September 1998."[23] At that conference, over 3,500 organizers, activists, and scholars, some of whom were formerly incarcerated, "developed the concept of the 'prison industrial complex' to name the expanding apparatus of surveillance, policing, and incarceration the state increasingly employs to solve problems caused by social inequality, stifle political resistance by oppressed communities, and serve the interests of corporations that profit from prisons and police forces."[24] Notably, this modern abolition movement was inextricably feminist—"The visible leadership of feminist activists and scholars, both in planning the conference and during the event itself, signaled that a powerful abolitionist framework required an antiracist, anticapitalist feminist practice."[25]

Like the past, today's abolition movement is in response to the untenable—the persistent act of violence against Black Americans at the hands of the state. Today's abolitionists publicly detail how prisons are designed to be brutal and inhumane and that the violence and oppression inflicted by policing and prisons are not aberrations that can be reformed away. Although scholars and activists have varying definitions of abolition, the thinking and organizing behind the movement largely coalesces around dismantling harmful systems and envisioning and building different ways to prevent and address harm and ensure safety. Yet as Roberts notes, "It is hard to pin down what prison abolition means. Activists engaged in the movement have resisted 'closed definitions of prison abolitionism' and have instead suggested a variety of terms to capture what prison abolitionists think and do—abolition is 'a form of consciousness,' 'a theory of change,' 'a long-term political vision,' and 'a spiritual journey.'"[26] Other descriptions of the movement from today's abolitionists include:

> Abolition is presence, not absence. It is about building life-affirming institutions.[27]—Ruth Wilson Gilmore
>
> [A]bolition is not merely the absence of police . . . it's eliminating the root causes of harm, and it's eliminating the kind of society that could rely on police to solve that harm.[28]—Derecka Purnell
>
> Abolition works to dismantle systems that have caused harm, namely police and prisons, and reallocate funds to social and economic resources, and to develop new systems of community-controlled public safety and restorative justice.[29]—Robin D. G. Kelley
>
> [A]bolition is more than closing prisons and ending policing as we know it. It is about the everyday questions and creation of solutions to the underlying reasons why people cause harm and are harmed.[30]—Marlon Peterson
>
> People like me who want to abolish prisons and police, however, have a vision of a different society, built on cooperation instead of individualism, on mutual aid instead of self-preservation. What would the country look like if it had billions of extra dollars to spend on housing, food, and education for all?[31]—Mariame Kaba
>
> Now and long before, abolition is and was a practice, an analytical method, a present-tense visioning, an infrastructure in the making, a creative project, a performance, a counterwar, an ideological struggle, a pedagogy and curriculum, an alleged impossibility that is furtively present, pulsing, produced in the persistent insurgencies of human being that undermine the totalizing logics of empire, chattel, occupation, heteropatriarchy, racial-colonial genocide, and Civilization as a juridical-narrative epoch.[32]—Dylan Rodriguez

Finally, Angela Davis specifically looks to W. E. B. DuBois' analysis of abolition democracy and expands upon it, stating:

> When I refer to prison abolitionism, I like to draw from the DuBoisian notion of abolition democracy. That is to say, it is not only, or not even primarily, about abolition as a negative process of tearing down, but it is also about building up, about creating new institutions . . . DuBois pointed out that in order to fully abolish the oppressive conditions produced by slavery, new democratic institutions would have to be created. Because this did not occur; black people encountered new forms of slavery—from debt peonage and the convict lease system to segregated and second-class education. The prison system continues to carry out this terrible legacy. It has become a receptacle for all of those human beings who bear the inheritance of the failure to create abolition democracy in the aftermath of slavery.[33]

These descriptions of today's abolitionist movement clearly demonstrate that the true vision of abolition, as in the past, is grounded in all that abolition hopes to create. The goals of abolition cannot be realized without dismantling oppressive structures, but the true power of abolition comes from the work that will be done to create a society where those structures would never exist.

The Movement to Abolish the Family Policing System

As the movement to abolish prisons and policing has grown since the 1970s, so have the policies and structures that maintain the carceral state. Shortly following passage of the Civil Rights Act in 1965 and the demonization of Black families and Black communities perpetuated by the Moynihan report and others, President Richard Nixon announced what became known as the "War on Drugs" in June 1971 when he declared "drug abuse" to be "America's public enemy number one."[34] This "War on Drugs" led to increased surveillance in communities of color, militarization of the police, harsher and stricter sentencing laws, and the rapid expansion of prisons across the United States, all predicated on the deeply rooted idea of Black criminality. During the 1980s and 1990s, the federal government dismantled the social safety net and further increased criminal punishments and the expansion of prisons.[35] As Dorothy Roberts notes, "prisons are the state's response to social crises produced by racial capitalism, such as unemployment and unhealthy segregated housing, and to the rebellions waged by marginalized people who suffer most from these conditions."[36]

The same is true for the family policing system. Since the 1960s, the family policing system has grown and responded within this larger ecosystem and now functions similarly to policing and prisons as a means of social control and punishment. As prior chapters have demonstrated, however, the family policing system has largely avoided its connections to the carceral state due to the perception that it protects vulnerable children from harm and helps vulnerable families in need. Yet consider its functions and the roles the family policing system plays in the lives of Black families and communities. As Chapter 4 demonstrated, today's family policing system largely functions as a system with enormous power to surveil, regulate, and punish families, all roles typically associated with policing rather than children's "welfare." Also consider the purpose of these roles. These roles have been used throughout the system's history for the purpose of maintaining White power and the subjugation of Black Americans as a means of maintaining an exploitable, oppressed working class for the purpose of furthering capitalist accumulation. For centuries, this has been the purpose of the police, this has been the purpose of prisons, and this is the purpose of the "child welfare" system, which we intentionally refer to as the family policing system due to its similarities in purpose, roles, and functions.

We recognize that conceptualizing the child welfare system as the family policing system and as part of the carceral state are new ideas for some. Yet we also understand that this recognition is long past due. For decades, parents and youth have described the devastation that results from family policing intervention. For decades, we have known the harm that results from family separation and placement in foster care. And for decades, we have known that this harm is inflicted disproportionately on Black children and families. However, the system and its supporters continue to uphold the system and spare no effort to assure us that the system itself is not the problem. Some will point to poverty or societal racism as drivers of the racist inequities that exist in the system, while absolving the system of any fault or harm.[37] Others will point to "unintended consequences" of a legacy of child welfare policies that have interacted with these societal factors to result in disproportionate harm to Black families and communities.[38] Yet when a system knows these harmful consequences are occurring, and it continues to operate in ways that inflict this harm, at what point do we question whether these consequences are unintentional? At what point do we acknowledge that the family policing system was designed to maintain the oppression of poor Black families and communities and is operating as intended? And at what point do we accept that ending a harmful, oppressive system is the only way to stop the harm and oppression it produces?

By viewing the family policing system through the lens of the harm and oppression it produces, and acknowledging the intentions behind this harm and oppression, the call for abolition is not a unique call. Although the original abolition movement in the United States ended the practice of chattel slavery, the oppression maintained through slavery simply evolved into oppression maintained by criminalization, incarceration, and the destruction of Black families and communities at the hands of the state. Each of these mechanisms of oppression are maintained through centuries of racist policies designed to ensure these mechanisms remain. Thus, the goal of the abolition movement is and has always been the same—freedom from oppression and the creation of a society where the systems and mechanisms for maintaining oppression no longer exist.

Just as the original abolition movement was never intended to end solely with the elimination of slavery, but rather sought to build a society in which Black Americans were free from injustice and oppression, the movement to abolish the family policing system, as well as the movement to abolish policing and prisons, has never been simply about ending these systems of harm. The movement to abolish the family policing system is and will always be a movement that seeks to create a society not simply where the family policing system no longer exists, but to create a society where the need for a family policing system is obsolete. Abolitionists seek to create a society in which a family policing system, and all systems of oppression, are no longer needed because in their place we have collectively created the conditions in which all children, families, and communities have everything they need to truly thrive. Abolitionists seek to create a society where all children and families have everything they need to experience safety in their homes and their communities, free of violence and harm, and free of the societal conditions that create violence and harm. As Erin Miles Cloud, cofounder of the Movement for Family Power, states, "Everybody wants safety for someone, some of the time. Abolitionists want safety for everyone, everywhere, all the time."[39] This is the work of abolition. And this is the work that begins by imagining something different.

The Limits of the White Imagination

We exist in the White imagination—an imagination built on the legacy of settler colonialism and the founding of this country by White male property owners, most of whom were enslavers. The White imagination created the systems that exist today for the purpose of maintaining the system of racial capitalism upon which this country was founded. These systems are designed to maintain financial and social inequality, to favor some people and undermine the well-being of others, and to require those experiencing incredible stress and oppression to comply with services that do not meet their needs in order to receive a fraction of what they truly need. They hold no accountability to Black families. They are built on political compromise and how White people view helping others, especially Black people. The White imagination envisions a world of scarcity, where poor people must constantly work to prove their value, where there is a specific view of what makes a good parent, and accommodations are not made for culture, identity, or disability, let alone the challenges of living in poverty. Inequality has only grown under the White imagination—surveillance of Black families begins prenatally; when Black parents search for help, they receive increased surveillance; and when they are unable to provide their children what they need, they are punished for their inadequacy and their failure. In the White imagination, a system can only provide help after it first finds fault within individuals, controls access to help, and demands correction for the individual inadequacy that created the need for help. If this first requires a punishment as a means of facilitating correction—such as incarceration or family separation—this is the consequence of inadequacy and failure. In the White imagination, the abolition of systems of punishment is unfathomable, because punishment is both appropriate and necessary to maintain the world order upon which the imagination was constructed.

The White imagination also constrains our ability to imagine what is possible—because in many ways, "what is possible" is beyond what we have the capacity to imagine. Within the White imagination, when we are confronted with a problem, we think of solutions that exist within what we know to be possible. Even when those solutions seem radical and difficult to achieve within our current reality, they exist within the reality of what we know to be possible. For example, when we consider the problem of poverty, we are able to think of what some would consider radical solutions to address this—universal basic income, living wages, guaranteed child allowances—in other words, if the problem we face is that people do not have enough wealth to survive, we can imagine strategies that build wealth. Yet we do not ask ourselves why we live in a society where people are required to have wealth in order to survive. And we do not ask ourselves why we allow a society that relies on economic inequality to continue. As family policing abolitionist Maya Pendleton has asked, "Why is it always build wealth, and never abolish capitalism?"[40] These are the limits of the White imagination.

In recent years, many people have come to understand the harms that result from carceral systems—whether those systems are prisons, policing, the family police, or others—and many understand and agree with the need to end those harms. Yet when the idea of abolishing a system that is responsible for harm is raised, a common response is "What would we replace it with?" In the White imagination, if we end one system that is responsible for harm, we must create a new system to replace it. Within the world of prison reforms, Mariame Kaba refers to this as the "Somewhere Else"—the kinder, gentler place where certain "criminals" or other "undesirables" can go that is not as harmful as prisons, but still keeps them far away from society.[41] For people charged with drug-related offenses, this might be a mandatory treatment facility, while for certain law breakers, this might be house arrest—both ideas that retain coercion and confinement.

Within the world of family policing reforms, this manifests in efforts such as *Thriving Families, Safer Children: A National Commitment to Well-Being,* a national effort sponsored by the United States Children's Bureau—the federal arm of the family policing system—and its philanthropic supporters to "transform child welfare into a child and family well-being system" that purports to focus on prevention while still retaining its functions of surveillance and family separation.[42] Or this manifests in efforts that seek to "reimagine" child welfare services to focus on prevention while simultaneously seeking to "improve policies and practices relating to reporting and investigating child maltreatment." This effort to "reimagine" also calls for the elimination of "non-therapeutic congregate care as a foster care placement setting," which will then "necessitate increased support for therapeutic foster care"—thus, family separations and foster care are maintained; but specifically for the purpose of being "therapeutic."[43] Here we see each of these efforts fully manifest the idea of the "Somewhere Else"—reforms that make the system appear more palatable to certain people, while quietly retaining all the aspects of coercion and punishment upon which the system is based.

A New Way of Imagining

In their book, *Prison by Any Other Name: The Harmful Consequences of Popular Reforms*, Maya Schenwar and Victoria Law question the logic behind reform movements that simply replace one form of coercion with another and pose the question, "What would it look like for there to simply be no Somewhere Else?"[44] This is the question at the core of every abolitionist effort. Yet answering this question requires us to break free from the White imagination that limits our ideas of what is possible.

Imagining a world where the family policing system is obsolete requires a new way of imagining—a way of imagining that exists outside the bounds of the world that have been constructed around us and outside the world we have been socialized to believe is our only reality. The work of this way of imagining is threefold—(1) it requires naming the harms of the system and the power interests that maintain the system, (2) disrupting the ways of thinking that maintain the idea the system is necessary, and (3) innovating continuously and investing creatively to build something better. This way of imagining requires recognizing that there is not one solution, but many. It also requires recognizing that we do not need to know any of these solutions before we begin. We only need to know that we *must* begin because the current reality cannot continue.

This way of imagining begins by asking: What would it look like for there to be no foster care? And what would it look like for there to be no "somewhere else," no alternative system disguised as a nicer, friendlier version of the one that exists today? Schenwar and Law describe this simply as "nothing." When we imagine a world without a "something else," they state, "'nothing' becomes a powerful alternative to imagine. It stunts the growth of a self-feeding machine bent on expansion."[45] Although this line of thinking is radical, it is necessary. Because if we cannot imagine a world with "nothing"—a world without a replacement for the family policing system—we will always be confined to imagining "something else"—and "something else" will always be confined within the White imagination.

Thus, when we ask—What would it look like for there to be no foster care? And what would it look like for there to be no somewhere else?—we empower one another and every community to begin to imagine the solutions that, if given the investment and power, will ensure children and families are safe and supported within their homes and communities, not "somewhere else." We also imagine new ways to ensure harm is prevented, and when harm occurs, responses are developed by and within communities to ensure safety and accountability. As Craig Gilmore says, "the power of abolition is precisely its ability to experiment and, in fact, its insistence on experimentation."[46] Abolition creates room for us to experiment with our imagination—to move our ideas of a better world to reality by testing what solutions might work to end harm and keep each other safe and healthy.

The White imagination will seek to identify a leader, a single definitive voice that will tell us the solution and the definitive plan—so we will see some be lifted up and their language taken and replicated—but the work of abolition is ultimately communal. It requires study and conversation and challenging one another so that the work is rigorous and generative and breaks free from the constraints of the White imagination. It is done in community and in coalition with those most impacted by the family policing system, including the development of systems of accountability to ensure the work is done in ways that do not replicate harm and oppression. This is because, in the new society we create, we are all dependent on one another for our well-being. As Ruth Wilson Gilmore has said in defining the idea of "radical dependence," "What we're doing is piecing together a society in which we're not afraid to be dependent on each other. Because abolition is also about radical dependency, not on some external force, but on each other."[47]

When we imagine, we also remember the inspiration and purpose of our movement—the safety and liberation of all people. As was true with the original abolition movement in the United States, abolition is about building a new society free of harm and oppression—a society where the systems and mechanisms for maintaining harm and oppression no longer exist. In their place are new institutions, new structures, and new social and political relationships that form a fundamentally reconstructed social, economic, and political order—one that exists for the purpose of maintaining a racially just society.

Thus, the work of imagining—and the work that abolition requires of us—necessitates that we work not only to dismantle, but that we begin the process of building something new—that we work not only to end the family policing system, but we work to build a society where the need for a family policing system is obsolete. This requires that we begin examining the root causes that perpetuate the need for a family policing system and begin creating something different.

As Chapter 6 demonstrated, reforms persist because they maintain the existing social order. This social order, upon which this country was founded—the social order that depends on White supremacy and the subjugation of Black, Latinx, and Indigenous populations—is racial capitalism.[48] From settler colonialism, genocide, and human chattel slavery, to the current state of the United States that replicates slavery through criminalization, incarceration, and family separation, the project of the United States is one built upon the idea of capitalist accumulation. Capitalist accumulation requires both the maintenance and subjugation of an exploitable labor class who are confined to poverty, which enables their exploitation. This labor class exists for the purpose of maintaining a system whereby those with wealth continue to gain wealth, and those whose labor produces wealth are maintained in a condition where wealth will never occur. Since the earliest origins of the United States, this condition has been maintained through violence—violence that is inflicted directly and violence that is inflicted through policy. Yet while the forms of this violence have shifted over time, its purpose has remained the same—the oppression and subjugation upon which wealth accumulation among the White elite depends. Thus, racial capitalism—or simply capitalism, as all capitalism is racial capitalism[49]—is both the root cause and the social order that perpetuates the need for a family policing system, and all carceral systems. Capitalism depends on violence and oppression to maintain the subjugation of Black, Latinx, and Indigenous populations, and the family policing system, prisons, and police are the systems through which this violence and oppression are enacted.

Thus, to fully realize abolition of the family policing system, and other carceral systems, we must imagine and begin the work of abolishing racial capitalism. This is the vision of the abolitionists who came before us. This is the vision of Frederick Douglass, W. E. B. DuBois, Sojourner Truth, and all those who envisioned a society not only where systems of harm and oppression were ended, but a new society that fully embraced the freedom and equality of all Black Americans. This society cannot exist within a social and economic system based on the idea of racial capitalism, given that racial capitalism will always require their subjugation, and racial capitalism will always maintain the systems that bring about this subjugation.

It is important to recall what many perceived as the failure of the original abolitionist movement in the United States. Although the system of human chattel slavery was ended, the conditions in society that led to the enslavement of Black Americans remained unchanged. Eventually slavery was simply replaced by another system of forced exploitable labor, facilitated by the Thirteenth Amendment, as well as the rapid expansion of racist policies for the purpose of maintaining Black Americans' subjugation. The dream of a racially just society built on the ideas of freedom and liberation was never achieved.

Similarly, if we limit our efforts solely to ending the family policing system without addressing the root cause that allows the family policing system to exist, our real dream for abolition will never be fully realized—there will always be a "somewhere else." If we allow the reformers to succeed with their plans for "transformation" and the family policing system is indeed "reimagined" into a system that looks different but where family separations still occur—if we do nothing to address the system of capitalism that purposely maintains poverty among Black Americans and will continue to disproportionately drive them into the "somewhere else,"—we will look back and stand aghast, just as Frederick Douglass did upon revisiting the South twenty years after the abolition of slavery. We will realize nothing has changed—family separations continue, Black Americans remain oppressed, racism continues to flourish, and the White child-savers who led the efforts for "transformation" and "reimagining" sit back and marvel at everything they've accomplished.

The Work that Can Begin Today

Dismantling the system of racial capitalism upon which this country was founded centuries ago is an enormous undertaking—one that abolition requires, yet one that is no less daunting. However, it is the immense nature of this undertaking that is intended to immobilize us. Capitalism depends on an idea of invulnerability in order to remain invulnerable, but there are strategies we can begin today—strategies we *must* begin to fully realize the vision of abolition. And we must begin today. Although abolition is about both dismantling and creating, the lack of movement toward building a new society where the family policing system is obsolete is often what prevents those who are skeptical of abolition from moving forward with dismantling.

This work can begin through a process of divesting and investing—divesting from the family policing system and the foster care industrial complex built around it, and investing in families and communities, beginning with those most impacted by family policing intervention. As of 2018, $33 billion ($33,000,000,000) are spent annually to maintain the family policing system; nearly half of these funds are spent solely to maintain out-of-home placements resulting from family separations.[50] As prior chapters have demonstrated, nearly 70 percent of these separations are due largely to issues resulting from poverty. What if, instead of forcibly separating children from their parents and then paying "foster parents" to care for others' children, we simply used those funds to ensure parents have everything they need for their children to grow and thrive safely in their homes? This is not a radical idea, and it does not even involve identifying new funding streams. By divesting billions of dollars from the existing family policing system and investing those funds in families and communities we can begin the process of dismantling a harmful, oppressive system while simultaneously strengthening and supporting the well-being of children, families, and communities. Decades of research demonstrate that providing direct material assistance to families significantly reduces both involvement with the family policing system and incidents of child maltreatment.[51] Thus, this is not only a strategy we can begin today, but also a strategy we know will be effective.

Critically, direct financial resources are part of repairing the damage of the past and supporting the work of the future—but money is and will never be enough. In addition to direct material supports, we can create broader structural changes needed to end poverty and advance the safety and well-being of children. These include a housing guarantee; free public transportation; and free, accessible, and meaningful child care, health care, and mental health care. Each of these will require robust policy changes, but these are policy changes that are needed and that are possible in the near-term.

In addition to divesting and investing financial resources, we can build on the strengths of families by shifting power away from harmful, oppressive state institutions and toward families and communities. Communities should have the responsibility for working with families to identify the resources families need, and these resources should be available outside of carceral systems in ways that meet their holistic needs while accounting for the larger systemic issues that serve as barriers to achieving their goals. Ultimately, what families need should be the standard used to determine the appropriateness of the services and supports they access.

Shifting power to families and communities also includes ensuring they have the resources to prevent harm from occurring, to address harm when harm occurs, and to promote healing. When harm does occur, communities should have responsibility for rendering healing and accountability while strengthening relationships among community members. Rather than relying on state-sanctioned interventions that cause further harm by separating families and fragmenting communities, divesting from the family policing system and investing in families and communities also includes building mechanisms that support families in autonomously identifying noncarceral solutions that support healing, safety, and the prevention of future harm.

In many ways, we are already seeing this occur. When the COVID-19 pandemic emerged, people ramped up their efforts to care for one another in community, providing each other with direct support through mutual aid efforts. As Mariame Kaba has said, "the key things to remember about mutual aid is it empowers communities to meet needs like housing, healthcare, food, and transportation. It is premised on solidarity, not charity. It rejects saviorism, hierarchy, and authoritarianism. Mutual aid exposes the failures of the current system and shows an alternative."[52]

Taken together, shifting power to families and communities, divesting from harmful state institutions, and investing in families and communities begins the process of moving toward a society where the family policing system is obsolete. Here it is important to recognize that the process of creating this new society does not imply the creation of a stronger welfare state—rather, this involves the creation of a new society where the concept of welfare no longer exists because all families and communities have everything they need to thrive. This is the work that moves us beyond the White imagination, and although the end we seek is radical change, this is the work that can begin today.

As we stated earlier, the White imagination constrains our ability to imagine all that is possible. It also constrains our ability to understand the strategies needed to achieve all that is possible because they are beyond what we have yet to imagine. However, we also understand that the need to identify these specific strategies is rooted in a culture of White supremacy that demands a solution and a definitive plan to achieve that solution before we can even begin the work of imagining. White supremacy culture seeks to control the solution and define whose expertise is centered in identifying that solution. We reject this. In pursuing abolition, we understand there is not one right way to achieve this—there are many paths, many futures, and many communities already imagining and building the alternatives to what exists today—and we will continue to imagine and build.[53]

How We Struggle

There is no monolithic abolitionist. In the era of human chattel slavery, the abolitionists were of many races, various religions, different genders, free and enslaved, poor and wealthy. They disagreed with one another, vied for the spotlight, and sought control. In the modern prison abolition movement, there also exist many different perspectives and identities. Yet abolitionists share a common goal—ending the oppression, harm, and exploitation of people. Thus, building on Ruth Wilson Gilmore's idea of "radical dependency," abolitionists like Angela Davis and Mariame Kaba emphasize the importance of *how* we engage in abolitionism, and *how* we interact with one another. The process is as important as the end goal in that abolitionists are trying to end not only oppressive institutions, but also oppressive interactions. "Indeed, one of the fundamental precepts of abolition is that winning a campaign is not the only measure of success: how we struggle, how our work enables future struggles, and how we stay clear about what we are fighting for matters."[54]

As we move forward, it is important to be prepared for and attend to points of rupture and facilitate ways of being with one another, in community, working toward our common goal. The work of abolition is not just about the work to abolish, but how we are in relationship with one another. This is both a lesson to take from the original abolitionists, but also a critical reminder of the need to be collectively prepared to face the backlash that has already begun and will continue. As Alicia Garza notes, "Change does not occur without backlash—at least, any change worth having—and that backlash is an indicator that the change is so powerful that the opposing forces resist that change with everything they have."[55]

Efforts to end the oppression and subjugation that are needed to maintain White power have been met with backlash and violence since the earliest origins of the United States. Throughout our history as a country, when White power is threatened it responds with White rage.[56] At various times throughout our history, that White rage has manifested through horrific violence from what was seen during the era of slavery where violence was used both to prevent rebellion and as a response to rebellion, to the violence inflicted on Black Americans during the civil rights movement of the 1960s. At other times throughout history, when overt physical violence was insufficient or less supported by the broader society, White rage has been enacted through policy. From the Black Codes to the Jim Crow Laws to the policies that presently maintain the carceral state, policy has been an essential tool used by the state to channel White rage for the maintenance of White power.

In recent years, we have seen both violence and backlash in response to the movement for Black lives and the movement to defund the police. Each of these movements challenge White power because they seek Black liberation—and each of these movements have been met with the White rage that is unleashed when White power is threatened. From both direct violence and threats of violence to policies that strengthen the police or threaten to withhold state funding should funds be divested from the police, the broader movement to abolish policing and prisons is now the subject of intense backlash and opposition.[57]

Although not yet as broad or intense, the backlash and resistance to abolition of the family policing system has been quick and has grown in intensity as the movement has gained supporters and momentum. We have seen this in opinion pieces that intentionally misrepresent the movement, in scholarly publications questioning the "science" behind abolition, to fearmongering over children who will be harmed that blatantly misunderstands the movement, to direct recommendations for new policies that will increase the surveillance of Black families.[58] Parent leaders within the abolition movement have described their experiences of harassment by family policing agencies and their supporters.[59] In some instances, this harassment has occurred in public spaces and on social media, where Black mothers criticizing the family policing system have been challenged by White academics.[60]

Yet as we have seen from prior movements that challenge White power, this backlash is to be expected. As prior chapters have demonstrated, the maintenance of White power is dependent on the subjugation of Black Americans, and the family policing system plays a crucial role in maintaining this subjugation. As the abolition movement grows and sees success, and White power is threatened, the backlash will intensify as White rage is increasingly activated. This will come directly from the system itself, as well as from those who support the system because they understand the role this system plays in the subjugation of Black people. It will also come from those with a vested interest in maintaining the status quo, particularly as we have seen from the White researchers and academics who depend on this status quo to justify their careers. We will also see the same tactics—deliberate attempts to confuse or misrepresent the movement, attempts to discredit the movement with rigid interpretations of "evidence" or lack thereof, and most unfortunately, individual attacks directed at those who are visibly engaged in the movement, particularly parents and youth who have been directly harmed by the family policing system.

The system knows the power the stories of these parents and youth hold, and the system understands the influence these stories can have on an un-informed public. Just as the stories of family separations during the time of chattel slavery became the catalyst that led to an indifferent public joining the abolitionist movement, the stories of the parents whose children were forcibly taken from their arms and the children who were carried away by family policing agents are the stories that once again will move the public to understand the harm and devastation brought by the system and the need for its abolition. The system and its supporters are very aware of this, and the system and its supporters are now activated to prevent this from occurring. They will flood the field with counternarratives and "success stories." Just as enslavers told stories of how well they treated their slaves and how happy and contented their slaves were, so too do supporters of the family policing system tell stories of how happy certain children are in foster care and how better their lives are because of it. They will present panels of youth who have achieved great success after leaving foster care while not mentioning the pain and devastation that preceded this success or the ramifications of trauma and separation that still impact them. Just as pro-slavery advocates said that enslaved people would be unable to care for themselves if they weren't enslaved, family policing advocates will tell stories of vulnerable children who were rescued from harm and are now "safe" in the care of the state. They will share stories of the most extreme cases of abuse to justify the need for the system and call for expansion rather than elimination. As we have seen since the original abolitionist movement, the stories have changed, but their purpose remains the same—to minimize the harm inflicted by the system, to present a narrative of benevolence, and to convince the public that although the system has challenges, the system must be maintained.

While this backlash is expected and will continue to grow as the move-ment grows, those of us in the movement must remember the impor-tance of staying in relationship with one another and remaining united in our common purpose. We must work together to challenge the narratives presented by the system and tell the true stories of trauma and devastation that result from family separation. We must continue to expose the system as a state-sanctioned mechanism of oppression that was designed for the main-tenance of White power. And we must continue to uplift the voices of the Black mothers who have led the movement to abolish this system since the beginnings of the movement. We have already seen the movement and our language begin to be co-opted by White-led think tanks who have aligned with aspects of the movement to convince the public that we all want the same thing. We do not. And we must remember that the work of abolition will not be complete by simply ending the family policing system—the work of abolition will only be complete when we abolish the society that supports the existence of a family policing system and all other systems of punishment and oppression. This is our true goal, and we must stay committed to this goal until it is realized.

The World We Wish to See

Ruth Wilson Gilmore has said, "Abolition is a way of seeing. Abolition makes you ask, when you look, what are you seeing, and what would you rather see?"[61] When we look at the family policing system today, we see a system built upon a model of surveillance, regulation, and punishment. We see a system that disproportionately surveils Black bodies, a system that disproportionately separates Black children from their families, and a system that responds to families in need with an intervention that causes those families more harm. We see a system that was created to ensure Black children and families exist in poverty and remain in poverty. We see a system that exists to establish a narrative that the condition of poverty inflicted on Black Americans by the state is the result of individual pathology among Black mothers. We see a system that was created as part of a broader national project to maintain a system of racial capitalism ruled by White elites that depends on the continued subjugation of Black Americans. And we see a system that replicates the harshest form of punishment used during slavery to ensure this subjugation continues.

What we would rather see is a world where children and families have everything they need to be healthy, to eat, to live safely, and to thrive in their homes and communities. We would rather see a world where families are interconnected with their communities and freely seek help without fear of judgment or punishment. We would rather see a world where the idea of a family policing system would never be brought into existence because the idea of forcibly separating children from their parents is so repellant. We would rather see a world that is not dependent on the subjugation of some to further the supremacy of others, a world that would look upon the horrors of human chattel slavery and agree that those horrors can never be repeated, a world where true equality is fully realized.

We would rather see a world where we are free.

Abolition is fundamentally about hope. Hope for another world, and the belief that another world is possible. This hope has existed long before us, and this hope will continue. Yet it is not a misguided hope or a dream of a utopia beyond our grasp. It is the hope for something we know is possible because the idea that it is impossible is not something we can accept. It is the hope that fueled centuries of those who came before us, and the hope that fuels all that is being done today. The world we wish to see is possible, and the work to bring this world into reality is being done by individuals and communities across the globe. Those of us who hope for freedom know that it is within our power to bring about the change we wish to see. We also know that our collective power is greater than those who wish to deny us freedom. As George Jackson says in *Blood in My Eye*, "A people can never be so repressed that they can't strike back in some way."[62] Using our collective power requires risks and will come with backlash from the White elites who control society, because "repression is indeed a part of revolution."[63] Yet we know that we will continue. We will continue because we must—because we understand that our current reality cannot continue. This is the work of abolition, and this is the work that continues until we are free.

Notes

1. Tema Okun, "White Supremacy Culture," 2022, https://www.whitesupremacycult ure.info.
2. Maya Schenwar and Victoria Law, *Prison By Any Other Name: The Harmful Consequences of Popular Reforms* (New York: The New Press, 2021), p. 198.
3. For examples, see Frederick Douglass, *The Life and Times of Frederick Douglass* (Boston: De Wolfe & Fiske Co., 1892); Linda Hirshman, *The Color of Abolition: How a Printer, a Prophet, and a Contessa Moved a Nation* (Boston: Mariner Books, 2022); and Manisha Sinha, *The Slave's Cause: A History of Abolition* (New Haven, CT: Yale University Press, 2017).
4. William Lloyd Garrison, "To the Public," *The Liberator,* January 1, 1831, https://www. masshist.org/database/1698.
5. For more on the economic interests related to chattel slavery, see Sven Beckert and Seth Rockman, Eds., *Slavery's Capitalism: A New History of American Economic Development* (Philadelphia: University of Pennsylvania Press, 2016).
6. Sinha, *The Slave's Cause*, p. 2.

7. Frederick Douglass, "What to the Slave is the Fourth of July" (speech, Rochester Ladies' Anti-Slavery Society, Rochester, New York, July 5, 1852), p. 20, https://upload. wikimedia.org/wikipedia/commons/b/b4/What_to_the_Slave_Is_the_Fourth_of_J uly.pdf.

8. Sinha, *The Slave's Cause*, p. 130.

9. Phillis Wheatley, "To the Right Honourable William, Earl of Dartmouth, His Majesty's Principal Secretary of State for North America &c," *Poems on Various Subjects, Religious and Moral* (London: A. Bell, Rockefeller, Aldgate, 1773), p. 73.

10. Frederick Douglass, "Our Work Is Not Done" (speech, Annual Meeting of the American Anti-Slavery Society, Philadelphia, December 3–4, 1863), https://rbscp.lib. rochester.edu/4403.

11. W. E. B. DuBois, *Black Reconstruction in America 1860–1880* (New York: The Free Press, 1935), p. 182.

12. Angela Y. Davis, *Abolition Democracy: Beyond Empire, Prisons, and Torture* (New York: Seven Stories Press, 2005), p. 91.

13. Allegra M. McLeod, "Prison Abolition and Grounded Justice," *UCLA Law Review* 62 (June 2015): pp. 1162–1163, https://www.uclalawreview.org/prison-abolition-groun ded-justice/.

14. See for example, "Testimony of Slaveholders," *The American Anti-Slavery Almanac* 1, no. 4 (1839): p. 39, which states, "Abolitionists are often charged with over-statements in describing the horrors of slavery, but when slaveholders voluntarily take the pencil, who will accuse *them* of high coloring in drawing the picture?"

15. Christina Gregg, "UMass Professor Manisha Sinha Re-examines Abolitionists' Role in Civil War," *The Massachusetts Daily Collegian,* April 27, 2011, https://dailycolleg ian.com/2011/04/umass-professor-manisha-sinha-re-examines-abolitionists'-role- in-civil-war/.

16. Nikole Hannah-Jones, "Democracy," in *The 1619 Project: A New Origin Story*, created by Nikole Hannah-Jones (New York: One World, 2021), pp. 29–30.

17. Christopher R. Adamson, "Punishment After Slavery: Southern State Penal Systems, 1865–1890," *Social Problems* 30, no. 5 (June 1983): pp. 555–569, https://www.jstor. org/stable/800272; Ruth Delaney, Ram Subramanian, Alison Shames, and Nicholas Turner, *Reimagining Prison* (Vera Institute of Justice, October 2018), https://www. vera.org/downloads/publications/Reimagining-Prison_FINAL3_digital.pdf; Nadra Kareem Nittle, "The Black Codes and Why They Still Matter Today," *ThoughtCo,* December 21, 2020, https://www.thoughtco.com/the-black-codes-4125744.

18. Frederick Douglass, "I Denounce the So-Called Emancipation as a Stupendous Fraud" (speech, Twenty-Sixth Anniversary of Emancipation, Washington, DC, April 16, 1888), https://www.historyisaweapon.com/defcon1/douglassfraud.html.

19. Sinha, *The Slave's Cause*, p. 3.

20. For histories of racial justice organizing and the prison system see Dan Berger, *Captive Nation: Black Prison Organizing in the Civil Rights Era* (Chapel Hill: University of North Carolina Press, 2016); Ronald Berkman, *Opening the Gates: The Rise of the Prisoners Movement* (Lexington, MA: Lexington Books, 1979); Heather Ann Thompson, *Blood in the Water: The Attica Prison Uprising of 1971 and its Legacy* (New York: Pantheon

Books, 2016); and Donald F. Tibbs, *From Black Power to Prison Power: The Making of Jones v. North Carolina Prisoners' Labor Union* (New York: Palgrave MacMillan, 2012).

21. Delaney et al., *Reimagining Prison.*
22. Ashley Nellis, *The Color of Justice: Racial and Ethnic Disparity in State Prisons* (The Sentencing Project, October 2021), https://www.sentencingproject.org/publications/color-of-justice-racial-and-ethnic-disparity-in-state-prisons/.
23. Dorothy E. Roberts, "Abolition Constitutionalism," *Harvard Law Review* 133, no. 1 (November 2019): p. 5.
24. Roberts, "Abolition Constitutionalism," p. 6.
25. Angela Y. Davis, Gina Dent, Erica R. Meiners, and Beth E. Richie, *Abolition. Feminism. Now.* (New York: Haymarket Books, 2022), p. 45. See also Chapter 1 and others for historical analysis on how women of color rejected the neoliberal reforms offered by "carceral feminism" for more radical abolition efforts.
26. Roberts, "Abolition Constitutionalism," p. 6.
27. Ruth Wilson Gilmore, "No Easy Victories: Fighting for Abolition," (lecture hosted by Critical Resistance, Chicago, IL, November 8, 2017), https://www.youtube.com/watch?v=FGPVPrJGXsY.
28. Derecka Purnell, "Making the Argument for Abolishing the Police" (interview, The Daily Show, September 30, 2021), https://www.youtube.com/watch?v=vUtpuU4mzOM.
29. Robin D. G. Kelley, "Change from the Roots: What Abolition Looks Like, From the Panthers to the People," in *Abolition for the People: The Movement for a Future Without Policing and Prisons,* edited by Colin Kaepernick (New York: Kaepernick Publishing, 2021), p. 187.
30. Marlon Peterson, "Who Is Being Healed?: Creating Solutions Is About Answering Questions Prisons Never Asked," in Kaepernick, *Abolition for the People,* p. 213.
31. Mariame Kaba, "Yes, We Mean Literally Abolish the Police," *The New York Times,* June 12, 2020, https://www.nytimes.com/2020/06/12/opinion/sunday/floyd-abolish-defund-police.html.
32. Dylan Rodríguez, "Abolition as Praxis of Human Being: A Foreword," *Harvard Law Review* 132, no. 6 (April 2019): p. 1578, https://harvardlawreview.org/2019/04/abolition-as-praxis-of-human-being-a-foreword/.
33. Davis, *Abolition Democracy,* pp. 69–70.
34. Richard Nixon, "Remarks About an Intensified Program for Drug Abuse Prevention and Control" (press conference, White House briefing room, Washington, DC, June 17, 1971), https://www.presidency.ucsb.edu/node/240238.
35. For a further elaboration of how neoliberal policies impacted Black families and communities beginning in the 1970s, see Emma Peyton Williams, *Regulating Families: How the Family Policing System Devastates Black, Indigenous, and Latinx Families and Upholds White Family Supremacy* (upEND Movement, June 2022), https://upendmovement.org/regulation/.
36. Roberts, "Abolition Constitutionalism," p. 16.
37. See as examples, Richard P. Barth, Jill Duerr Berrick, Antonio R. Garcia, Brett Drake, Melissa Jonson-Reid, John R. Gyourko, and Johanna K. P. Greeson, "Research to

Consider While Effectively Re-Designing Child Welfare Services," *Research on Social Work Practice* 32, no. 5 (July 2022): pp. 483–498, https://doi.org/10.1177/104973 15211050000; Elizabeth Bartholet, "The Racial Disproportionality Movement in Child Welfare: False Facts and Dangerous Directions," *Arizona Law Review* 51, no. 4 (2009): pp. 871–932, https://arizonalawreview.org/bartholet/; and Brett Drake, Jennifer M. Jolley, Paul Lanier, John Fluke, Richard P. Barth, and Melissa Jonson-Reid, "Racial Bias in Child Protection? A Comparison of Competing Explanations Using National Data," *Pediatrics* 127, no. 3 (March 2011): pp. 471–478, https://doi.org/10.1542/peds.2010-1710.

38. See as examples Sydney L. Goetz, "From Removal to Incarceration: How the Modern Child Welfare System and Its Unintended Consequences Catalyzed the Foster Care to Prison Pipeline," *University of Maryland Law Journal of Race, Religion, Gender, and Class* 20, no. 2 (2020): pp. 289–305, https://digitalcommons.law.umaryland.edu/cgi/viewcontent.cgi?article=1352&context=rrgc; and Mark F. Testa and David Kelly, "The Evolution of Federal Child Welfare Policy through the Family First Prevention Services Act of 2018: Opportunities, Barriers, and Unintended Consequences," *Annals of the American Academy of Political and Social Science* 692 (November 2020): pp. 68–96, https://doi.org/10.1177/0002716220976528.

39. As cited in "A Future Without Police? Andrea Ritchie on Crime and Abolition," Undistracted with Brittany Packnett Cunningham Podcast, August 18, 2022, https://podcasts.apple.com/us/podcast/a-future-without-police-andrea-ritchie-on-crime/id1534591370?i=1000576462454.

40. Authors' communication with Maya Pendleton, May 2021.

41. As cited in Schenwar and Law, *Prison by Any Other Name*, p. 17.

42. "First-of-its-Kind National Partnership Aims to Redesign Child Welfare into Child and Family Well-Being Systems" (press release, Administration for Children and Families, September 9, 2020), https://www.acf.hhs.gov/media/press/2020/first-its-kind-national-partnership-aims-redesign-child-welfare-child-and-family.

43. "Reimagining Child Welfare: Recommendations for Public Policy Change," American Academy of Pediatrics, April 16, 2021, https://www.aap.org/en/advocacy/child-welfare-report/.

44. Schenwar and Law, *Prison by Any Other Name,* p. 200.

45. Schenwar and Law, *Prison by Any Other Name,* p. 201.

46. "'Abolition Is Inherently Experimental' Craig Gilmore on Fighting Prisons and Defunding Police," Millennials Are Killing Capitalism, September 30, 2020, https://millennialsarekillingcapitalism.libsyn.com/abolition-is-inherently-experimental-craig-gilmore-on-fighting-prisons-and-defunding-police.

47. Ruth Wilson Gilmore, "Eyes on Abolition" (lecture, University of Houston Graduate College of Social Work, October 5, 2020), https://www.youtube.com/watch?v=cdByv0fWjSI.

48. For further readings on racial capitalism, see the works of Cedric J. Robinson, many of which are compiled in H. L. T. Quan, Ed., *Cedric J. Robinson on Racial Capitalism, Black Internationalism, and Cultures of Resistance* (London: Pluto Press, 2019).

49. See Cedric J. Robinson, *Black Marxism: The Making of the Black Radical Tradition* (London: Zed Press, 1983).

50. Kristina Rosinsky, Sarah Catherine Williams, Megan Fischer, and Maggie Haas, *Child Welfare Financing SFY 2018: A Survey of Federal, State, and Local Expenditures* (Child Trends, March 2021), https://www.childtrends.org/publications/child-welfare-financ ing-survey-sfy2018.

51. See as examples, Lawrence M. Berger, Sarah A. Font, Kristen S. Slack, and Jane Waldfogel, "Income and Child Maltreatment in Unmarried Families: Evidence from the Earned Income Tax Credit," *Review of Economics of the Household* 15, no. 4 (December 2017): pp. 1345–1372, https://doi.org/10.1007/s11150-016-9346-9; Maria Cancian, Mi-Youn Yang, and Kristen S. Slack, "The Effect of Additional Child Support Income on the Risk of Child Maltreatment," *Social Service Review* 87, no. 3 (September 2013): pp. 417–437, https://doi.org/10.1086/671929; and Alexandra Citrin, Megan Martin, and Clare Anderson, "Investing in Families through Economic Supports: An Anti-Racist Approach to Supporting Families and Reducing Child Welfare Involvement," *Child Welfare* 100, no. 1 (January 2022): pp. 51–79.

52. As quoted in Dan White, "Hope, Mutual Aid, and Abolition," *UC Santa Cruz News Center,* February 16, 2021, https://news.ucsc.edu/2021/02/kaba-mlk-coverage-2021.html.

53. Abolitionist actions to transform society are happening daily. Examples can be found at One Million Experiments, https://millionexperiments.com, and Interrupting Criminalization, https://www.interruptingcriminalization.com.

54. Davis et al., *Abolition. Feminism. Now.,* p. 34.

55. Alicia Garza, "2014–2019: Black Lives Matter," in *Four Hundred Souls: A Community History of African America, 1619–2019,* edited by Ibram X. Kendi and Keisha N. Blain (New York: One World, 2021), pp. 382–386.

56. For more on White rage, see Carol Anderson, *White Rage: The Unspoken Truth of Our Racial Divide* (New York: Bloomsbury, 2016).

57. For examples, see Mihir J. Chaudhary and Joseph Richardson, Jr., "Violence Against Black Lives Matter Protestors: A Review," *Current Trauma Reports* 8 (May 2022): pp. 96–104, https://link.springer.com/article/10.1007/s40719-022-00228-2; Summer Lin, "Black Lives Matter Shirt Worn in Class Sparks Death Threats, California Teacher Says," *The Sacramento Bee,* August 27, 2020, https://www.sacbee.com/news/ california/article245307265.html; Paulina Villegas, "Texas Governor to Sign Law Preventing the Defunding of Police, Setting Up Another Clash with Cities," *The Washington Post,* May 24, 2021, https://www.washingtonpost.com/nation/2021/05/ 24/texas-greg-abbott-defund-police/.

58. See Barth et al., "Research to Consider While Effectively Re-Designing Child Welfare Services"; Sarah A. Font, *What Lessons Can the Child Welfare System Take from the COVID-19 Pandemic?* (American Enterprise Institute, January 2021), https://www. aei.org/wp-content/uploads/2021/01/What-Lessons-Can-the-Child-Welfare-Sys tem-Take-from-the-COVID-19-Pandemic.pdf?x91208; Naomi Schaefer Riley, "Wanted: Sanity on Foster Care," *City Journal,* October 20, 2020, https://www.city-journal.org/radical-activists-want-to-abolish-foster-care; Naomi Schaefer Riley,

"Child Welfare Is Becoming a Joke," *Quillette,* September 16, 2022, https://quillette.com/2022/09/16/child-welfare-is-becoming-a-joke/; Naomi Schaefer Riley, Brett Drake, Sarah A. Font, and Emily Putnam-Hornstein, *What Child Protection Is For* (American Enterprise Institute, September 2021), https://www.aei.org/wp-content/uploads/2021/08/What-Child-Protection-Is-for.pdf?x91208.

59. Eileen Grench, "NYC Child Welfare Officials Helped Get Her Fired Over Social Media Posts. Activism Got Her Back on the Job," *The City,* February 11, 2021, https://www.thecity.nyc/work/2021/2/11/22277355/nyc-child-welfare-acs-fired-over-social-media-posts.

60. See as examples https://twitter.com/RPBarth/status/1558235325574660103; https://twitter.com/RPBarth/status/1559266335648989184;   https://twitter.com/RPBarth/status/1504242540387745792.

61. Ruth Wilson Gilmore, "Eyes on Abolition" (lecture, University of Houston Graduate College of Social Work, October 5, 2020), https://www.youtube.com/watch?v=cdByv0fWjSI.

62. George L. Jackson, *Blood In My Eye* (Baltimore: Black Classic Press, 1972), p. 33.

63. Jackson, *Blood In My Eye,* p. 29.

Index